Translated Texts for Historians

300–800 AD is the time of late antiquity and the early middle ages: the transformation of the classical world, the beginnings of Europe and of Islam, and the evolution of Byzantium. TTH makes available sources from a range of languages, including Greek, Latin, Syriac, Coptic, Arabic, Georgian, Gothic and Armenian. Each volume provides an expert scholarly translation, with an introduction setting texts and authors in context, and with notes on content, interpretation and debates.

Editorial Committee
Phil Booth, St Peter's College, Oxford
Sebastian Brock, Oriental Institute, University of Oxford
Averil Cameron, Keble College, Oxford
Marios Costambeys, University of Liverpool
Carlotta Dionisotti, King's College, London
Jill Harries, University of St Andrews
Peter Heather, King's College, London
Robert Hoyland, Institute for Study of the Ancient World,
     New York University
William E. Klingshirn, The Catholic University of America
Michael Lapidge, Clare College, Cambridge
Neil McLynn, Corpus Christi College, Oxford
Richard Price, Royal Holloway, University of London
Claudia Rapp, Institut für Byzantinistik und Neogräzistik,
     Universität Wien
Judith Ryder, University of Oxford
Raymond Van Dam, University of Michigan
Yuhan Vevaina, Oriental Institute, University of Oxford
Michael Whitby, University of Birmingham
Ian Wood, University of Leeds

General Editors
Gillian Clark, University of Bristol
Mark Humphries, Swansea University
Mary Whitby, University of Oxford

A full list of published titles in the **Translated Texts for Historians** series is available on request. The most recently published are shown below.

For full details of **Translated Texts for Historians**, including prices and ordering information, please contact: Liverpool University Press, 4 Cambridge Street, Liverpool, L69 7ZU, UK (*Tel* +44-[0]151-794 2233. Email janet.mcdermott@liverpool.ac.uk, http://www.liverpooluniversitypress.co.uk).

Translated Texts for Historians
Volume 74

The Canons of the Quinisext Council (691/2)

Translated with an introduction and notes
by RICHARD PRICE

Liverpool
University
Press

First published 2020
Liverpool University Press
4 Cambridge Street
Liverpool, L69 7ZU

British Library Cataloguing-in-Publication Data
A British Library CIP Record is available.

ISBN 978-1-78962-236-2 (Hardback)
ISBN 978-1-78962-813-5 (Paperback)

Typeset by Carnegie Book Production, Lancaster
Printed and bound by CPI Group (UK) Ltd, Croydon CR0 4YY

CONTENTS

PREFACE

The Quinisext Council of 691/2 enjoys (or should one say suffers from?) a plethora of names. 'Quinisext' means 'fifth-sixth', and translates its Greek name 'Penthektê'. This expresses its claim to complete the preceding Fifth and Sixth Ecumenical Councils (of 553 and 680–81) which, as is pointed out in its address to the emperor, had failed to issue any disciplinary canons. Other names are 'Trullan' or 'in Trullo', after the domed hall in the imperial palace in Constantinople (called Trullos or Trullon) in which it was held.[1] Rather than indulge in elegant variation, I have kept to 'Quinisext'.

The Quinisext Council issued, as is well known, the largest body of ecclesiastical legislation of any of the general councils. Although its quality is variable, and Byzantine canon law is inferior to Byzantine civil law in both precision and comprehensiveness, the historian may still judge that it contributed more to the well-being of the Christian Church than the more prestigious pronouncements on arcane questions of doctrine by the numbered ecumenical councils, pronouncements that, in the main though with exceptions, contributed heat rather than light and contributed to tensions rather than resolving them.[2] The social historian, keen to discover how Christians led their lives, finds it helpful to be reminded of how, according to canon law, they were at least supposed to lead their lives; the more some things were forbidden, the more the very need for legislation reveals that they were being practised.

The Acts of the ecumenical councils do not contain minutes relating to the presentation and discussion (if any) of disciplinary canons. Most often they do not even mention the conciliar session at which they were approved; they were handed down purely as a self-standing document.[3]

---

1 If it is to be called the Trullan Council, it should be called the Second Trullan Council, since Constantinople III (680–81) was held in the same location.

2 See Price (2017) for a critical assessment of these councils.

3 This is true of the canons of Chalcedon and Nicaea II (787). However, at the Council of Constantinople of 869–70 the canons occur within the proceedings of the final session, immediately before the council's *horos*.

It is this that makes the 'acts' (if they may be so called) of the Quinisext Council so slim a document, for they consist of only three elements: an address to the emperor Justinian II (*logos prosphonetikos* in Greek) by the assembled bishops, the text of the 102 canons, and a subscription list, giving the names of 226 bishops who subscribed and doubtless attended the council. The address will have been delivered at the end of the council, but I follow the manuscripts (and Ohme's latest edition) in placing it first, as an introduction to what follows, revealing both of its purposes and the ideology behind it.

The text I translate is the critical edition with full apparatus recently produced by Heinz Ohme and published in the *Acta Conciliorum Oecumenicorum* series (Berlin, 2013). This involved an immense labour on his part, since the manuscripts of this major canonical text, of greater practical importance for churchmen than all the other conciliar acts, are extremely numerous. Ohme has also produced a stream of publications discussing and analysing this text, and placing it in both its immediate historical context and the history of the development of Byzantine canon law. This is the first set of acts of which I have produced a translation and commentary where the work has essentially been done for me already. The need for my work arises solely from the fact that the text is of interest to many historians who either cannot or are reluctant to read works in German. For this reason I have received every encouragement from Professor Ohme himself, who indeed gave me copies of almost all his relevant publications; he was also so kind as to respond to a number of specific queries I sent to him. My commentary contains constant references to his work, and is often dependent on it where no specific reference is made. In particular, in my commentary on the individual canons, which is hugely indebted to his own commentary in the *Fontes Christiani* series, I have not thought it necessary to refer to him at all often, since this is so obvious a source, and all my readers who can also read German will refer to his commentary at the same time as they use mine.

This book is accordingly dedicated to him, in gratitude for his work not only on the Quinisext Council but also on the monothelete controversy, to which my work on the Lateran Synod of 649 and the Third Council of Constantinople (680–81) is likewise greatly indebted.

I wish to record my debts to some other scholars. Averil Cameron had the goodness to read through my text and offer useful comments, Michael Whitby yet again checked my translation, and Stephanie Forrest replied at length to my queries about Armenia in this period. As for research materials, the library resources of London – the British Library, the Institute of Historical Research, the Warburg Institute, the Institute of Classical Studies Library, and the Senate House Library, through which books in the Heythrop College Library are still accessible – provided all I needed, and I thank their always helpful staffs.

ABBREVIATIONS

ACO	Acta Conciliorum Oecumenicorum, Series prima
ACO²	Acta Conciliorum Oecumenicorum, Series secunda
AHC	*Annuarium Historiae Conciliorum*
BMGS	*Byzantine and Modern Greek Studies*
Byz	*Byzantion*
ByzZ	*Byzantinische Zeitschrift*
CCSL	Corpus Christianorum Series Latina
CJ	*Codex Justinianus* (*Iustinianus*)
COGD	Conciliorum Oecumenicorum Generaliumque Decreta (Turnhout)
CSCO	Corpus Scriptorum Christianorum Orientalium
CSEL	Corpus Scriptorum Ecclesiasticorum Latinorum
CTh	*Codex Theodosianus*
DHGE	*Dictionnaire d'histoire et géographie ecclésiastiques*
DOP	*Dunbarton Oaks Papers*
DThC	*Dictionnaire de Théologie Catholique*
ep.	*epistola*
GCS	Die Griechischen Christlichen Schriftsteller der ersten Jahrhunderte
GOTR	*Greek Orthodox Theological Review*
HE	*Historia Ecclesiastica*
JRS	*Journal of Roman Studies*
LP	*Liber Pontificalis*
MGH *Epp.*	Monumenta Germaniae Historica, *Epistolae*
nov.	*novella*
OCP	*Orientalia Christiana Periodica*
ODB	*Oxford Dictionary of Byzantium*
or.	*oratio*
PG	Patrologia Graeca
PGL	*A Patristic Greek Lexicon*, ed. G.W.H. Lampe
PL	Patrologia Latina

PmbZ 1	Prosopographie der mittelbyzantinischen Zeit, Erste Abteilung (641–867)
PO	Patrologia Orientalis
RAC	*Reallexikon für Antike und Christentum*
RÉB	*Revue des Études Byzantines*
SBN	*Studi Bizantini e Neoellenici*
SC	Sources Chrétiennes
StPat	*Studia Patristica*
SVSQ	*St Vladimir's Seminary Quarterly*
TM	*Travaux et Mémoires*
TRE	*Theologische Realenzyklopädie*
TTH	Translated Texts for Historians
ZKG	*Zeitschrift für Kirchengeschichte*

INTRODUCTION

1. THE COUNCIL AND ITS SETTING

The Context of the Council

Our knowledge of the reign, the policies, the personality, of the emperor Justinian II (born *c.* 668/9, reigned 685–95 and 705–11) is limited. The sources for his reign are both slender and hostile.[1] The preceding decades had been the most traumatic period in the history of the Roman empire, with the loss of by far the greater part of its territory – Syria, Palestine, Egypt, most of the Balkans – and for many years almost annual Arab raids into Asia Minor.

And yet his lifetime had already seen the beginning of a Byzantine recovery. The defeat of the long Arab siege of Constantinople (674–8) had marked the first, and decisive, halting of the Arab advance. It was in this context that Justinian, at the age of only sixteen, found himself on the premature death of his father Constantine IV suddenly elevated into autocratic power and unlimited responsibility. By a most fortunate conjunction this was also a period of sudden Arab weakness: rebels in Persia, Mesopotamia and Arabia controlled more than half the caliphate. The new caliph 'Abd el-Malik (685–705) needed to make rapid peace with the empire in order to direct his attention to enemies on his eastern flank.[2] This enabled the young Justinian immediately on his accession to

---

1 Ohme (1992a) 370–71, citing Head (1972) 14–18. Note, however, that Justinian's name appears in some later calendars of saints, doubtless because of his role in the convening and work of the Quinisext council. The absence of a mention of the council in the accounts of the reign of Justinian II in the chronicles of Nikephoros and Theophanes must reflect not doubts about the council, but a wish not to associate with it a name of an emperor they so detested. Theophanes 361–2 (trans. Mango and Scott 504) actually cites, under the last year of Constantine IV, two passages from the Quinisext canons as part of a (defective) chronological argument.

2 Treadgold (1997) 325–31.

conclude a highly favourable treaty with the caliph, involving a substantial annual tribute to be paid to the emperor and an equal division of the tax revenues of Armenia and Iberia (Georgia) as well as of Cyprus.[3] He felt able to embark on a series of campaigns to reclaim lost territory. In 688 a successful expedition under his personal direction restored Roman control over the Balkan territory between Constantinople and Thessalonica.[4] A large number of Slavs were transported from this region into Bithynia, sufficient in number to provide an army of 30,000, which Justinian was able to employ in his recovery of territory in Armenia.

The series of expeditions that Justinian sent, or on occasion led in person, into Armenia in the period between his accession and the Quinisext Council will be treated below (pp. 29–30) as providing a context for the anti-Armenian canons that the council issued. He extended the region under Byzantine control eastwards across the Euphrates. In the same period, and shortly before the Quinisext Council, he moved 'the population' of Cyprus (surely not more than a substantial chunk of it) to a site, now given the name Nea Iustinianupolis, near Kyzikos in Hellespontus.[5] If we add to this the transport of a great number of Slavs into the same region shortly before, it becomes clear that this region had been seriously depopulated by the Arab occupation during the four-year siege of Constantinople in the 670s.

On the religious front Justinian attempted to put an end to continuing discussion of the decrees of the Third Council of Constantinople (680–81), which had defined the theological nicety of two wills in Christ, though without making clear what this was supposed to mean, and, much more contentiously, imposed posthumous anathematization on all four patriarchs of Constantinople between 610 and 666.[6] The unpopularity of this may be judged from the way in which the council dragged on for almost a whole

3 Theophanes, *Chronicle* 363, trans. Mango and Scott, 506. The implication is that these regions would not be under the direct rule of either power but pay tribute to both.

4 Theophanes, *Chronicle* 364 gives the date of 687/8. Many of his dates for this period are one year too early, but this one is shown to be correct by both an inscription – for which see Theophanes, trans. Mango and Scott 508, n. 1 – and also an edict of Justinian II (in Vasiliev 1943 and Grégoire 1944/5), which commemorates his military victory in defence of Thessalonica by transferring a state storehouse of salt to the ownership of the Church of St Demetrios, to come into effect 'in September of the present second indiction': that is, September 688.

5 Theophanes, *Chronicle* 365, trans. Mango and Scott 509. For this settling of the Cypriots in Hellespontus see Canon 39 below (pp. 119–21).

6 The theological poverty of the Definition of Constantinople III arose from its ignoring Maximos the Confessor and his account of will in Christ.

year before Constantine IV managed to dragoon the bishops into doing his will and also from the mediocre attendance – only fifty (of which only 38 were bishops) at the crucial eighth session (at which the monothelete Patriarch Makarios of Antioch was condemned) and still no more than 165 (of whom not all were bishops) at the final eighteenth session; to this we may contrast the 226 (or possibly 227)[7] at the Quinisext Council and the 307 at the Second Council of Nicaea a century later. Justinian's determination to put this chapter behind him is recorded in his *keleusis* (instruction) – a letter to Pope John V of 687, giving an account of a meeting in Constantinople to which he summoned the patriarchs and bishops in the city, the senate, representatives of the people and the chief military commanders for a reading of the Acts (doubtless not in full!) of the council of 680–81, and for the handing in of all copies of the Acts in private hands.[8] His aim, we may deduce, was to confirm the work of this council, but still more to exclude any further debate relating to it. Instead he proceeded five years later to a new council, the one later called the 'Quinisext'. This council claimed to be ecumenical, but stopped short of calling itself the 'seventh council'. It had a very different and far more constructive agenda than its predecessor, namely the issuing of just over one hundred disciplinary canons relating to behaviour and religious practice, far more numerous that those of any previous ecumenical council.

Why another church council? Justinian chose to stress the Christian foundation of his rule.[9] According to Theophanes, he named the army he raised from among the Slavs transported to Anatolia 'the chosen people'.[10] The most striking display of this was in his coinage. For the first time in Byzantine coinage, he introduced the figure of Christ onto the obverse of the gold coins he issued, with himself appearing on the reverse.[11] This

---

7 The numbers in the list that are provided in the ACO edition amount to 226 names. But it is possible, even likely, that a name has dropped out and that the true total is 227. See p. 180, n. 319 below.

8 In ACO² II.2, 886–7. John V had in fact died six months earlier. See Ohme (2009) 24 with n. 124 for a council synopsis which says that Justinian also summoned a synod of 130 bishops to confirm Constantinople III.

9 Note his savage persecution of the Paulicians, for which see Petrus Siculus, *Historia Manichaeorum*, PG 104, 1281–4.

10 Theophanes 366, trans. Mango and Scott 511. These Slavs were presumably new in the faith. Justinian was unwise to trust them: when sent to Armenia, most of them deserted to the Arabs (Theophanes, ibid.).

11 Haldon (1994) 106 dates this to around 690/1.

implied that he saw himself as Christ's representative on earth and as the divinely protected agent of Christ's kingship.[12]

This is the setting in which we need to examine the convening of the council, which was carried out, as in the case of all councils claiming to be ecumenical, by the emperor himself.[13]

The Purpose of the Quinisext Council[14]

The only direct evidence for Justinian II's purpose in convening the Quinisext Council of 691/2 is the *logos prosphonetikos* or address by the bishops to the emperor (pp. 71–74 below) which was delivered at the end of the council but in the conciliar proceedings comes before the canons issued in its name.

This address to the emperor describes the unremitting battle between the agents of God, 'the luminaries and teachers of the church', and the devil. At present, it relates, the people of God are living negligently, and the devil has 'stolen their virtue'. Later in the text special reference is made to 'remnants of pagan or Jewish perversity' that have sullied the church's purity. The remedy adopted by God is described as follows (p. 73 below):

> Christ our God, who steers this greatest of vessels, the whole world, has raised you up as our wise helmsman, pious emperor and true champion … Wisdom has appointed you to be the eye of the world, as with the purity and lustre of your mind you give a clear light to those who are subject to you. To you she has entrusted her church and taught you to ponder her law day and night, so as to equip and edify the peoples under your hand.

This sad state of affairs had been compounded (the text continues) by the fact that the two previous ecumenical councils, Constantinople II (553) and Constantinople III (680–81), 'did not compose sacred canons, as the other four holy ecumenical councils had done, by which the congregations are led to forsake a worse and inferior pattern of life and converted to a better and superior one'. The text continues (p. 73):

12 Note the description, in an edict of Justinian's father Constantine IV confirming the decrees of Constantinople III, of God as his 'co-ruler', ACO² II.2, 854, 11.

13 That the council was called on the emperor's initiative is shown (if any proof is necessary) by the council's *logos prosphonetikos*.

14 Ohme (1992a) provides his own general introduction to the council, lucid and comprehensive.

In consequence the holy nation and royal priesthood for which Christ died has been torn asunder and dragged down by many disorderly passions, torn and sundered little by little from the divine sheepfold. In ignorance and forgetfulness it has fallen away from the feats of virtue, and, to use the apostle's words, spurned the Son of God, treated as common the blood of the covenant by which it had been sanctified, and insulted the grace of the Spirit. But your wish was to gather it together as a people for his possession.

The attribution to the emperor of a primary role in preserving or restoring the proper state of the church had a solid biblical foundation in the role attributed to the kings of Judah, such as Josiah (4 Kgs 22–23), in maintaining and, when necessary, purifying the cult. This found expression as soon as there was a Christian emperor. In 313, almost immediately after his conversion, Constantine the Great wrote to Aelafius the vicar of Africa in the following terms:[15]

I confess to your gravity ... that I think it not at all right that quarrels of this kind be concealed from us, as a result of which the most high Godhead might be moved not merely against the human race but also against me myself, to whose care he had committed the management of all earthly affairs, and in his anger determine otherwise than hitherto. For I shall be able ... to hope in all respects for prosperity and success from God almighty when I perceive that everyone in fraternal harmony worships the most holy God in the catholic religion.

This passage expresses a key belief that, almost four centuries later, may be attributed equally to Justinian II, even if it is not explicitly stated in this address, namely that the prosperity of the empire and its success against its enemies depended on the goodwill of God, and that this goodwill was conditional on the good estate of the church, its orthodoxy and sound order.[16] This meant that the emperor, as the one to whom God had entrusted the 'management of all earthly affairs', even if by the late seventh century the territory under his actual control was hugely reduced, had a responsibility to God and to his subjects to use his power to promote the good estate of the church.[17] The emperor's belief that his victories in

15 CSEL 26. 204–6; trans. Coleman-Norton (1966) I, 55–6.

16 This explanation had the advantage for the state of shifting blame from the emperor himself. That large parts of the population were more inclined to blame the reigning emperor, however, is shown by the frequency of revolt and usurpation, such as the two successful revolts against Justinian II.

17 Ohme (2013) LXXII–III makes the contrasting suggestion that, in view of the loss to

the years immediately preceding the Quinisext Council were due to divine favour finds expression in an extant inscription of 688, where he attributes his victory over the Slavs to the will of God and the intercession of St Demetrius, and recognizes that this obliged him to express his gratitude by beneficence towards the church.[18] The holding of the Quinisext Council expressed both his gratitude and his need to earn yet further divine favour through improving the state of the church. This means that we should not separate the convocation of the Quinisext council from Justinian's modest but successful attempts in the years immediately before the council to recover lost territory, as if they belonged to quite separate spheres of operation. The two were part and parcel of a single policy – to make the empire God's instrument in the world, assured by God of triumph over the devil and his human agents or dupes.[19]

Justinian's sense of his unique responsibility is tellingly expressed in one novel feature of the Quinisext Acts, and that is the placing of his subscription to the canons in the very first place, above the pope, above the patriarchs, above all the bishops. This was a startling novelty; it is particularly striking in view of the fact that his father Constantine IV had placed his signature at the end of the subscriptions to the Definition of Constantinople III.[20] It is not obvious what the explanation is. Ohme sees this novel stress on imperial authority as motivated by a need to compensate for the lack of any papal involvement.[21] It can also be accounted for as expressing a sense that it was really Byzantium not Rome that was the normative centre of the Christian world, even if the pope's personal primacy was not denied. It is also possible, however, that the bishops (doubtless through the patriarch of Constantinople) themselves took the initiative in inviting the emperor to sign first, as happened at the Council of Constantinople of 869–70.[22] At that council the emperor (Basil I) declined; here at the Quinisext Council Justinian obliged. The reason

---

the empire of so many provinces and dioceses to 'barbarians', it was no longer adequate, as hitherto, for most matters of church law to be settled in imperial edicts. But the oriental patriarchs still viewed the emperor as their liege sovereign, even if his political authority had been usurped by invaders; indeed, the position of the imperial signature at the head of the subscription list expressed this.

18 The text is in Vasiliev (1943) 5–7.

19 See below (pp. 71–6) the council's *logos prosphonetikos* with my commentary.

20 ACO² II.2, 796, 26–8.

21 Ohme (2013) LXXIV.

22 Acts of Constantinople IV, ed. Leonardi, 354, 1215–19.

for this may have been his character rather than an intention to make a particular point.[23]

It would be a mistake to reduce this concern for godly good order to a calculation that this would contribute to the stability of society and the unity of the empire in worldly terms. If the latter had been Justinian's aim, he would surely have been concerned to weld all parts of the empire to his own person through judicious toleration. When in his *keleusis* to Pope John V he addressed him as 'ecumenical pope' with an implicit downplaying of the claim by the patriarch of Constantinople to be 'ecumenical patriarch', he was showing diplomatic finesse. But when under his direction the Quinisext council directly attacked certain Roman practices (see p. 37 below), he showed that his priority was correct Christian practice rather than winning favour in Rome. Likewise, when in the midst of his attempts to secure Roman control of Armenia, he either initiated or at least adopted at this same council a condemnation of a range of practices in the Armenian church, he showed that it was God rather than men whose support he valued.

In his campaigns to recover lost territory, in his summoning of an ecumenical council, in his lavish building programme, in founding a city with his name (Nea Iustinianupolis), even in the small detail that the Khazar wife he took during his exile was renamed Theodora, we may see him as consciously imitating the one whose name he bore – Justinian I.[24] He would probably have known enough about his great predecessor to be aware that Justinian I's aim in ecclesiastical matters had been not to appease opponents but to advance Byzantine orthodoxy and its universal recognition.[25]

The Date of the Council

The published proceedings of the council, since they do not mention any actual sessions or include any dated documents, fail to provide any direct or precise information as to its date. Fortunately, a date can be deduced from its Canon 3, which refers to '15 January last in the now past fourth indiction and the year 6199' (p. 83 below) – that is, 15 January 691 – and Canon 17,

---

23 For Justinian's vanity consider the position in the subscription list accorded to his new foundation Nea Iustinianupolis, which is placed immediately after the patriarchs and before all the other bishops (p. 178 below).

24 See PmbZ 1, §7282 for the fact that his wife took the name 'Theodora' only at her marriage and the accompanying baptism.

25 Price (2009) I, 19–23.

which refers likewise to 'the month of January in the fourth indiction now past' (p. 99). This implies a date for the council in the following indiction year. Here, unfortunately, there is an ambiguity in that the standard Byzantine indiction year ran from 1 September until 31 August, but at the end of the seventh century use was also made of an alternative system in which the indiction year ran from 21 March until 20 March.[26]

What time of year was preferred for a church council? Quinisext Canon 8 lays down an annual synod in each province to be held 'between the holy feast of Easter and the end of the month of October'. In practice, there was a preference for the Easter season or the autumn. We may note that the Council of Chalcedon sat in October, Constantinople II (553) in May, Constantinople III (680–81) opened in November, while Nicaea II (787) sat in late September and early October. Plausible dates for the Quinisext Council would therefore be October 691 or a few weeks after Easter 692, which fell on 14 April.[27]

Attendance at the Council

In its *logos prosphoretikos* (address) to the emperor, the council lays direct claim to the status of an ecumenical council, as it does also in its Canons 3 and 51. It certainly satisfied the two most important criteria for such a council: it had been summoned by the emperor, and it took care to be faithful to the tradition.[28] There was, however, a further criterion for ecumenicity that was not an absolute *sine qua non* (the Council of Hiereia of 754 happily dispensed with it) but was certainly helpful to appeal to, which was representation at the council in question of all the members of the pentarchy (Rome, Constantinople, Alexandria, Antioch, Jerusalem), principally through the presence of their heads (at least through their legates) and partly through attendance by bishops under their jurisdiction. It can be presumed that Justinian sent a summons to the council to the pope, inviting him (according to convention) to come in person or (more

26 Peri (1995) 18–20 and Ohme (2006a) 186, n. 89.

27 Esbroeck (1995/6) 104–5 (and also Esbroeck 1992, 92) draws attention, however, to the entry in various synaxaria for 15 July that runs, '[The commemoration] of our emperor of pious memory Justinian the Younger in [the Church of] the Holy Apostles', and argues that the only thing that Justinian ever did that could have earned him this commemoration was the holding of the Quinisext Council. But the location of this commemoration and the midsummer date make this an implausible reference to the council.

28 See Price (2018) I, 49–51 for the primacy of these two criteria.

realistically) at least to send legates. He will have written in the same vein to the metropolitans in Italy (the bishops of Ravenna and Calaris) and in Illyricum, which was under Roman jurisdiction. In the event, none of these came to the council – save the metropolitan of Crete – and the pope sent no legates.

Attendance at the Quinisext Council, despite the absence of any attendance list, is revealed in full by the list (issued by the council) of episcopal subscriptions to the canons it decreed. This list contains 226 (or 227) names. Pre-eminent among these were four members of the pentarchy – the patriarchs of Constantinople, Alexandria, Antioch and Jerusalem – the absence of papal representatives, however, being glaring. Of the other bishops, 187 were from the patriarchate of Constantinople, 24 from the patriarchate of Antioch, 1 from that of Jerusalem, and 10 from East Illyricum (the Balkans south of the Danube, minus the north-west and Thrace), formally under the jurisdiction of the Roman see.

The excellent attendance from the patriarchate of Constantinople is not, of course, surprising. It is, however, to be noted that it was significantly higher than that at Constantinople III (680–81), with its unpopular agenda of adopting dyotheletism (the doctrine of two wills in Christ) and an attendant humiliation of the patriarch of Constantinople (who was not, initially, in its favour) and anathematization of four previous patriarchs of Constantinople.[29]

The figure of 24 bishops, plus George their patriarch, from the patriarchate of Antioch is deceptive, since all 24 were from the north-western, Anatolian provinces of Isauria and Cilicia. As for George, he had attended Constantinople III as a presbyter representing the patriarchate of Jerusalem. His transfer to Antioch as its patriarch can only have arisen as an appointment made in Constantinople, like that of his predecessor Theophanes.[30] The fact that the suffragans who accompanied him at the Quinisext Council were all from the north-west corner of his patriarchate, still under Byzantine control, reveals the limits of his authority in Arab-held areas.

What of the patriarchs Peter of Alexandria and Anastasios of Jerusalem, also included in the Quinisext subscription list? The same questions

---

29 See Price (2018/19) 129–34.

30 See PmbZ 1, §1990 for George and §8082 for Theophanes. That George *apokrisiarios* of Jerusalem and George patriarch of Antioch were one and the same person is stated in the Acts of Constantinople III, ACO² II.2, 830, 13–16 (necessarily an addition to the original text).

arise: who appointed them, and where did they reside? It is possible that the peace treaty between Justinian II and the caliphate at the start of his reign (see pp. 1–2 above), or the earlier accord after the defeat of the Arab siege of Constantinople (674–8), enabled the holding of canonical elections in these two sees; but this is only a possibility. The fact that in the final sessions of Constantinople III (in September 681) those in charge of the sees of Alexandria and Jerusalem were still only 'caretakers' shows that no patriarchs had, at least by this date, been elected or appointed. Patriarchs there were by the time of the Quinisext Council, and probably by 687, when 'the most holy and blessed patriarchs' who attended a major meeting of officials of church and state presided over by Justinian II may well have included those of Alexandria and Jerusalem. The emperor's *keleusis* which describes this meeting says that it was also attended by 'the God-beloved metropolitans and bishops residing here in the imperial city'.[31] This suggests that the patriarchs who attended were also resident in Constantinople. That those of Alexandria and Antioch travelled backwards and forwards between their sees and Constantinople is in any case unlikely; and, if resident in Constantinople, they are likely to have been appointed there. As regards Anastasios of Jerusalem, the contrast between his listing in the extant Quinisext Acts and the lack of mention of him in the precise description of these same Acts in the *Liber Pontificalis* makes it possible that he arrived late and signed the Acts only after the original edition of the proceedings had been sent to Rome;[32] but this would not prove that he travelled from Jerusalem. The fact that George of Antioch, as argued above, appears to have been appointed in Constantinople and to have had to stay there makes it unlikely that the patriarchs of Alexandria and Jerusalem were more fortunate. As for the one other bishop from Palestine in the Quinisext subscription list, Mamas of Tiberias, the most natural explanation for his presence is that he was a refugee.

This is not to dismiss these oriental patriarchs as bogus. They need not have been as spurious as the representatives of the oriental patriarchates at Nicaea II (787)[33] and at the pro- and anti-Photian Constantinopolitan councils of the 860s, at least according to their opponents. The problem was that, while ecumenical councils required representatives of the oriental patriarchates, it was difficult for these patriarchates under Arab rule to

---

31 ACO² II.2, 886, 18–20.
32 Ohme (2009) 14–15 or (2010a) 69. For the passage in the *LP* see pp. 35–6 below.
33 See Price (2018) I, 198–202.

hold elections *in situ*.[34] We should ask too whether patriarchs or bishops from far-away Palestine and Egypt would have chosen to make the long journey to Constantinople. In all, though we must admit our ignorance, the more likely answer is that these patriarchs were resident in or near Constantinople and had been appointed by the emperor himself.

Even so, this is not to say that they were merely honorary patriarchs *in partibus infidelium*, without contact with their titular sees. If they were appointed by the emperor, it was because proper elections could not be held; and in this situation their patriarchates, which continued to regard the Byzantine emperor as their liege lord, need not have regarded them as bogus or supposititious. The fact that the patriarchates of Alexandria and Jerusalem were represented at Constantinople III one by a 'caretaker' and the other by the representative of a caretaker shows that they were not mere appointments in Constantinople and resident there, or they would have been given the title of patriarch.

To what extent were the patriarchs appointed and resident in Constantinople known and recognized in their patriarchates? Evidence is lacking, but there is the odd pointer to contact between some at least of these patriarchs in exile and their sees. The strong and informed monothelete reaction in Syria to the condemnation of monotheletism at Constantinople III suggests that Patriarch Makarios of Antioch, the spokesman of the monotheletes at the council, who certainly resided in or near Constantinople and was almost certainly appointed there, was in contact with his church in Syria and able to inform them of the fortunes of their party in the imperial capital.[35] There is other scattered evidence of contact in this period between Constantinople and the oriental patriarchates.[36] Moreover, there is no reason to suppose that the patriarchs in Constantinople despaired of ever returning to the Orient to take charge of their sees: after the stemming of the Arab advance with the failure of the siege of Constantinople in the 670s a recovery of the lost Byzantine provinces in the Near East became an object of aspiration.[37]

---

34 The *Life* of Andrew of Crete says that he was enrolled in the clergy of Jerusalem by 'Theodore the patriarch of the places there'. This will be the Theodore who is described as 'caretaker' of the see of Jerusalem in the Acts of Constantinople III. That he is called 'patriarch' in this *Life* is not evidence that he himself laid claim to this dignity. See PmbZ 1, §362 (Andrew) and §7316 (Theodore).

35 As remarked by Brock (1984) 71. See also Brock (1992).

36 Read, though with caution, Trombley (1983).

37 This found expression in the *Apocalypse* of Ps.-Methodius, dating to *c.* 691: that is, in precisely this period. See Humphreys (2015), 43–4.

In contrast, the absence of Roman representation at the council was glaring. A fig leaf that attempted to disguise this fact was the high position given in the list of subscriptions to that by the bishop of Gortyna, the metropolis of Crete, who describes himself as 'the representative of the whole synod of the church of Rome', a position he had indeed held (together with four others) at the final two sessions of Constantinople III.[38] At Constantinople III the 'representatives of the Roman synod' were envoys from a synod held in Rome shortly before, and took with them to Constantinople a decree issued by the synod. Of course the phrase 'representative of the whole synod of Rome' could equally mean simply the representative of the college or fellowship of bishops under direct papal jurisdiction and need not refer specifically to an actual 'synod' in our sense of the word; but manifestly the claim that Basil was still, as at Constantinople III, the representative of all the bishops under Rome was clutching at a straw.

The hope of obtaining more substantial western endorsement of the council is shown by the inclusion in the conciliar subscription list of both the see of Rome and of other major sees either Italian or in East Illyricum (which was subject to Roman jurisdiction), namely Sardinia (Caralis), Ravenna, Thessalonica and Corinth. It is simply the names of these sees that are given. Where the actual names of the pope and these bishops would have been if they or their representatives had attended the council, spaces were left – presumably in the hope that their signatures would be obtained after the council, to express their acceptance and confirmation of its decrees. These spaces were never filled.[39]

If these subscriptions by Rome and major sees in what we may call the Roman patriarchate were sought after the council, it may be presumed that the bishops of these sees had been invited to attend, as in the case of the earlier ecumenical councils.[40] We have no information as to why the pope chose not to send legates, or why the metropolitans under him in Italy and Illyricum, though invited, chose not to attend.[41] It was in any case not

38 ACO² II.2, 706, 731, 754, 780.

39 See pp. 195–7 for further discussion of this peculiarity, unique in conciliar acts.

40 That the pope was not invited has been suggested or presumed, but against this see Ohme (1990) 373–6 or (in English) Ohme (1995b) 39–40. The notion that the council was anti-Roman from its original conception is simply a mirror image of later Catholic criticism of this council.

41 Ohme (1995b) 40 surmises that the pope may have learnt from his apocrisiarius in Constantinople about the coming work of the council and thought it best to keep his distance.

to be expected that bishops in Italy would make the long and at this date dangerous journey to attend an eastern council that was not addressing a major doctrinal issue.[42] The absence of the bishop of Thessalonica is hard to account for, especially since Justinian II had recovered the coastline between Thessalonica and Constantinople only a few years previously, in 688, when he conferred a special endowment on the Church of St Demetrius, which is commemorated in an extant inscription that links the names of the emperor and of the city's archbishop, Peter.[43] The absence of the bishop of Corinth may have arisen from his timidity at the thought of the potential danger of a crossing of the Aegean in insecure times; or he may simply have felt that he had more immediate problems to attend to at home than those addressed at the council.[44]

Nevertheless, a number of bishops from East Illyricum chose to attend – ten in all, including the bishop of Gortyna. This rather poor attendance is not to be attributed to discouragement from Rome, since this region, although under nominal papal sovereignty, had in practice and for a long time been more beholden to Constantinople.[45] The real reason will have been the parlous condition of a region that had largely slipped from Byzantine control. Of the ten bishops from this region, five were from the islands of Crete and Lemnos, one from the coast of Epirus, three from near Thessalonica, and only one from an inland region, namely Stoboi, and this bishop cannot have been resident in his diocese, which had ceased to exist.[46]

Papal legates, if sent, might have been coerced into agreeing to canons unacceptable, or at least irrelevant, to the West.

42 Ravenna's aspiration to autocephaly and escape from Roman jurisdiction, together with Constantinople's varying attitude towards this, may also have contributed in some way (Ohme 2009, 62), but the evidence is lacking.

43 Vasiliev (1943).

44 For debate over the state of Corinth at this time see Ohme (1990) 231–3.

45 Already at Chalcedon the bishops from East Illyricum joined the Palestinians in interrupting the reading of Pope Leo's Tome, while the other bishops present remained silent (ACO II.1 [277–8] §24, trans. Price and Gaddis, II, 25). Note too the presence of Illyrian bishops at Constantinople II, despite the non-attendance of Pope Vigilius, actually in Constantinople at the very same time and therefore impossible to ignore; see Price (2009) II, 294.

46 Ohme (1990) 227–8 points out that Stoboi had been deserted from the end of the sixth century, and that therefore the title of 'bishop of Stoboi' can only have been an honorary one.

The Proceedings of the Council

The documentation of the council is less than that for any other ecumenical council of the fourth to eighth centuries: we have the canons it issued, a subscription list, and a *logos prosphonetikos* addressed to the emperor and containing no information as to how the council had achieved its work. This is not, as has sometimes been presumed, because the text of the conciliar proceedings has been 'lost'. Rather, we may be confident that it was never issued. For the disciplinary canons issued by other ecumenical councils of this period – Chalcedon and Nicaea II – were likewise issued without any publication of attendant proceedings. For the issuing of canons was different in kind from the judicial or quasi-judicial character of the other decrees of these councils, with their trial and condemnation of individuals and the implicit condemnation of categories of heretics in their doctrinal decrees; decrees of this kind required attendant proceedings, as proof that proper procedure had been followed.[47]

The question then arises whether disciplinary canons were even discussed at councils, or simply presented to the assembled bishops for their approval by acclamation and/or individual subscription. After all, a large assembly of bishops was scarcely a practical forum for a scrutiny of numerous canons on disparate points of detail. We then have to ask: who drafted them? The Canons of Chalcedon form a coherent sequence, consistent in style and concerned above all to boost the authority of the patriarch of Constantinople. It may be presumed that they were composed by Patriarch Anatolius of Constantinople, with the assistance, doubtless, of competent members of the patriarchal staff, very possibly before the council had even met, and simply presented to the bishops for formal approval.[48]

Was the same true of the Quinisext Canons? Were they composed in advance of the council by the patriarchate, most probably by patriarchal

---

47   See Chrysos (1983).

48   I suggested in Price and Gaddis (2005) III, 92 that they were issued after the council and in the name of the council, but without any need for actual conciliar approval. But the emperor Marcian, when he asked the council to issue certain draft canons (which were then incorporated in the sequence), referred specifically to the need for conciliar endorsement (Session VI. 16). It is true that the famous Canon 28 on the status of Constantinople *was* debated, both in the final official session and at a previous meeting of bishops under the patriarch's chairmanship: but it was a case of unique importance and contentiousness, and was not presented to the council as one of the series of canons (originally 27 in number) but as a separate decree.

and imperial officials working in collaboration? Did the bishops travel to Constantinople and foregather in the *trullos* of the palace, only to find that what was asked of them was simply that they should give their assent by acclamation and subscription to a collection of canons that had been drawn up in advance? If they had an inkling of this, would they have bothered to make the journey – save those who resided in Constantinople (including, probably, all the oriental patriarchs) or were within easy reach of it? We have noted that the council was reasonably well attended, and its members included bishops from as far east as Armenia and Cilicia. Imperial summons to councils did not in themselves ensure attendance: consider the poor attendance at Constantinople III and the derisory attendance at Constantinople IV (the anti-Photian council of 869–70), whose first session was attended by only fifteen bishops or patriarchal representatives, plus the papal representatives, while in the final subscription list the fifteen had arisen to only 106.[49]

But the comparison is not a fair one. The attendance at the Quinisext council was good – 226 (or 227) patriarchs and bishops – but not outstanding. It fell well short of both Nicaea II, attended by around 340 patriarchal representatives and bishops, and the Council of Constantinople of 879–80, attended by 386.[50] Both Constantinople III and Constantinople IV had distinctly unpopular agenda – in 680–81 the adoption of Roman dyotheletism in preference to the monotheletism long, and still, preferred in the patriarchate of Constantinople, and in 869–70 the condemnation of the widely supported Photios.[51] The very fact that the Quinisext council would have lasted only a few days at the most (one session to approve the canons and perhaps one or two others of a celebratory nature) could have been an attraction for the bishops: who would have wished to attend the whole of Constantinople III, whose sessions were spread out over ten months? Justinian II doubtless attracted bishops to his council by recourse to both carrot and stick, both favours and the threat of his displeasure.

49 Heinz Ohme in correspondence argues against me that the bishops may not have known what awaited them, and that the task was not merely the composition of new canons but a new attempt at codifying canon law and a renewed confirmation of Constantinople III (contained in Canon 1).

50 Hefele–Leclerq (1911) 587 and Dvornik (1948) 194. This figure again excludes the patriarch himself.

51 See Price forthcoming in *AHC*.

The Drafting of the Canons

If the canons were, in all probability, composed before the bishops saw them, who (we may ask) had drawn them up? The canons that were critical of either Rome or Armenia and therefore had relevance for the relations between the empire and key players on the insecure borders of the empire must have been drawn up by the emperor or his staff or at least at their direction: the patriarch of Constantinople would not have taken the initiative in this sensitive area. The general notion of producing a substantial collection of canons, some new, some reaffirming traditional regulations, must also have originated from the emperor, as the one who convened the council. It is conceivable that he had given instructions for the production of precisely 102 canons, made up of the first two, that set out the key sources for doctrine and canon law, and then the round number of 100 canons on particular matters.[52] No earlier church council had produced so substantial a body of legislation.[53] The actual compilation of these canons will presumably have fallen to the patriarch and his staff, not without liaison with state officials.[54] How competently was this carried out?

Any reader of these canons will be struck by how varied they are in length, skill of drafting, and quality of reflection – notably more so than those of the comparable canons of other councils, whether Nicaea, Chalcedon or Nicaea II. Of course the need for detailed argumentation was felt in only a few cases, and where there was simply a reassertion of traditional rules casuistry and originality were not called for. But the variations remain striking. Ioannis Konidaris drew attention to the contrast between Canon 44, which, though on a serious matter (monks guilty of fornication or living with a woman), is exceedingly brief, while Canon 45, on a matter of minimal importance (nuns who arrive for their clothing in luxurious and showy attire), is verbose.[55] Inconsistency in drafting may likewise be illustrated by the contrast between Canon 32, which presents

---

52 Note the artificiality of the division between Canon 14 and Canon 15, which would more naturally have formed a single canon. Were they separated in order to achieve the neat total of 100 for the canons on particular matters?

53 The 'Canons of the Council of Carthage' in Byzantine canonical collections are of almost twice the length, but they were a compilation from various sources.

54 The relation between the patriarchal staff and the imperial administration in the work of church councils and the production of their acts is unclear and needs investigation. It is obscure in this case, since we have no proceedings for the conciliar sessions.

55 Konidaris (1992) 281.

a lengthy and learned discourse on the need at the eucharist to add water in the chalice, and the extreme brevity of Canon 57 on the impropriety of offering milk and honey on the altar, which consists of a mere ten words that do not even form a complete sentence. For an example of sloppy drafting take Canon 78, which wishes to insist (presumably) that everyone must learn the creed, but does so merely by repeating verbatim an old canon laying down that candidates for baptism must be taught the Creed, which had been made obsolete by the general adoption of infant baptism. There are cases, too, where the canons merely cobble together pieces of earlier legislation without providing much-needed clarification. For example, both Canon 87 on marital infidelity and Canon 93 on wives of soldiers who remarry on the supposition (but without proof) that their husbands have died string together various sentences from the canons of Basil of Caesarea without attempting to draw up coherent guidelines.

This point should not be exaggerated. The canons forbidding illicit forms of clerical marriage are well drafted and on a major matter of discipline. The same goes for the canons (discussed below) that explicitly condemn practices of the Roman Church. Indeed, the whole sequence of canons (3–39) on the norms for bishops and clergy is weighty and coherent. But the rest of the canons have an utterly miscellaneous character, jumbling together matters of importance and trivial matters, and omitting many matters of greater moment.[56]

In all, the irregularities in what the canons cover and in the intelligence and clarity with which they deal with the matter in hand point to the lack of an overall plan, and the work of a variety of officials and clerks of very variable ability. One is reminded of the proverb 'Too many cooks spoil the broth'.

56 Contrast the judgement of Humphreys (2015) 64: 'Trullo produced not a jumble of existing canons, but an officially sanctioned selection from an authorized set of sources, designed and organized systematically; that is, Trullo was codifying in a manner highly reminiscent of Justinian I's codification of civil law.'

2. EASTERN CANON LAW AND THE
QUINISEXT COUNCIL[57]

The Quinisext council issued no dogmatic teaching, yet claimed to be ecumenical. To buttress this claim, its very first canon reaffirms the dogmatic teaching of the preceding six ecumenical councils, as a way of creating continuity with them and presenting itself as their heir and successor.

The second of the Quinisext canons gives the first official list of the sets of canons recognized in Byzantine canon law.[58] Place of honour is given to the 85 'Apostolic Canons',[59] on the presumption that they were the earliest conciliar canons, approved (as they claim to be) by the original apostles at 'Council of Jerusalem', which is mentioned in the Acts of the Apostles 15 and is of possible, though far from certain, historicity.[60] These had been taken from Ps.-Clement, *Apostolic Constitutions* VIII. 47, and adopted into the growing Byzantine corpus of canon law in the mid-sixth century, despite the doubts recurrently expressed (as in this canon) over heretical elements in the *Constitutions*, which show them to have originated in an Anomoean, or semi-Arian, context in the 380s. These canons concentrate on the rights and duties of clerics and their pastoral and sacramental responsibilities. Though claiming to be older and more authoritative than all the conciliar canons, they betray knowledge of the canons of several fourth-century councils and seek to reconcile conflicting traditions. The importance of this collection may be instanced from its Canon 74, which lays down that the deposition of a bishop requires a synodical decision after he has received three summonses – a rule that the Councils of Ephesus and Chalcedon scrupulously followed in their respective condemnations of Nestorius and Dioscorus.

After the Apostolic Canons there follows in Quinisext Canon 2 a list of the councils, both ecumenical and local ones, whose canons had been

---

57 This section of the introduction draws on Ohme (2012).

58 For the gradual formation of the corpus of eastern canon law see Wagschal (2015) Chapter 1, 'The Shape of the Law'. A rapid guide is provided by his chronological list of the various collections from the fourth until the end of the ninth centuries on pp. 55–6.

59 Only the first fifty were recognized in the West.

60 The account in the Acts of the Apostles of the apostolic 'Council of Jerusalem' is generally judged basically authentic, although at the same time problematic. Its purpose is to give weight to the specific contents of a supposed decree on the admittance of Gentiles to the church. It claims that this decree was welcomed by St Paul, but since there is no mention of it in the Pauline letters (though the story of the council may have been suggested by Galatians 2) the whole account should be considered dubious.

accepted in the Greek Church. Most of them were already to be found in a collection of conciliar canons with continuous numbering that was used at the Council of Chalcedon (451), namely (to give them in their conventional order) Nicaea (325), Ancyra (314), Neocaesarea (c. 315), Gangra (early 340s), Antioch (c. 330) and Laodicea (between 340 and 380);[61] and apart from these the canons of Constantinople I (381–2) were also cited as author-itative at Chalcedon.[62] To these were added in the mid-sixth century during the long reign of Justinian I canons extracted from decrees of Ephesus (431) and the canons of Chalcedon, and by the end of the sixth century those of Sardica (342), Carthage (419)[63] and Constantinople (394).

The Canons of Nicaea derived a particular authority from their promul-gation at the first ecumenical council and link with the first Christian emperor, Constantine the Great. They lay stress on the role of the province in ecclesiastical administration: new bishops are to be elected by all the bishops of the province (Canon 4), and the bishops of each province should meet together in a synod of the province twice a year, particularly to review excommunications imposed by individual bishops (Canon 5). The foundations of the patriarchal system were laid by the explicit recognition that the bishop of Alexandria enjoyed jurisdiction over the whole of Egypt and Libya, comparable to the authority of Rome in much of Italy (Canon 6). The authority of the local church was further enhanced by a rule forbidding clergy from transferring from one city to another (Canons 15 and 16).

The Canons of Chalcedon, originally 27 in number, form a particularly coherent group, both in style and in their manifest concern to promote the interests of the bishop of Constantinople. They lay down that monks, like clerics, are to be subject to their bishop and not to go round the city stirring up trouble (Canons 4, 8 and 23). Any cleric or monk who conspires against his own bishop is to lose his rank (Canon 18). Bishops and clerics must remain tied to a particular diocese and are not to move from city to

---

61 The Acts of Chalcedon number Canon 4 of Antioch as 83 and Canon 5 of Antioch as 84 (ACO II.1, 459–60), which implies that the first five of these councils were included in the edition with continuous numeration, while Laodicea would have come after them. Later canonical collections abandoned the continuous numbering. It is not preserved in any of the extant manuscripts.

62 At its final session, as the basis for the new canon on the authority of the see of Constantinople, in Price and Gaddis (2005) III, 86–7.

63 This collection, as incorporated subsequently in the canon law of both East and West, included many canons that were added in the sixth century from earlier African decrees. See Ohme (2012) 75.

city – Constantinople, of course, being the main draw (Canons 5–6, 10 and 20). Clerics in contention with other clerics or their own bishop are not to have recourse to the civil courts (Canon 9). Appeals by a bishop or cleric against the metropolitan of the province are to be heard either by the 'exarch' (certainly of Thrace, Asia and Pontus; and possibly of Syria and Egypt)[64] or the bishop of Constantinople (Canons 9 and 17). Separate from these canons in the Acts of Chalcedon is the new canon establishing the primacy of Constantinople in the East and formalizing its authority over the churches of Thrace, Asia and Pontus, but in later Byzantine collections it was added to them as Canon 28.

There follows in this Quinisext Canon 2 a list of canons extracted from the writings of individual church fathers, namely Dionysius of Alexandria, Peter of Alexandria, Gregory the Wonderworker, Athanasius of Alexandria, Basil of Caesarea, Gregory of Nyssa, Gregory Nazianzen, Amphilochius of Iconium, Timothy I of Alexandria, Theophilus of Alexandria, Cyril archbishop of Alexandria, and Gennadius of Constantinople. The acceptance of these texts into the code of canon law was a gradual process which may well have begun before Chalcedon. The list given in the Quinisext canon derives from that in the original edition of the *Syntagma in 14 Titles* of *c.* 580, and is likely to have been almost identical (though the precise content of the *Syntagma* prior to the Quinisext Council is uncertain), since the overwhelming majority of these fathers and their canons receive no mention in the Quinisext Canons themselves.[65] Indeed, of all the fathers listed in its Canon 2 only one is ever cited or echoed in the rest of its canons, namely Basil of Caesarea.[66] This can be explained by Basil's particular standing, and the uniquely substantial character and quality of his canons – spread over three letters addressed to his friend and ally Bishop Amphilochius of Iconium (*epp.* 188, 199, 217) and amounting to 84 canons (supplemented by some canons extracted from other letters of Basil's). Basil drew on many canons that were already circulating, but incorporates his own mature reflection on moral and canonical questions.

---

64 This is dismissed by Ohme (2012) 63, n. 193 as 'improbable', since it would imply that the patriarch of Constantinople had the right to hear appeals from Syria and Egypt, but in view of the deposition of Dioscorus of Alexandria and the weak position of Maximus of Antioch Anatolius of Constantinople may have intended this possibility to be left open.

65 For the *Syntagma in 14 Titles* see Wagschal (2015) 39–40.

66 Ohme (2012) 86 mentions that the only patristic texts in the collection of canons in the *Synagoga* of John Scholastikios (patriarch of Constantinople 565–77) were 68 canons of St Basil.

He covers not only rules to be followed, but also the forms and stages of penance appropriate for particular sins.

On what topics did the Quinisext Canons draw on Basil? The repeated specification that clerics are to be deposed for grave offences but not excommunicated as well, on the grounds that a single offence should not receive two penalties, had been stated and justified in Basil's Canon 3. Quinisext Canons 3 and 26 cite his Canon 27 on the penalty for a priest who had entered into an unlawful marriage. Canon 40 cites his Canon 18 on the minimum age for entering religious life, even though it proceeds to modify his ruling. Canon 44 on monks guilty of fornication manifestly echoes his Canon 19, though without explicitly citing it. Canon 54 on prohibited degrees of marriage cites him as the sole authority on the subject (several of his canons treat it). Canon 87 on husbands or wives who desert their spouse and marry another cites several of his canons. Canon 91 cites him on abortion. The final Quinisext canon (Canon 102) quotes his Canon 3 on the need to balance 'strictness' and 'custom', giving greater weight to the latter. What here in Basil relates specifically to a particular offence, namely deacons guilty of fornication, is here elevated into a general principle relating to the choice of penalty in all categories of sin.

The Quinisext legislation is concerned to demonstrate its continuity with older canons. But it felt able to modify their precise rulings, when the basic moral or canonical principle was not threatened. Canon 3 allows those in priestly orders who have married a widow or married after ordination to be restored to active ministry, but only as a one-off concession and not as a general rule. Canon 8 relaxes the older requirement that provincial synods should be held twice yearly, appealing to the special circumstances of disruption arising from barbarian raids. Canon 11 extends the restrictions on contacts between Christians and Jews. Canons 31 and 59 impose a universal rule banning the celebration of the eucharist or baptism in private houses. Canons 53 and 54 extend into new degrees of affinity the prohibition of marriage between those related by marriage or by a spiritual bond.

In addition, a number of the Quinisext Canons lay down rules on topics that had not hitherto been covered in ecclesiastical legislation. Canon 23 impose deposition on those who exacted fees for distributing communion, treating it as a variety of simony. Canon 27 was the first enactment in eastern canon law requiring clergy always to wear clerical dress. Canon 43 rules that past offences should never in themselves exclude an applicant from being received into a monastery, though (as Canon 40 reiterates) they are never to be admitted without scrutiny of their suitability. Canon 46 lays down that nuns should never sleep outside their monastery. Other new enactments, relating specially to the concerns of the seventh century, will be discussed in the following section.

3. THE MESSAGE OF THE CANONS

In the logos *prosphonetikos* addressed by the council fathers to the emperor the council explained its work as necessitated by the failure of the two preceding councils, Constantinople II (553) and Constantinople III (680–81), to issue disciplinary canons. As a basis for its work, the council had to look back to the 28 canons issued by the Council of Chalcedon (451).[67] The great majority of these canons are cited, echoed or expanded in the Quinisext canons.[68] Generally the provisions of the Chalcedonian canons are simply reasserted, but occasionally there are modifications. Quinisext Canon 72 extends the ban decreed in Canon 14 of Chalcedon against marriage to heretics by those in minor orders: it is now made to extend to all laymen. Canon 16 of Chalcedon had forbidden monks to marry, while allowing bishops to grant dispensations, presumably in cases where the entry into religious life had been involuntary; Quinisext Canon 44 treats the 'marriages' of monks as fornication and imposes the corresponding penance. Canon 8 bows to necessity in troubled times by reducing the requirement for provincial synods that had been laid down by Canon 19 of Chalcedon from twice to once a year; in contrast, Quinisext Canon 18 tries to restrict the provisions of Canon 20 of Chalcedon for clergy who fled from dioceses disrupted by enemy raids, doubtless because this had been misused by clergy moving from one see to another out of ambition or avarice rather than necessity.

One notable feature of the Quinisext Canons is the condemnation of ecclesiastical practices alien to those followed in Byzantium. Much attention by canonists and historians has been devoted to the canons openly critical, or implicitly critical or allegedly critical, towards practices of the Roman Church. This we deal with below, in the context of the Roman reaction to the Quinisext Council.[69] May it suffice in the present context to

---

67 COGD 1, 138–51, trans. Price and Gaddis (2005) III, 92–103 and (Canon 28) 75–6.

68 Herrin (2009) 165–6 provides a list of the Canons of Chalcedon, indicating which Quinisext canon or canons relate to each.

69 See pp. 37–9 below.

say that our conclusion, following Ohme, is that it is only the two canons that explicitly mention Roman practices in order to criticize them that can fairly be read as intentionally directed against Rome – Canon 13, which rejects the Roman rule imposing clerical continence, and Canon 55, which condemns the Roman practice of fasting on Saturdays. Other canons which clash with Roman ideas, such as Canon 36 on Constantinople's primacy in the East and Canon 82 banning the representation of Christ as a lamb, are evidence, certainly, of Constantinople's concern to publicize its own status and promote what it considered proper practice, but not of conscious opposition to Rome.

Indicative of an actual tolerance towards distinctively Roman practices is Quinisext Canon 30, which accepts the Roman rule of clerical continence in the case of 'barbarian lands', probably meaning Slavic parts of the Balkans under western influence, albeit with the derogatory comment, 'We have conceded this to them on no other ground than their timorousness of mind and their bizarre and irresolute behaviour.' Even in the rare cases where the council attacks Roman practices, it can scarcely have expected Rome to submit meekly and adopt those of Byzantium.

The canons which condemn Armenian practices are also dealt with below.[70] Justinian II was keen to achieve Byzantine control of more of Armenia, and the church under his leadership wished to extend this to the curtailing of traditional Armenian practices that genuinely shocked Byzantine susceptibilities, such as not mixing water in the chalice and a hereditary priesthood. This stopped short, however, of an attempt to impose a full range of Byzantine practices. For instance, the Armenians were not commanded to adopt the Byzantine (and western) celebration of Christ's nativity on 25 December.

Historians have also pointed to the continuation within Byzantine territory of local languages and traditions, largely traditional, but increased by the influx of Slavs not only in the Balkans but also in Hellespontus, into which Justinian II transferred a significant Slavic population – sufficient to produce an army of 30,000 men and therefore likely to have numbered around 150,000.[71] Did Byzantine cult and culture feel under threat? It would be more in accord with beliefs at the time to lay the emphasis on fear of divine displeasure, whence the ban imposed by the Quinisext Canons

---

70 See pp. 31–2.
71 For ethnic diversity in Anatolia see Charanis (1959) 25–6. For the Slavs see Theophanes 366, trans. Mango and Scott 511.

(and discussed below) on various supposedly pagan customs. But none of this amounts to convincing evidence of a mounting Byzantine intolerance of diversity *in se*.

The conclusion is invited that the Quinisext legislation was not primarily motivated by a desire for centralization or standardization, or by a conscious attempt to make Byzantine practice the norm for the whole Christian world. Rather, its prime concern was to condemn practices that seemed aberrant – a natural aim of any council concerned to correct abuses. It is true, of course, that if propriety is defined too strictly a demand for it will have consequences similar to those of a demand for uniformity.[72] But the demand for propriety remains distinct from an attempt to impose uniformity of practice, both in the extent of the demands made and most certainly in its motivation.

Much of the Quinisext legislation was simply the reaffirmation of traditional norms. The elements of innovation in content or emphasis may be set out under the headings of clerical morals, the marriages of laymen, and the suppression of pagan or semi-pagan practices.[73]

The traditional ban on simony was reasserted, just as it was at most councils, including Chalcedon (Canon 2) and Nicaea II (Canons 5 and 19). The problem was much exacerbated by the simultaneous approval of gifts made on ordination though not in payment for ordination, as if the two were easy to distinguish.[74] Novel, however, was Quinisext Canon 23 against the clergy demanding payment for giving communion. A number of canons deal with clerical marriage. Canons 3, 6 and 26 reimpose the ban on the ordination of those who have married a second time, or married a widow or a woman with an infamous past, and on the continuance in major orders of those who marry after ordination. In dealing with past cases Canon 3 modifies the strictness of the legislation, allowing such clergy to be reinstated in office after a period of penance, on condition they had already repented and ended their illicit union by a deadline in January 691.[75] The need for these canons on clerical marriage points to slippage

---

72 Take Quinisext Canons 55–6, which attach a surely excessive value to uniformity of practice as regards the Lenten fast.

73 See also the admirable treatment of the distinctive concerns and emphases of the Quinisext Canons in Humphreys (2015) 62–73.

74 See Canons 5 and 19 of Nicaea II with the annotation in Price (2018) II, 613–14 and 621–22.

75 See too Canons 4 and 5 on sexual misconduct by members of the clergy.

in the observation of the traditional rules in the anarchic conditions of the seventh century.[76]

The canons show a new degree of concern over clerical lifestyle and over maintaining a proper distinction between clerical and lay roles. Several canons in this domain made novel demands. Canon 27 requires clergy always to wear clerical dress. Canon 24 forbids them from going to the theatre or hippodrome. Meanwhile, a number of canons insist on proper behaviour by the laity in church. Canon 64 forbids laymen from lecturing or preaching in church, while Canon 69 insists that they are never to enter the sanctuary; nor, according to Canon 58, are they to give themselves communion when a priest or deacon is present. Canon 101 forbids them from showing off their status by producing gold or silver vessels on which, rather than in their hands, to receive holy communion. Canon 66 insists that the laity must devote Easter week to the pious frequentation of churches, and not to secular amusements. Canon 80 requires them to attend Sunday worship never less than once every three weeks. According to Canon 90 they are to express their awareness of the full significance of Sunday worship as a celebration of the Resurrection by never kneeling (in church) on a Sunday.

As for reverence for church buildings, several canons insist that laymen are not to profane sacred space by using it as if it were their own home (Canons 74, 76, 88, 97). We should note, however, that this is not pushed too far: Canon 88 says that when a traveller has no option but to lodge in a church and it would endanger the animal's life and perhaps in consequence even his own if he left his beast of burden outside, he may bring the animal into the church, since 'the sabbath was made for man, not man for the sabbath'.

It is not surprising that concern over the marriages of the clergy extended to fresh legislation on the marriages of the laity, which shows particular concern over marital impediments (Canons 53–54, 72, 87, 92–93, 98). A few of the canons constitute an unexpected intrusion by church legislation into the lifestyle of the laity: Canon 96 forbids men from having elaborate hairdos, while Canon 71 forbids those studying civil law from going to the theatres or wearing unusual dress.

These restrictions on the laity, with a particular stress on reverent behaviour in church, involved both sexes; few of the Quinisext canons are gender-specific. Yet the charge has been made that the council was particularly concerned to impose restrictions on women.[77] This depends

---

76 Contrast the silence about these offences in the canons of Nicaea II.
77 As in Herrin (2013).

on a particular reading of Canon 70, which forbids women from 'talking' (or 'speaking') in church. This has sometimes been taken as prohibiting them from taking part in the recital of liturgical texts such as the creed or in making the responses, but this is highly improbable. The citation in the canon of a passage from St Paul about women who wish to 'learn' points to the correctness of Balsamon's interpretation of this canon, as forbidding distraction during the liturgy through audible discussion of the Scripture readings (see p. 147 below). The implied charge that women were more likely to do this than men reflects a traditional male attitude towards female garrulity; at the same time it opens a welcome window on the assertiveness and lively minds of Byzantine women.

A quantity of canons condemn practices that were viewed as semi-pagan or superstitious.[78] This accords with the mention of a need to suppress 'remnants of pagan perversity' in the *logos prosphonetikos* (p. 74). Canon 50 condemns playing with dice, probably because it was viewed as involving superstitious beliefs about good fortune. Canon 51 condemns both mimes and shows involving hunting or dancing on the stage, presumably because of their pagan associations. Canon 61 condemns soothsaying and the use of amulets of various kinds. Canon 62 attempts to abolish popular feast-days of pre-Christian origin. Canon 65 forbids bonfires on nights of a full moon. Canon 71 forbids traditional customs of pagan origin followed by students of civil law. Canon 94 forbids the use of pagan oaths. In condemning these as 'pagan' survivals the bishops were attending to the original context and purpose of such practices; but in a Christian context and as practised by perfectly ordinary Christians it would be a mistake to regard them as signs of the survival of actual pagan *beliefs*; nor need we suppose that the bishops made the mistake of supposing they were, except, perhaps, in a few small isolated pockets.[79] The presumption was that the population (apart, perhaps, from some doubtfully converted Slavs) was solidly Christian; we hear nothing of campaigns of evangelization.[80]

---

78 See Rochow (1978), who characterizes these practices as 'pagan so-called'.

79 Trombley (1978) 4–5 mentions such a pocket in Maina in the Peloponnese, still pagan until the late ninth century, according to Constantine Porphyrogenitus, *De administrando imperio*, p. 237.

80 Haldon (1990) 332–7 and 350–51. Compare the still prevalent notion that Russian folk religion was a synthesis of Christianity and paganism, the so-called *dvoeverie* or double belief, criticized in Rock (2007). In a Christianized culture survivals from paganism become integrated into Christian belief or simply secularized.

A feature of the Quinisext canons of particular interest for the historian of this phase in Byzantine history is the evidence they provide for disruption to church life, and indeed life generally, as a result of the barbarian invasion or raids and resultant urban collapse that historians recognize as key features of the seventh century.[81] Canon 35 insists that on the death of a bishop the property of the diocese is be looked after by his clergy and not purloined by the metropolitan, except if 'no clerics are left' – that is, if the diocese had been virtually abandoned. Canon 37 insists on the full diocesan rights of a bishop even if, because of barbarian inroads, he is unable to reside in his see. Canon 39 treats the special case of the metropolitan of Cyprus, and a significant part of his flock, who had now been moved to a new home in the province of Hellespontus. Canon 49 treats monastic property misappropriated by laymen, most probably through the monks having taken to flight. Canon 93 treats the case of a wife who remarries on the disappearance of her husband, presumed to be dead, only to discover subsequently that her first husband is still alive (as in Tennyson's *Enoch Arden*).

I have left to the end the most famous of all the Quinisext Canons and the one most cited in the controversy that was to convulse the empire in the following century and a half – the celebrated Canon 82, which lays down that Christ is to be represented not in the form of a lamb ('Behold the lamb of God', John 1:36) but in human form. Justinian II and the bishops he convened will not have foreseen the coming iconoclast era; their concern was rather with the impropriety of representing Christ with the figure of the passover lamb of ancient Jewish cult now that with the coming of Christ in the flesh type and symbol have been superseded by fulfilment and reality. This canon was to become the single most cited text for justifying images of the humanity of Christ (his Godhead being incapable of representation) during the controversy that erupted a generation later.

The stress in this canon on representing Christ 'in truth' drew attention to the question, that had been simmering for two centuries, as to exactly *how* Christ was to be represented. At this date images of Christ aimed increasingly at offering a portrait. But what had Christ looked like? A standard representation was desirable if images of Christ were to be immediately recognizable. But at the time of the Quinisext Council there was still no agreed answer. This is shown with particular clarity in the gold coinage of Justinian II, the first emperor to place the head of Christ

81 See Liebeschuetz (2001).

on his coins, an innovation that is to be linked with this canon and may well have been exactly contemporary.[82] In his first reign (685–95) Christ was represented in what has since become the standard form – with a beard and long hair flowing down both sides of his face. But in Justinian's second reign (705–11) Christ was depicted with short curly hair, as in a famous passage of Theodore the Lector (writing in c. 500).[83] By the ninth century the former of these two images was dominant, but it is striking that in the *Letter of the Three Patriarchs*, dating to the second half of the ninth century, it is to the coins of Justinian's second reign that the detailed account that is given of Christ's appearance corresponds.[84]

If these are the details of the Quinisext legislation, what was its overall purpose? Manifest in both its rules relating to the clergy and those relating to the laity is the concern for purity – purity before God and above all in the performance of the Christian cult. We are reminded of the letter of Constantine the Great cited above, which states as his prime desire that 'everyone in fraternal harmony should worship the most holy God in the catholic religion' (p. 5 above). The priority accorded to worship is notable. That the lives of Christians should reflect their faith is naturally insisted upon in the Quinisext canons, but the central focus is on the proper worship of God, and the need this imposes for a spotless priesthood and for a people who play a full and orderly role in worship, uncontaminated by survivals, however unconscious, of the pagan origins of the Greco-Roman world.

In the light of this, the question of the authorship of the canons may be reconsidered. Where the production of canons was but a secondary element in the work of a council, as at Chalcedon and later at Nicaea II and Constantinople IV, the presumption is that they had been compiled before the bishops were consulted: the only practical procedure was for officials of church and state to draw up canons according to directives from the emperor and the patriarch of Constantinople; the role of the bishops would then consist of no more than giving their approval by acclamation and subscription. In case of the Quinisext Council we might prefer to suppose that the bishops played a less passive role (though see pp. 14–15 above).[85] But

---

82 Spieser (2015) 451, n. 139.

83 Theodore the Lector, *HE*, ed. Hansen, 108, 1–2. See Spieser (2015) 421–60, with figs 117 and 129 for the two contrasting images on the coins of Justinian II.

84 *Letter* 7.d, p. 31, 11–20, in Munitiz's edition.

85 Compare the Council of Lateran IV (1215), which issued the most important collection of medieval western canons. The council had only three sessions; there cannot have been

once we appreciate that the canons, as a body, have a distinctive emphasis and purpose, this can only have come from the emperor who convened the council. The actual task of creating and wording a long sequence of canons will, of course, have fallen to his agents and officials in collaboration with the staff of the patriarchate. We noted above (pp. 16–17) that this task was performed with striking variations in competence. But the overall result has coherence, and reflects the aims of the emperor as they are expressed in the *logos prosphonetikos* that is placed in the Acts before all the canons. This address locates the work of the council in the broad context of the needs of the people of God under the direction of the emperor to whom God had entrusted the well-being of both church and empire.

4. JUSTINIAN II AND ARMENIA

The first Arab raid into Armenia was in 640, and for the rest of the century this land was contested between Byzantium and the Arabs.[86] We first hear of a new Byzantine military province, the Armeniakon theme, in 666/7, under which the chronicler Theophanes mentions an attempted revolt against Constans II by its *strategos* Saborios.[87] This theme lay in eastern Anatolia and Armenia west and north of the Euphrates.[88] It was in this region that resided the nine Armenian bishops who attended the Third Council of Constantinople (680–81).[89] For the beginning of the reign of Justinian II Theophanes provides the following information relevant for the history of Armenia:

(p. 363)[90] In his first year (September 685 to September 686) Justinian made an advantageous treaty with Abimelech (this is the caliph 'Abd

scope for the bishops and religious who attended to discuss the canons that were presented to them for their approval.

86 For a survey of Armenian history in this period, and the problems facing the historian, see Greenwood (2008).

87 Theophanes Confessor, *Chronicle* 348–9, trans. Mango and Scott 488.

88 Note the presence at Constantinople III of the bishop of Melitene, the metropolis of Armenia I and near the Euphrates (ACO² II.2, 756, 8). This suggests Byzantine control of the whole of the province at this particular date, after the confused and unsettled situation in the third quarter of the seventh century.

89 The Armenian church, in schism from Constantinople since the Second Council of Dvin (554/5), had returned to communion with the Chalcedonian church in 632.

90 These page numbers are those of de Boor's edition (1883), given in the margins of the Mango–Scott translation.

el-Malik), involving a substantial regular tribute to be paid to the emperor and an equal division of the tax revenues of Armenia and Iberia. This suggests a division of Greater Armenia, east of the Euphrates, into a sphere under Roman sovereignty (doubtless short of real control) and an Arab one.

(p. 363) Later under the same year (although the chronology is unreliable) Theophanes writes: 'Justinian sent the *strategos* Leontios with a Roman army to Armenia. He slew the Saracens that were there and subjugated Armenia to the Romans – likewise Iberia, Albania, Bukania and Media – and, after imposing taxes on those countries, sent a great sum of money to the emperor.'

This would have constituted a breach of the treaty, but Theophanes himself records under 691/2 that this breach occurred later, as I discuss below. The error must consist in the presumption that a campaign in Armenia must have been against the Saracens (Arabs). This can be corrected through recourse to information provided by the *History* of Step'anos Tarōnec'i, composed in *c.* 1000, where we read of Justinian in his third year (687/8) sending an army to drive the Khazars out of Armenia, while at the same time the Arabs invaded the south-east of the country and routed an Armenian army. For Justinian's fourth year this work records an expedition led by Justinian II in person, who set up new princes in Armenia and Albania and took back to Constantinople some of the princes or their sons as hostages, leaving an army of 30,000 in support of the princes he had appointed. This same source adds that the emperor also took back to Constantinople, and 'under arrest', the catholicos Sahak III with five of his bishops.[91]

This journey of Sahak with other bishops to Constantinople is confirmed in what are the very last pages (apart from a rhetorical flourish) of an Armenian chronicle, uniquely pro-Chalcedonian, that survives only in a Greek translation, the *Narratio de rebus Armeniae*, composed soon, perhaps immediately, after the events it records.[92]

> [144] In his [Justinian II's] fifth year [689/690] he summoned the catholicos Isaac [Sahak III] with the bishops to Constantinople, and united them to those who profess two natures in our Lord and God, Godhead and manhood, without fusion or separation in one hypostasis, and they swore in writing no longer to speak against this. [145] When they returned, those left in Armenia took offence at their leadership because they had come to a common mind with

91 Step'anos Tarōnec'i, *Universal History*, trans. Greenwood, 166.
92 Garitte (1952) 398 dates the work to 'around 700', but Esbroeck (1992) 84 argues from the lack of any mention of the Quinisext Council that it must have been written before it.

the Romans, [146] and they now engaged in argument and contention with Isaac and those who had accompanied him, saying, 'If you do not turn and anathematize them, we shall not accept you into our land.' [147] But they, loving glory from men rather than glory from God, again anathematized first themselves, for having come to an agreement with the Romans, and then the Romans as well, and were seen to be incurable in their wickedness.[93]

According to this account, Sahak and his bishops, during their visit to Constantinople, accepted the Chalcedonian Definition with its teaching of two natures in Christ and promised to promote it back in Armenia, but reneged on this promise on their return home. This found expression in a substantial extant discourse by Sahak III, in which he insists that after the incarnation there is only one nature, one will and one operation in Christ, thereby rejecting both Chalcedon and Constantinople III, which Justinian II had confirmed in his *Keleusis* of 687.[94] The context of this discourse, shortly before the Quinisext Council, is most clearly shown in its argument that water should not be mixed with the wine in the eucharist, citing a text of John Chrysostom, as we shall see in a moment.[95]

It is in this context of a renewed Byzantine interest and interference in the affairs of Armenia that we should consider those Quinisext canons that are directed against Armenian practices, sometimes specifying their Armenian character and sometimes not. The following canons condemn practices that are explicitly said to be Armenian:

Canon 32 condemns the practice of not mixing water in the chalice.
Canon 33 condemns the restriction of priesthood to the sons of priests.
Canon 56 condemns the practice of eating dairy products on the
    Saturdays and Sundays of Lent.
Canon 99 condemns the cooking and eating of meat in church.

Two further canons may have had Armenia in mind: Canon 63, which condemns 'false' accounts of martyrs, possibly relating to Monophysite hagiography read in Armenia, and Canon 81, which condemns the Monophysite version of the Trisagion.

Canon 32 is of particular interest, since it is manifestly a response to the argument advanced by Sahak in defence of the Armenian practice of

---

93 *Narratio de rebus Armeniae*, ed. Garitte (1952) 46–7.
94 A full translation of Sahak's *Discourse* is in Esbroeck (1995). See 374–6, §12 for his insistence on one nature and one will in Christ. Justinian's *Keleusis* is in ACO² II.2, 886–7.
95 Trans. in Esbroeck (1995) 434–6, §§87–89.

not mixing water with the wine in the chalice. It argues at length against his citation of a passage of John Chrysostom, pointing out (correctly) that Chrysostom's argument was directed not against mixing water with the wine but against those (the 'Hydroparastatai') who poured only water and no wine into the chalice.

At this point mention should be made of the presence at the Quinisext Council of a number of Armenian bishops, namely the bishops of Arabissos and Kukusos in Armenia I, those of Sebasteia, Koloneia, Nikopolis, Satala and Sebastopolis in Armenia II, and those of Dadima and Kitharizon in Armenia IV.[96] The great majority of these sees lay within the Roman theme of Armeniakon, that is, west (and north) of the Euphrates. The only exceptions are the two sees in Armenia IV, east of the Euphrates; this is the only one of these provinces that lies outside the region represented at Constantinople III (680–81). The presence of bishops from this province thereby reflects an expansion of the area under Byzantine control in the intervening period, doubtless in the campaigns under Justinian II that are recorded by Theophanes and Stepʻanos Tarōnecʻi and which I mentioned above. Even so these bishops remain representative not of the Armenian episcopacy as a whole, but overwhelmingly of those in western Armenia.[97]

Did these Armenian bishops make any contribution to the council beyond meekly adding their signatures to its decrees? The anti-Armenian canons doubtless represent a desire by the central government and the Constantinopolitan patriarchate to restore what they considered to be proper practice and suppress corruptions, as I discussed above (pp. 23–24). But it is also possible that the bishops from western Armenia, under Byzantine control and significantly Hellenized, had a more than passive role at the council, out of a wish on their part to advance an Armenian adoption of Byzantine norms. Did they during the preparations for the council prompt the production of these canons or at least provide the information about Armenian aberrations that these canons display? Finally, we may presume that the intention of Justinian II and the Quinisext Council was that the 'correct' practices it laid down would be adopted throughout Armenia and not only in the region currently under Byzantine control.[98]

---

96 See their listing on p. 193 below.

97 Esbroeck (1992) 81.

98 Esbroeck (1992) 81–4 places the Synod of Theodosiupolis (Karin) and its canons (full text in Esbroeck 1995, 439–45) at this point: that is, as the Armenian response to the Quinisext Council. But more recent scholarship considers them a later forgery. Certainly

For the events that followed, we must turn to the twelfth-century *Chronicle* of Michael the Syrian:[99]

> Justinian emperor of the Romans would not allow Cyprus to be shared by the Romans and the Arabs, and removed the Cypriots in the seventh year of his reign [691/2]. On learning this 'Abd el-Malik [ibn Marwan] reproached him strongly for breaking the treaty and not waiting until the end of its term. This is why Muhammad[100] invaded Roman territory. The Romans opened battle near Kaisareia in Cappadocia. The Slavs[101] took the side of the Arabs and went off with them to Syria, numbering around 7,000.

This offers an account of a serious Byzantine defeat that is also mentioned by Theophanes, who locates it, however, at Sebastopolis.[102] Theophanes here is incoherent, in that he makes the Byzantines initiate the war by advancing on this city, which in fact lay in the extreme north-west corner of Roman Armenia. He lays great stress on Justinian's perfidy in breaking through military action the treaty with the Arabs agreed at the start of his reign. Clearly, however, it was the Arabs who had initiated the war by advancing deep into Roman territory, albeit with the excuse that Justinian had broken the treaty by transporting a large number of Cypriots to Hellespontus.

Under the following year (692/3, p. 366) Theophanes records that Sabbatios, the 'patrician of Armenia', 'on being informed of the defeat of the Romans, delivered Armenia to the Arabs'.[103] However, in 702/3 according to the same source the Armenians rebelled against the Saracens, killed those of them in Armenia, and invited the Romans into their country again.[104] But, as Theophanes continues, Muhammad[105] promptly subjugated Armenia yet again to the Arabs. The tug of war between the Romans

---

the way in which (apart from the issue again of water in the chalice) there is no coincidence between the specific issues they raise and the Quinisext canons points to a quite different context for their origination.

99 Michael the Syrian, *Chronicle* XI. 15, vol. 2, 470.

100 Muhammad ibn Marwan, the brother of 'Abd el-Malik (the caliph).

101 This is the army mentioned by Theophanes 366 of 30,000 men, recruited from the Slavs Justinian had moved to Bithynia (see p. 2 above). It is manifestly the same army which, according to Step'anos Tarōnec'i (see above), had already been stationed in Armenia.

102 Theophanes, *Chronicle* 366, trans. Mango and Scott 511–12.

103 Theophanes 366. The reference must be to Armenia east of the Euphrates (Armenia IV), not to the territory of the Armeniakon theme.

104 Theophanes 372, trans. Mango and Scott, 519 *fin*.

105 This will be Muhammad ibn Marwan again.

and the Arabs over Armenia (beyond the Armeniakon theme) continued unabated.[106] Meanwhile, in church affairs the definitive separation of the Armenian from the Byzantine Church occurred in 726.[107]

5. THE ROMAN REACTION[108]

The Quinisext Council completed its work, we may presume expeditiously, and the bishops then dispersed. The council had been attended and its canons signed by 226 (or 227) bishops, a notably larger number that the previous council of Constantinople III, whose definition had been signed by only 165 bishops.[109] But then the work of Constantinople III, with its posthumous anathematization of four previous patriarchs of Constantinople, had been at least controversial and probably deeply unpopular in the imperial capital. The one glaring omission in the authentication of the new council's work was the absence of papal representation at the council and the consequent absence of Roman endorsement of its decrees, a difficulty that has remained until this day.

In contrast to the iconoclast Council of Hiereia (754), where no Roman representatives attended and no subsequent Roman approbation of the council was sought, Justinian II attempted after the council to obtain papal confirmation retrospectively. This is shown by the listing of the see of Rome, with a blank space for the pope's signature, at the head of the episcopal subscription list (p. 178 below). Justinian is likely to have been thinking of the First Council of Constantinople (381), which no Roman representatives attended and yet was subsequently accepted by Rome as ecumenical. The citation from an address to Theodosius the Great at the final session of Constantinople I that comes at the end of the Quinisext Council's *logos prosphoretikos* (pp. 77–78 below) was perhaps intended as a reminder of this fact.

The story of the Roman reaction to the Quinisext Canon is told in instalments in the *Liber Pontificalis*, beginning in the biography of Pope Sergius I (687–701):[110]

---

106 Greenwood (2008) 346.
107 Esbroeck (1992) 79.
108 For an account of this by Ohme in English see Ohme (1995b) 22–30.
109 For the 227 figure see p. 180, n. 319 below.
110 *LP* 86.6–7, ed. Duchesne, I, 372–3.

In his time the emperor Justinian ordered a council to be held in the imperial city, at which the legates of the apostolic see also convened and were deceived into subscribing. He too was under pressure to subscribe, but he absolutely refused since certain chapters contrary to ecclesiastical observance had been inserted in them [the conciliar proceedings]. As if they were conciliar decrees, they were written on six rolls, with the subscriptions of the three patriarchs, that is of Constantinople, Alexandria and Antioch, and of the other bishops who had convened there in time,[111] confirmed by the emperor's hand. Placed in a despatch-case, he sent them to be confirmed and subscribed at the top by the pontiff Sergius as the head of all the bishops. This blessed pontiff, as has been said, absolutely refused to assent to the emperor Justinian, nor did he allow these rolls to be accepted or opened for reading. Instead he abhorred and rejected them as invalid, preferring to die sooner than consent to erroneous novelties.

This requires annotation, first on four incidental points of detail. Who were 'the legates of the apostolic see' who 'were deceived into subscribing'?[112] At Constantinople III a high position in the subscription list and the dignity of 'legate' of the Roman see was accorded to the bishops of metropolitan status under Roman jurisdiction.[113] In the Quinisext subscription list the metropolitan sees under Rome are likewise placed high up in the subscription list (though now intermingled with the senior metropolitans of the patriarchate of Constantinople). The title 'representative of the whole synod [college or fellowship] of the holy church of Rome' is given only to Bishop Basil of Gortyna, but the *Liber* must also have been thinking of Bishop Sisinnius of Dyrrachion, the only other metropolitan under Rome who attended the council and subscribed. Basil of Gortyna had signed the subscription list of Constantinople III with the same title of representative of the church of Rome, a dignity he had been given in the final two sessions of Constantinople III, but was a piece of fiction a decade later, manifestly included in his subscription to imply Roman acceptance of the canons, even if the pope had not yet formally expressed this.[114] This supposed evidence of Roman approval has been adduced by Orthodox controversialists ever since.

---

111 As Ohme (2010a) 69 notes, *in tempore* has this meaning and not merely 'at the time'. See Lewis and Short, *A Latin Dictionary*, p. 1852: 'in tempore' means 'at the right time' or 'in time'.

112 One may doubt whether any 'deceit' was involved. The very fact that they attended the council, without (manifestly) being sent by Rome, suggests Constantinopolitan sympathies.

113 ACO² II.2, 778–80.

114 See p. 179, §8 below, and Acts of Constantinople III, ACO² II.2, 706, 731, 754, 780. The meaning of 'synod' in the context of the Quinisext Council will simply have been that of episcopal college or fellowship.

Note secondly that the writer of this description of the documents of the Quinisext Council as they were received in Rome must have had them in front of his very eyes, and describes them with precision. His mention of 'six rolls' of conciliar acts is ambiguous: did he mean that the Acts were written on six rolls or that six copies of the Acts had been sent to Rome?[115] The Acts are not a very long text, and could have been fitted onto one long roll, if we compare them to the Acts of Constantinople III, which were accommodated on eight or nine rolls, every one of which could have been longer than the Quinisext Acts. On the other hand, the *Refutation* of the iconoclast *Horos* of 754 (read out at Nicaea II), a text virtually identical in length to the Quinisext Acts, was spread out over six rolls, as we are told explicitly in the conciliar Acts.[116] When Patriarch Tarasios had Quinisext Canon 82 read out at Nicaea II, he stated that both it and the bishops' subscriptions came on the same roll:[117] how else would the signatures confirm the authenticity of the canon? The same consideration will surely have applied in the case of the copy, or rather copies, of the Quinisext Canons that were sent to Rome immediately after the council.[118] Why were six copies called for? Presumably, once the pope had signed them, one copy was to stay in Rome, one to be stored in the imperial archives, and one copy to go to each of the four eastern patriarchates. Six copies surely implies that these were indeed the original rolls, with the original signatures, including the copies destined for the oriental patriarchs, who in all probability were resident in Constantinople or at least not far away.[119]

Note thirdly the absence of Jerusalem from the list of oriental patriarchs present at the council.[120] Ohme, laying emphasis on the statement that the bishops who subscribed had arrived 'on time', suggests that the Patriarch of Jerusalem arrived late – too late to attend the council or sign his name on the copy of its proceedings sent in haste to Rome.[121]

---

115 See Ohme (2010a) 66–8 and (2013) lvii–lviii with n. 221.

116 These indicate where each roll began; see Price (2018) II, pp. 439, 450 and following.

117 ACO² III.2, 344–6, trans. Price (2018) I, 289–90.

118 Ohme's judgement remains, however, that this problem (one copy in six rolls or six copies) must 'remain open' (ACO² II. 4, lviii).

119 See pp. 9–10 above.

120 There is one, but only one, MS of our Acts that likewise omits Anastasios of Jerusalem: Ohme's Codex A. See his edition XVI, LIX (n. 225) and 63. This scarcely constitutes real MS support for the omission of Jerusalem in the original subscription list, for which the *LP* remains our only, but adequate, evidence.

121 Ohme (2009) 14–15 or (2010a) 69. As he observes, this raises the question of whether other signatories may similarly have arrived late.

Fourthly, we are told that Pope Sergius refused to have the rolls of the conciliar acts 'opened for reading'. This must have been intended as a dramatic expression of their unacceptability. At the same time he must have known what he was rejecting, most probably from the papal apocrisiarius in Constantinople.[122] Could the apocrisiarius have procured, and sent, a copy of the complete text? If his report simply mentioned key points likely to be unacceptable to Rome, we in our turn should not hunt through the Acts looking for every possible detail that a jaundiced Roman eye could have objected to.

The major point here, of course, in this section of the biographical notice for Pope Sergius is his refusal to subscribe to the Quinisext Canons, and the passion in his declaration that he would 'rather die than consent to novel errors', with reference to 'certain chapters contrary to ecclesiastical observance'. This expresses papal fury at the canons that were contrary to Roman practice. No Roman document tells us exactly which of the 102 canons these were.[123]

Western commentators have identified a whole sheaf of canons in the Quinisext collection that could have been seen as offensive to Rome.[124] But, as Ohme has pointed out, we need to ask which of these were found offensive at the time, rather than have been found unacceptable subsequently in the context of the developing code of western canon law.

It is obvious that Rome will have objected to canons that explicitly mention and condemn her own practice. This is true of two of them, and only two. Canon 13 specifies and rejects the Roman rule of priestly continence. It does not merely note that the eastern practice is different, but orders the deposition of any churchman 'who in opposition to the apostolic canons presumes to deprive anyone of those in sacred orders, we mean presbyters or deacons or subdeacons, of union and fellowship with his lawful wife'. Meanwhile, Canon 55 not only rejects the Roman practice of fasting on the Saturdays of Lent, but states explicitly that its own contrary ruling applies 'even in the case of the Church of Rome'.

Other differences from Rome are more accidental and less pointed. The inclusion of Pope Honorius among condemned heretics in Canon 1 has shocked papalists of more recent times, but his condemnation at

---

122 Ohme (1990) 55.

123 The following discussion is indebted to Ohme (1995a).

124 Ohme (1995a) 309–10 lists as the ones cited in this context more than once by scholars Canons 1, 2, 3, 13, 30, 36, 55, 67, 82.

Constantinople III only a decade before had been accepted by the Roman Church. The list of approved canonical sources in Canon 2 does not correspond to the western one, in that no western sources are mentioned save the canons of Sardica and Carthage. The eastern ignoring of all other western synods would irritate a western canonist, but was traditional in the East, and can scarcely have contributed significantly to Pope Sergius' anger; and the condemnation in this canon of 'other canons concocted with false ascriptions by some who attempted to pervert the truth' applies simply to pseudepigraphal ones and not to papal decretals or to other canons approved at western synods. Canon 36 renewed the famous Canon 28 of Chalcedon, with its ascription to Constantinople of 'the same privileges' as those of Rome. It had been rejected at the time by Pope Leo the Great on the ground not that it directly threatened Roman primacy (which indeed the new Canon 36 explicitly affirms) but that it gave Constantinople a status above Alexandria and Antioch; but after the Arab conquest of Egypt and Syria any attempt to reassert the formerly higher status of these two oriental sees would have been wholly unreal, even if formal Roman acceptance of the eastern primacy of Constantinople dates only centuries later, to the time of the Latin empire of Constantinople, when the purpose was to enhance the status of the new Latin patriarch of this see. Canon 67 renewed the prohibition in the Book of Acts of the eating of blood; Rome was more tolerant, but this was not an issue to go to war over. The famous Canon 82 which condemns artistic representations of Christ as a lamb is most unlikely to have had any Roman examples of this in mind, and a pope as self-confident as Sergius will not have seen it as a threat.

A few of the canons that depart from Roman practice and have been interpreted as anti-Roman express in contrast an actual toleration of Roman practice. Take Canon 3, on the treatment of clergy who had already entered into second marriages and not repented by a deadline previously set.[125] The canon attributes 'strictness' to the church of Rome and 'mercy' to that of Constantinople, before setting out a compromise, involving forgiveness for those who have already repented, with an eye to a restoration in future of the stricter discipline constantly maintained at Rome. Meanwhile, in the context of the explicitly anti-Roman Canon 13, Canon 30 deserves mention: it allows 'priests in barbarian lands' (meaning parts of the Balkans) to practise marital continence, which seems

125 Ohme (1995a) 337–8.

a concession to a practice presumably adopted under Roman influence, and attributes their behaviour to 'their timorousness of mind and their bizarre and irresolute behaviour'. Despite this derogatory language, the very fact that the Quinisext Council was ready to tolerate this infringement of its Canon 13 shows that correcting Roman 'errors' was not its priority.

In all, it is only the two canons that explicitly criticize a Roman practice that can fairly be designated as directed against Rome, and which contribute to an understanding of Pope Sergius' fierce reaction to the council. It may well seem strangely exaggerated.[126] Ohme therefore draws our attention, in an extremely important discussion, to a different category of objections.[127] Open to objection above all was the way in which the council declared itself ecumenical despite the lack of Roman participation, and reduced the role of Rome to that of a see that was expected to approve in all meekness canons that it had played no part in formulating.[128] In addition, there were details in the subscription list attached to the canons that will have caused offence to a punctilious and suspicious eye, if we may presume that Sergius' attention had been drawn to at least some of them. While in the address to the emperor at the close of Constantinople III, issued just a decade before, an account of the previous ecumenical councils gives the name of both the emperor and the pope for each council, Quinisext Canon 1 mentions the emperors who convened them, but without any mention of popes.[129] Then in the Quinisext subscription list the newly created Nea Iustinianupolis was placed above Thessalonica, the seat of the papal vicar in East Illyricum. In addition, while in the subscription list to the Definition of Constantinople III the metropolitans under Rome were placed before those under Constantinople, in the Quinisext subscription list the Roman and Constantinopolitan names are intermingled; likewise, while in the list of 681 the Illyrican suffragans had been placed before even the autocephalous archbishops of the Constantinopolitan patriarchate, they were now intermingled with the suffragans of this patriarchate.[130] This could have been interpreted by

126 Sergius' declaration that he would rather die than sign the canons suggests a conscious self-identification with Pope Martin I, who has suffered deposition, exile and death through his condemnation of imperial monotheletism.

127 Ohme (1992a) 396–400 and (1992b) 122–6.

128 Constantinople II (553) had provided a precedent, but a humiliating one that Rome had no wish to follow. Constantinople I (381) was not a direct parallel, since ecumenical status was attributed to it only at Chalcedon, decades later.

129 Compare the Acts of Constantinople III, ACO² II.2, 808–12, to pp. 77–9 below.

130 For this part of the final subscription list of Constantinople III see ACO² II.2, 778–84.

Rome as a claim by Constantinople to authority over East Illyricum.[131] But, above all, the emperor's subscription was placed first of all, even before the space left empty for the pope to fill in his own. This is in marked contrast to Constantinople III, where Constantine IV signed after all the papal and patriarchal legates and bishops.[132] To look ahead to the anti-Photian and pro-Roman Constantinople IV (869–70), after the bishops' approval of the conciliar *horos* by acclamation and the reading out of an address by the emperor Basil (in his presence) the Roman legates, as the senior churchmen present, as a courtesy to an emperor who had fulfilled the wishes of the apostolic see, asked the emperor to sign the *horos* first of all. He replied that he would have preferred to sign last of all, but as a compromise he would sign after the Roman legates and patriarchal legates, but before the bishops.[133] The discussion suggests knowledge of the precedent at the Quinisext Council and a decision by the emperor not to follow it.[134]

It should finally be noted that the derogation of the dignity of the Roman see that all these factors constituted will have come as a particular shock and indeed insult after the triumph of the papacy at Constantinople III, where the church of Constantinople was humiliated by the anathematization of four of her previous patriarchs, and where the doctrine of two wills and operations in Christ was imposed by the emperor on a reluctant Byzantine church in order to align it with the teaching and the authority of the Roman see. Yet the account of this council in Quinisext Canon 1 makes absolutely no mention of Roman involvement. The fury of Pope Sergius surely owed much to this.

---

131 Ohme (1995b) 36–7. The very fact that several of the Illyrican bishops attended the Quinisext Council, despite Rome's abstention (just as had happened at the earlier Constantinopolitan council of 553) points to the looseness of their obedience to their lawful overlord. And note how already at Chalcedon the Illyrican bishops had joined those of Palestine in interrupting with objections the reading of Leo the Great's Tome, ACO II.1 [278], trans. Price and Gaddis (2005) II, 25–6.

132 Nicaea II, which was not attended by the emperors, does not provide a comparable example. That the emperors added their signatures when the conciliar definition, already signed by all the bishops, was presented to them can be taken for granted, although the 'Session VIII' which purports to be the formal record of this occasion is a later fiction. See Price (2018) II, 655–60.

133 Acts of Constantinople IV, ed. Leonardi, 354–7.

134 Ohme (2010a), 246–51. In all probability the emperor Michael III also signed first, right at the head of the subscription list, at the pro-Photian council of 861; see Ohme (2013) LXXIII. But this, of course, was not a precedent that Basil I, hostile to Michael's memory, would have chosen to follow.

The passage from the account of Pope Sergius in the *Liber Pontificalis* given above proceeds to narrate the emperor's reaction to Sergius' hostility:[135]

> In scorn for the above-named pontiff the emperor sent the *magistrianus* Sergius to Rome, and he carried off the God-beloved John bishop of Portus and Boniface counsellor of the apostolic see away to the imperial city. Then he sent Zacharias, his ferocious *protospatharius*, with orders to bring the aforesaid pontiff as well to the imperial city ... But the hearts of the Ravennate soldiery were aroused, as well as those of the Pentapolitan duchy and the surrounding region, not to allow the pontiff of the apostolic see to go up to the imperial city. When a crowd of soldiers foregathered from every side, Zacharias the *spatharius* was terrified, and fearing that he might be killed by that mass of soldiers ... in his terror he took refuge in the pontiff's bedroom, begging the pontiff with tears to have mercy on him and not let anyone take his life ... They did not cease guarding the patriarchate until they had expelled the above-named *spatharius* from the city of Rome with blows and insults.

Why did Justinian wish to see John of Portus and Boniface? John had been the senior representative at Constantinople III of the Roman synod that had preceded the council, while Boniface had been much involved in the monothelete debate and was fluent in Greek.[136] Justinian must have presumed they could reveal the motives and intentions of the Roman see. Then, when informed of the pope's resolute resolve, he attempted unsuccessfully to secure his person.

In 695 Justinian found himself deposed, mutilated[137] and sent into exile in the Crimea. In 705, however, with the help of the Khazars he was restored to the throne, which he held until his overthrow and murder in 711. On his restoration he immediately took up the uncompleted business of relations with Rome and western approval of the Quinisext Canons. The *Liber Pontificalis* takes up the tale in its account of the new pope John VII (705–7):[138]

> The emperor Justinian ... returned to the imperial city ... On entering the palace and recovering his sovereignty, he at once addressed himself to the rolls he had previously sent to Rome in the time of the lord pontiff Sergius of

---

135 *LP* 86.7–9, ed. Duchesne, I, 373–4.

136 Ohme (2009) 20–21 or (2013) LX–LXI.

137 The Byzantine fondness for mutilation is not to be interpreted as barbarism but as a rather too literal application of the dominical teaching in Mt 18:8–9.

138 *LP* 88.4, Duchesne, I, 385–6.

apostolic memory, in which were written various chapters that were contrary to the church of Rome. He despatched two metropolitan bishops, sending through them a *sacra* in which he adjured and pressed the pontiff to convene a council of the apostolic church, and to confirm those of them that pleased him, and to quash and annul those that were the contrary. But he, taking fright out of human weakness, sent them back to the prince through the aforesaid metropolitans without amending them at all.

That this was one of the first acts of Justinian on recovering his throne is evidence of the exceptional importance he attached to the matter. As for Pope John's reaction to the emperor's apparently generous invitation for him actually to 'annul' whichever of these canons displeased him, an unexpected window into John's concerns is provided by a fresco he commissioned in the church of S. Maria Antiqua to represent the 'worship of the Lamb' in the Book of Revelation (7:9–17), where the expected Lamb of God is replaced by a Christ figure, whose head and hair has the uncommon form (round face, short and curly hair) that is found on the gold coinage of Justinian's second reign. This shows awareness of, and respect for, Quinisext Canon 82.

Ohme is puzzled by the contrast between this evidence of John's submissiveness and his failure to fulfil Justinian's request that he should exercise his judgement on the Quinisext canons.[139] The stress in the *Liber Pontificalis* on his timidity may suggest that he was distrustful of the emperor's invitation for him to 'quash and annul those [of the canons] that were the contrary', suspecting a trap. It may be relevant that at this same juncture Justinian had sent to Rome the disgraced and blinded Patriarch Kallinikos, who had taken part in Justinian's deposition in 695: this could have been (mis)understood as a threat.[140] Alternatively, he may have realized that apparent permission to annul a few of the canons did not meet the principal Roman objection, which was the required acceptance by Rome of the main body of a long set of canons which reflected Byzantine policy and Byzantine customs, at a time when Rome had already developed, though papal decretals, its own substantial body of canon law.

The final chapter in the story belongs to another pontificate and to the end of the second reign of Justinian, from October 710 to October 711.

---

139 Ohme (1990) 62–6.

140 Sansterre (1984) 18. In fact it is simply to be compared to the fate of Makarios of Antioch, the leader of the monotheletes at Constantinople III, who after his deposition was sent as a prisoner to Rome.

The *Liber Pontificalis* narrates how Justinian summoned Pope Constantine (708–15) to Constantinople and how the pope made the journey in slow stages to 'the seventh mile-stone from Constantinople'.[141] The account continues:[142]

> The emperor Tiberius, son of Justinian Augustus, came out to this spot with the patricians and the entire senate, Patriarch Cyrus, the clergy, and a crowd of people, all rejoicing and keeping festival; the pontiff and his dignitaries entered the city on imperial saddle-horses ... When the lord emperor Justinian heard of his arrival, he was filled with great joy [and arranged a meeting between them in Nicomedia] ... On the day they saw each other, the most Christian Augustus, crown on head, prostrated himself and kissed the feet of the pontiff.[143] They then rushed together in mutual embrace; and there was great joy among the people as everyone beheld the great humility of their good prince. On the Sunday he celebrated mass for the emperor; the prince received communion at his hands and besought the pontiff to pray for his sins. After confirming all the church's privileges, he gave the pope leave to return home.

Nothing is said here about the Quinisext Council and its canons. The 'privileges' mentioned are most likely to have been unrelated, namely Roman jurisdiction over the see of Ravenna and fiscal privileges for the papal patrimonies in Sicily and southern Italy.[144] However, the account of Pope Gregory II (715–31) in the *Liber Pontificalis* contains the following information:[145]

> He was promoted to the order of the diaconate and set out with the holy pontiff Constantine for the imperial city. When he was asked by the emperor Justinian about certain chapters, [he gave] an excellent reply and resolved every question.

Although this may well exaggerate Gregory's success and influence,[146] it reveals that the Quinisext Canons were discussed on the occasion of this meeting. We are not told what the terms were that secured reconciliation

---

141 Ohme (1992a) 379 notes that this was the first time a pope had visited Constantinople since 547 and the last until the twentieth century.

142 *LP* 90.5–6, Duchesne, I, 390–1.

143 Although the *Liber* does not mention it, it is likely that the pope reciprocated this gesture of respect.

144 Ohme (1990) 75.

145 *LP* 91.1, Duchesne, I, 396, col. 2.

146 Sansterre (1984) 14 notes that the older version of the biography of Gregory in the *Liber* does not include this reference to a discussion of the canons. By the time it was added, perhaps in the 740s, the temptation to exaggerate Gregory's earlier distinction will have been strong.

between Rome and Constantinople at this juncture.[147] The brief reference to the matter in the life of Gregory II just cited confirms that the issue was still the Roman attitude to the Quinisext canons. All commentators presume that the solution was, as it had to be, a compromise. As to the contents of this compromise we are left guessing. What did Rome gain? Doubtless, imperial acceptance that Rome would be dispensed from the canons that contradicted Roman practice. This was not particularly generous, since Byzantium had no means of imposing these canons on the West. What did Rome yield? Constantine did not add his signature to the Quinisext Canons; if he had, there would not be the embarrassing gap near the beginning of the subscription list in the manuscripts where the pope's name should have been. Nor were the Quinisext canons adopted into western canon law: they were not translated into Latin, and remained for a long time unknown in the West. That, however, Constantine made significant concessions short of this is made probable by the silence about the matter in the *Liber Pontificalis*, which suggests that the Roman curia was embarrassed by what looked like a betrayal of Sergius' intransigent stand. The probable answer is that Constantine gave a verbal assurance that, once it was agreed that the Roman see would not have to adopt those of the Quinisext canons that were contrary to Roman practice, he recognized their validity. In practice this meant that the canons would have full authority in the Greek East but would be used only selectively, or in practice ignored, in the West.

This raises a question that I have not met discussed: where in this context did the West end and the East begin? East Illyricum was theoretically subject to Roman jurisdiction, although in practice this was delegated to the bishop of Thessalonica as papal vicar, and the bishops of this region could not but experience the influence of an imperial capital much nearer to them than Rome. This question was to some degree hypothetical, since by far the greater part of this region had at this date been lost to the empire, but Justinian had shortly before recovered control of the coastal region from Constantinople to Thessalonica.[148] His subsequent imposition of Byzantine authority over this recovered territory will surely have included the imposition of the Quinisext canons, as part of Byzantine law. What of the mainly Greek-speaking region of Sicily and southern Italy, a region dear

---

147 Ohme (1990) 69 remarks that the pope's readiness to undertake so long and unusual a journey implies that agreement between Rome and Constantinople had already been reached before he set out.

148 See p. 2 above.

to Byzantium, as is illustrated by Constans II's move to this region near the end of his reign and its transfer to the patriarchate of Constantinople in around 730? We may surmise that these difficult questions of detail were left unanswered.

In all, the compromise amounted to an amicable parting of the ways. It was recognized that Byzantine canon law would enshrine Byzantine practice endorsed by eastern councils and under the supervision of the imperial will, while in the West the voice of Rome would continue to be the undisputed authority.[149]

Let us conclude with a general question. Why did Justinian II try so hard to obtain Roman confirmation of his council? Why was Roman approval considered of such importance? His outlook will have been shaped by the memory of the Third Council of Constantinople, a decade previously, a council that was not only attended by a number of papal legates but also (with the strong support of his father Constantine IV) dominated by them. As the *logos prosphonetikos* makes clear, Justinian saw his council as a completion of the work of the earlier council. In this perspective some degree of Roman involvement, even if only in the form of subsequent ratification, will have appeared essential.

But *was* it essential? The Second Council of Constantinople (553) condemned neo-Origenism and the Three Chapters with complete confidence in its authority, despite being boycotted by Pope Vigilius, who was in Constantinople at the time and had (in his *First Constitutum*) condemned the council's work while it was still sitting. It is true that almost nine months after the council Vigilius (in his *Second Constitutum*) yielded to the council by formally condemning the Three Chapters.[150] But in this document he did not formally confirm, or even mention, the decrees of the council.[151] It was important for Justinian that Rome adopted his own policy, but he clearly did not regard formal Roman confirmation as essential for the council's own authority and its claim to ecumenicity. Similarly, the

149 The letter of Pope Gregory II to Patriarch Germanos I (dating, if authentic, to the 720s) attributes conciliar authority to Quinisext Canon 82 (ACO² III.2, 434, 11–18, trans. Price 2018, 330), but this part of the letter (though other parts may be genuine) is a later, Byzantine, interpolation. See Price (2018) I, 251–2.

150 Price (2009) I, 52–5.

151 In his brief letter to Patriarch Eutychius, written before the *Second Constitutum*, he approves 'as brethren and fellow priests' those who 'have condemned or condemn' the Three Chapters (Price 2009, II, 217–18). This was not a formal confirmation of the decrees of the council.

iconoclast Council of Hiereia (754) condemned images and confidently styled itself 'ecumenical' without the presence and support of either Rome or any of the oriental patriarchates. This was because, as is apparent even at Nicaea II, where the appeal to the pentarchy gave backing to its rejection of Hiereia, two different criteria of ecumenicity received greater emphasis – fidelity to the Christian (primarily patristic) tradition and convening by the emperor.[152]

If this was the evolving Byzantine understanding of the key criteria for ecumenicity, it was not of course to be expected that Rome would agree. It represented a shift away from understanding ecumenical councils as the work of the ecclesiastical hierarchy, enabled by imperial convocation and with their decrees receiving the force of imperial law, to one of understanding them as expressive of the emperor's role as God's viceroy on earth, where his approval gave them full authority even without papal participation and even before the pope had added his signature to their decrees.[153]

6. LATER RECEPTION IN EAST AND WEST

The Quinisext Canons in Byzantium in the Following Centuries

The status of the Quinisext Council according to its own claim to be ecumenical encountered a degree of questioning and even contestation in the subsequent period of Byzantine history. This had nothing to do with the lack of papal backing for the council. It arose in the first place from the council's inferior status compared with the earlier ecumenical councils in that it had not issued any dogmatic decrees. A standard definition of an ecumenical council, drawn up soon after Constantinople II (553), stated that the only councils that counted as ecumenical, in contrast to local councils, were the five to which the bishops were summoned by the emperor and which they attended either in person or through their representatives, and which in addition issued dogmatic decrees.[154] This statement was in the first place a generalization on the basis of the five ecumenical councils to date. But it exerted influence as virtually a definition of what constituted

---

152 Price (2018) I, 49–51.
153 Ohme (1995b) 41–3.
154 Cited in Munitiz (1974) 174–5.

an ecumenical council.[155] This was reflected at the Quinisext Council itself, for its Canon 1 attributes to the First Council of Ephesus (431), which in fact issued no dogmatic decrees, the 'issuing of teaching' on Christology and the status of the Virgin as Theotokos, as if the ecumenical status of Ephesus depended on the attribution to it of dogmatic decrees.[156] The Quinisext Council styled itself 'ecumenical', but it could not, when taken on its own, claim to be on the same level as the six preceding ones.

How does the council's own *logos prosphonetikos* (address to the emperor) deal with this question? It points to the incompletion of the work of Constantinople II and Constantinople III, for they defined doctrine but fell short of the first four councils by failing to issue disciplinary canons, and 'left the faithful dragged down by disorderly passions' (p. 73 below). The new council fills this gaping omission, thereby elevating the two previous councils into full equality with the great councils of the fourth and fifth centuries; neither the fifth and sixth councils nor the new council *in Trullo* were to be taken and judged on their own. This found expression in the later name 'Quinisext', or 'Penthekte' in Greek – not a seventh council, as an ecumenical council in its own right, but one that perfected the fifth and sixth.

Actual contestation of the authority of the Quinisext Council arose during the iconoclast controversy in reaction to its Canon 82, which, while primarily intended to ban representations of Christ as a lamb (the 'lamb of God'), incidentally recommended representations of him in human form. Iconoclasts naturally questioned the status of this canon and the council that had issued it. The reaction of the iconophiles, for whom this canon was of prime importance, was to claim full ecumenical status for the Quinisext Council by presenting it as not a new council exercising authority in its own right but as a continuation of the Third Council of Constantinople, held a decade earlier (680–81).[157] This was clearly argued by Patriarch Tarasios at the Second Council of Nicaea (787), in the following terms:[158]

---

155 Anastasius Bibliothecarius in his defence of the ecumenicity of the Council of Constantinople of 869–70 found it necessary to argue that a council which had not defined doctrine could still be ecumenical (in the Acts of this council, ed. Leonardi, p. 16). The absence of definition of doctrine also accounts for the lack of mention of it in the substantial councils' synopsis dating to the end of the ninth century published by Hoffmann and Brandes (2013).

156 For the falsity of the attribution to Ephesus of a definition that the Virgin was Theotokos see Price (2019) 68–71.

157 Ohme (1990) 316–20.

158 ACO² III.2, 346, trans. Price (2018) I, 290–91.

Some people suffering from ignorance take offence at these canons, saying, 'Are they really of the Sixth Council?' Let these people know that the holy and great Sixth Council was convened under Constantine against those who asserted one operation and will in Christ. After anathematizing the heretics and giving a clear explanation of the orthodox faith, they returned home in the fourteenth year of Constantine. After four or five years the same fathers reassembled under Constantine's son Justinian and issued the afore-mentioned canons; so let no one dispute about them. For those who signed under Constantine were the same as those who signed the present document under Justinian, as is clear from the full identity of the signatures.

The argument is weakened by two apparent errors. The actual lapse of time between Constantinople III and the Quinisext Council is halved. This may well have arisen from ignorance rather than deceit: the Acts of the council are not dated, and Tarasios may have confused it with the meeting of ecclesiastical and state dignitaries in Constantinople in 687 that had resulted in Constantine IV's *keleusis*.[159] The statement that the two councils had 'the same signatories' was, if taken literally, a gross overstatement, for in fact the number of bishops who attended both councils was 57, in contrast to the 156 names in the final subscription list of the Sixth Council and still more at the Quinisext Council.[160] But Tarasios cannot have intended to state something that could instantly be ridiculed by anyone who checked the documents. Rather, he must simply be pointing to the visual identity of actual signatures in all the cases where the same bishop signed both documents.[161] The erroneousness of Tarasios' two claims when taken literally was soon exposed by supporters of iconoclasm.[162] But his main point remains defensible: there was a degree of real continuity between two councils, with many bishops at the Quinisext Council having personal memories of the sixth.

Tarasios was speaking as a resolute champion of iconophilism. The importance he attached to the Quinisext Council found expression in the

159 In ACO² II.2, 886–7. Or alternatively with a distinct episcopal council apparently held around the same time and for the same purpose (confirming Constantinople III), for which see Ohme (2009) 24 with n. 124.

160 Ohme (1990) 317–18 gives a figure of 55 bishops present at both Constantinople III and Quinisext. But now that, in his ACO critical edition of 2013, 'Justinian of Tyana' has been corrected to 'Justin of Tyana' (who attended Constantinople III) and 'Constantine bishop of Pisinus' has been expanded to two entries, namely 'Constantine bishop of Neokaisareia ... John bishop of Pisinus' (since this John attended Constantinople III), the number goes up to 57.

161 Ohme (1988) 336–7.

162 Ohme (2013) LXIV–LXVII.

canons issued by the same Second Nicene Council. Its Canon 1 states that 'we embrace the divine canons gladly and keep their injunctions intact and unshakable ... [including] those published by the six holy ecumenical councils'.[163] The canons published by the Sixth Council in this statement must be the Quinisext ones. Likewise its Canon 6 lays down that 'the sacred fathers of the Sixth Council decreed that [a provincial synod] should most certainly, and with no excuse allowed, take place once a year to correct abuses', which is a reference to Quinisext Canon 8.[164]

In assigning the Quinisext Canons to the Sixth Council as a powerful weapon in the iconophile armoury Tarasios was to be followed by the two leading iconophiles of the first half of the ninth century, Nikephoros and Theodore the Stoudite, both of whom recognized, following Tarasios and the Acts of Nicaea II, that these canons had indeed been issued after the Sixth Council, but insisted that this in no way prevented them being attributed to it.[165] Meanwhile, the iconoclasts' rejection of Canon 82 did not lead to a general rejection of the Quinisext canons during the period of iconoclast ascendancy. The *Ecloga* issued by Leo III in 741 carried over into imperial law a number of rules taken from the Quinisext canons.[166] And an edition of the *Syntagma Canonum in 14 Titles* has been traced which included the Quinisext canons and was in use as an official and authoritative text certainly by 787 and probably throughout the eighth century.[167]

From now on the Quinisext Canons had a secure place in Byzantine canonical collections.[168] This culminated in the so-called Photian recension of 883, which remained definitive thereafter.[169] Our earliest canon law manuscript, the ninth-century Codex Patmensis 172, contains these canons as part of an edition of the *Syntagma in 14 Titles*. The attribution of the Quinisext Canons to the Sixth Council continued in later Byzantine canonical texts, such as the corpus of 883, and the emperor

---

163 COGD 1, 318, 268–74, trans. Price (2018) 610.

164 COGD 1, 326, 478–82, trans. Price (2018) 614–15.

165 For Nikephoros see PG 100, 848A. For Theodore, take in combination PG 99, 996B and 1136C, which assign the canons to the Sixth Council without qualification, and PG 99, 1304D and 1609A, where he dates them to 'after' the Sixth Council.

166 Troianos (1992) 96. For the relation between the Quinisext canons and the *Ecloga* see Humphreys (2015) 84–129.

167 Ohme (2009) 26–31 and (2013) LXX–LXXIII. Note too the inclusion of the Quinisext Canons in a 'volume', most probably an extensive collection of canons, produced at Nicaea II, ACO² III.2, 346, 13–14, trans. Price (2018) I, 290.

168 Including the canonical synopses analysed in Wagschal (2015) 44–5.

169 Wagschal (2015) 47–50.

Leo VI the Wise (886–912) made extensive use of these canons in his own legislation, likewise attributing them to the Sixth Council.[170] This is not to say, however, that from the start the Quinisext Canons were put on a par with the early classic collections, such as the Canons of Basil and the Canons of Nicaea and Chalcedon. It was indeed firmly 'there' as a source to be used and applied with discretion. It was, however, only in what we may call the golden age of Byzantine canon law – that of the great twelfth-century canonists, Aristenos, Balsamon and Zonaras – that the canons of the council of 691/2, now called Penthekte (Quinisext, Fifth-Sixth), as completing the work of both the fifth and sixth ecumenical councils, came fully into their own.[171] The commentary which these three great canonists composed on each of the Quinisext canons cast fascinating light on the reception, interpretation and application of these canons in the later Byzantine world.

The Quinisext Canons in the West

How soon were any of the Quinisext Canons cited with respect in the West? Pope Hadrian I's *Epistula ad Carolum regem* of 792/3 cites Canon 82, with its promotion of images of the manhood of Christ, as issued by the 'holy Sixth Council'.[172] He was clearly happy to appeal to this canon in the context of his dispute over images with the Franks; this was not the context in which to question the Quinisext Canons' ecumenicity. This canon he will have known from its frequent citation in the Acts of Nicaea II (787), which had immediately been translated into Latin, and most probably earlier still from a now lost letter to him from Tarasios predating Nicaea II.[173] Hadrian's letter in reply to Tarasios', in the Greek translation included in the Acts of Nicaea II, cites the patriarch's expression of adhesion to the canons 'of the Sixth Council', that is, the Quinisext Canons:[174]

---

170 Wagschal (2015) 56. Laurent (1965) 23–4.

171 Ohme (1990) 332–44 and Wagschal (2015) 71 and 76–7. Texts took time to achieve classic status, in contrast to the modern RC Codes of Canon Law, 1917 and 1983, which at once superseded previous collections.

172 Hadrian I, *Epistola ad Carolum regem* 35, MGH *Epp.* 5, p. 32.

173 Price (2018) I, 176–7, n. 140. Although this letter is lost, a doubtless very similar letter from Tarasios to the oriental patriarchs is preserved in the Acts of Nicaea II. This gives the full text of Canon 82 and ascribes it to 'the Sixth Council', ACO² III.1, 240, 12–26, trans. Price (2018) I, 213.

174 ACO² III.1, 176, 4–9, trans. Price (2018) I, 176.

We have found in the aforesaid letter of your holiness, after the fullness of faith and of the profession of the sacred creed and all the holy six councils, a wonder worthy of welcome and commendation on the subject of the sacred and venerable depictions, containing the statement, I also accept the work of the same holy Sixth Council with all the canons it published according to divine law.

What is striking here is the way in which Hadrian avoids saying that he himself accepts 'all the canons' as the work of the Sixth Council, but attributes this attitude to Tarasios instead.[175] This, however, was misunderstood by Anastasius Bibliothecarius, who comments as follows in the preface to his translation of the Acts of Nicaea II, written in 873 and addressed to Pope John VIII:[176]

> *The principal see accepts at this council* the rules which the Greeks say were issued by the Sixth Council with the proviso that it in no way receives those of these which contradict earlier canons or the decrees of the holy pontiffs of his see or sound precepts, even though hitherto all of them remain totally unknown among the Latins, since they have not been translated and are not to be found in the archives of the other patriarchal sees, even though they use the Greek language.

The stress on the lack of a Latin translation reflects the change since the seventh and eighth centuries, when many of the popes were Greek or Syrian by birth and will have been fluent in the Greek language. Manifestly Popes Sergius I, John VII and Constantine I could read the Quinisext Canons in the original Greek. But by the late ninth century the lack of a Latin translation created a barrier. The final assertion in this passage is surprising: how could Anastasius have known about the contents of the archives of the oriental patriarchates? But what is manifest in view of his hostility to these canons is his embarrassment over their acceptance by the Roman see 'at this council': the reference must be to Nicaea II, and specifically to Hadrian's letter, understood as constituting an acceptance of the Quinisext Canons.[177] Anastasius must have misread the passage I have given above, taking the sentence 'I accept the work of the Sixth Council

---

175 At Session IV of Nicaea II Tarasios argued in detail that the Quinisext Council had full authority as a continuation of the Sixth Council. ACO² III.2, 346,17–348.3, trans. Price (2018) I, 290–91.

176 ACO² III.1, 1,31–2,5. The italics, of course, are mine.

177 The phrase *in hoc concilio* has misled a number of modern scholars into assigning to some western council a formal acceptance of the Quinisext Canons by the Roman see. That

with all its canons' as a statement not of Tarasios' judgement but that of Hadrian itself.

Anastasius' critical attitude towards Byzantium at this date relates to the Photian schism and the dispute about jurisdiction over Bulgaria that erupted at the end of the anti-Photian council of 869–70.[178] But a more irenic attitude towards the Quinisext Council and canonical divergences between East and West soon prevailed. A canon of the Council of Constantinople of 880 reads:[179]

> Every see has had by tradition certain ancient customs; they should not be used as grounds for mutual strife and polemics. The Church of Rome for her part keeps the customs proper to herself, and it is appropriate that this be so; meanwhile the Church of Constantinople observes certain customs of her own, which she has received from the beginning, and likewise the oriental sees.

The error made by Anastasius Bibliothecarius over Pope Hadrian I's supposed adoption of the Quinisext Canons re-emerged at the end of the eleventh century when it was repeated by the leading canonist Ivo of Chartres and in the mid-twelfth by his successor and follower Gratian, both of whom quote precisely this statement ('I accept the work … ') and attribute it to Pope Hadrian himself.[180] Gratian in his voluminous *Decretum* cited many of the Quinisext Canons, always attributing them to the 'Sixth Council': 2, 4, 6, 7, 9, 11, 13, 15, 17, 23, 25–8, 31, 32, 35 and 36.[181] He did not have access to the complete text of the Quinisext Canons: all those he cites were taken from the similar compilation by Ivo of Chartres, who may well have had access to a complete Latin translation of the canons. The restriction to the first part of the Quinisext Canons, that relating to the clergy, arose from the particular importance of this area of canon law to western canonists, though it also reflects the fact that the later sections were

it refers to Nicaea II was pointed out long ago in MGH, *Epp.* VII, 417, n. 5 and recently by Brunet (2011) 191.

178 This had led to Anastasius taking a not merely reserved but fiercely condemnatory attitude to the Quinisext Canons as 'being, almost all of them, utterly contrary to ancient tradition' in a letter of 871, in MGH, *Epp.* VII, 414,33–5. But by 873, under the new pope John VIII, as the passage I have quoted above shows, the Roman attitude to Constantinople had already softened.

179 Mansi 17, 489B.

180 See the citations from them in ACO² III.1, 177, apparatus. For an introduction to Gratian's work see *Dictionnaire de droit canonique* (Paris), vol. 4, 611–27.

181 I repeat the list given in Dură (1995) 247, who provides references to where in the *Decretum* each of these canons is cited.

of less relevance in the West, highly miscellaneous, and (on the whole) less well drafted.

It is important to take into account the title that came to be assigned to Gratian's work: *Concordia discordantium canonum* – 'the concord of discordant canons'.[182] It is not a collection of canons that confirm each other, but of canons sometimes in conflict, where a canonist has to exercise judgement. Ideally he will find a way of reconciling them, but where this is impossible he will give preference to those which have stronger support and cohere better with the rest of the tradition. Otherwise we would be startled to find him citing, in only slightly abridged form, one of the canons explicitly critical of Roman practice, namely Canon 13 on clerical continence, even including the sentence, 'Therefore, if anyone in opposition to the Apostolic Canons presumes to deprive any of the presbyters and deacons or subdeacons of union and fellowship with his lawful wife, he is to be deposed.' But he adds the annotation, 'This is be understood in context. The eastern church, for which the Sixth Council laid down a rule of life, does not accept a vow of chastity by ministers of the altar.'[183] Equally notable, in an article on precedence among the patriarchal sees which, in accord with the traditional ranking, assigns the second place to Alexandria, is the presence in Gratian's work of several eastern canons which assign this position to Constantinople – Canon 5 of Constantinople I (381), Canon 21 of Constantinople IV (869–70) as well as Quinisext Canon 36.[184] The first two of these are cited without annotation, while the Quinisext canon is followed by a comment which merely says that this canon could be interpreted as assigning the second place to Constantinople and Alexandria equally.

In all, it is manifest that Gratian cites Quinisext canons because, attributed as they were to an ecumenical council, they had *prima facie* authority; but, where they clashed with more numerous or more weighty canons or with the doctrine and practice of the Roman Church, he saw no problem in simply setting them aside as testimony to Byzantine canon law but without universal validity. Behind this lay a recognition that disciplinary canons are not immutable or of uniform validity, and also the fact that the western church has never given the same degree of authority

182 This title is not likely to have been given by Gratian himself. See *Dictionnaire de droit canonique* 4, 611–12.
183 Gratian, *Distinctio* 31. 13, PL 187, 174–5.
184 *Distinctio* 22, PL 187, 121–6.

to the later ecumenical councils as to the first four. Gratian's master, Ivo of Chartres, was quite explicit that even the decrees of ecumenical councils do not have universal and lasting validity until they have been approved by the pope – which, of course, the Quinisext Canons never were.[185]

Gratian's collection was never adopted in the West as an official text, but it was widely used by professional canonists, right down to the promulgation of the first official Code of Canon Law of the Catholic Church in 1917. Taken from Gratian, Quinisext Canons 52 and 101 were, for example, cited at Trent in support of the Catholic doctrine of the eucharist.[186] It was Gratian's *Decretum* that kept the memory of the Quinisext Council alive in the West.

7. MANUSCRIPTS AND EDITIONS

Those who wish to read an authoritative account of the editions of the Greek (and Latin) texts of the Quinisext Acts that preceded the new one in the ACO series by Heinz Ohme may be referred to their treatment in Ohme's introduction to this edition;[187] and the account I give here is wholly based on this treatment. The first printing of the Greek text was in 1540; 1612 saw the publication of the *editio Romana*, which was reprinted in Mansi's celebrated edition (Vol. 11, 921–1006). More recent editions, in particular the oft-cited editions by Rhalles and Potles (1852–9) and P.-P. Joannou (1962), made improvements but were based on a very limited selection of manuscripts.

Unlike the sixth ecumenical council, Constantinople III, whose acts have survived in only three Greek manuscripts (one of them incomplete), those of the Quinisext Council are legion – because of the practical importance of its canons in the life of the church and the incorporation of them in collected editions of Byzantine canon law such as the *Syntagma of Fourteen Titles* or the *Nomocanon*. The total number of manuscripts of the canons issued by the council, and dating from the ninth to the sixteenth century, amounts to 218. Ohme reports that the textual tradition of the canons themselves 'is outstandingly stable and contains scarcely any

---

185   Fournier (1898) 3.
186   Dură (1995) 249.
187   Ohme (2013) LXXXVI–XC.

surprises'; in contrast, the text of the subscription list 'shows significant variations and raises a variety of questions'.[188] For his edition he selected 72 manuscripts, including all those, sixty in number, which contain not only the canons but also the subscription list, in whole or in part.[189] Ohme's new ACO edition offers a significantly improved version of the subscription list – an advance beyond his earlier edition of the list published in 1990 – above all through using Π (Codex Patmensis 172), our oldest manuscript, dating to the end of the ninth century,[190] where the number of episcopal subscriptions rises from 220 to 226.[191]

A number of comparatively late manuscripts offer a list of the canons with a brief summary of the subject matter of each, as an initial table of contents. The preceding critical edition of the text, that of P.-P. Joannou (1962),[192] integrated these summaries into the text, as headings to each canon in turn. Ohme's new edition does not adopt this procedure. For the purposes of the present translation, however, while also providing these summaries as a list of contents, I have decided to imitate Joannou (followed in this respect by the editions of Nedungatt of 1995 and of Ohme's Fontes Christiani edition of 2006) in including them in the text as well, as headings that will be found useful by the reader. But it is important to be aware that these headings are secondary and late. Nor do they always correspond precisely to the canons they introduce: note especially the heading to Canon 101, which speaks of communion in the mouth, which was not universal before the twelfth century, while the canon itself speaks only of the older practice of communion in the hand.[193]

---

188 Ohme (2013) IX.
189 Ohme (2013) XCII.
190 This makes it the oldest of all our Greek canonical manuscripts (Flogaus 2009, 26, and Wagschal 2015, 25). It includes the Quinisext text within the *Syntagma in 14 titles*.
191 Ohme (2013), XXVII, n. 75.
192 Joannou (1962a) 101–241.
193 See, below, p. 174, n. 302.

DATE LIST OF CANONS, AD 314–870

Ancyra	314
Neocaesarea	*c.* 315
Nicaea	325
Antioch	*c.* 330
Sardica	342
Gangra	early 340s
Laodicea	between 340 and 380
Basil of Caesarea	374–5
Constantinople I	381–2
The Apostolic Canons	380s
Constantinople	394
Carthage	419
Ephesus	431
Chalcedon	451
Quinisext	691/2
Nicaea II	787
Prima Secunda	861
Constantinople IV	869–70

THE HEADINGS OF THE QUINISEXT CANONS

1 Ordinance about preserving without innovation or impairment the faith handed down by the six holy ecumenical councils
2 Confirmation of the apostolic canons, the traditions of the fathers, and the previous councils

About the Clergy

3 About the seating of presbyters who have entered into two marriages or contracted marriage after ordination or taken a widow or divorcee
4 About penance for one who has had intercourse with a woman consecrated to God
5 That those of priestly rank should not live with a maidservant as companion
6 That presbyters or deacons are not permitted to contract marriage after ordination
7 That deacons should not take precedence over presbyters
8 That every year there should be a synod of the bishops in each province wherever the metropolitan decides
9 That a cleric is not allowed to keep an inn
10 That a priest should not take interest or a hundredth part
11 About not associating or conversing with Jews or receiving medical treatment from them
12 That a bishop should not live with his wife after consecration
13 That presbyters, deacons and subdeacons should keep their wives
14 That a presbyter should not be ordained before the age of 30 or a deacon before that of 25 or a deaconess before that of 40
15 That a subdeacon should not be ordained before the age of 20

16 That the number of seven deacons in Acts should not be applied to those in the church

17 That a cleric should not be enrolled in another church without the consent of his own bishop

18 About clerics who on the pretext of an barbarian inroad or some other circumstance have emigrated, and that they should return to their own church after the departure of the [barbarian] nation

19 That those who preside in the churches should instruct the clergy and people with words of piety according to the tradition of the holy and inspired fathers

20 That a bishop should not teach publicly in a city not his own that has another bishop

21 About clerics who have incurred canonical charges and are repentant

22 About those who are ordained for money

23 That those who give out communion should not make charges of any kind

24 That one in priestly orders or a monk should not attend horse races

25 That the rural and country parishes of each church remain under the bishops who possess them

26 That one who has entered into an unlawful marriage in ignorance should retain only his chair

27 That no one enrolled in the clergy should wear inappropriate clothing

28 That the offering of grapes should not be combined with the bloodless sacrifice of the offering

29 That the holy [mysteries] of the altar are to be celebrated by men who are fasting

30 That those who have promised continence by agreement should not live with their wives

31 That the liturgy should not be performed in domestic chapels without the permission of the bishop

32 That it is necessary in the bloodless sacrifice to mix water with the wine

33 That it is a Jewish practice to enrol in the clergy only those of priestly descent

34 About bishops and clerics who conspire and band together

35 That the property of a bishop should not be removed or appropriated after his death by the metropolitan

36 About the ranking of the patriarchs

37 About bishops residing outside their own dioceses because of barbarian incursions

38 That in a newly founded city the ordering of the churches should be in accord

39 About the bishop of the island of Cyprus

About Monks and Nuns

40 About monks and monasteries and that those who choose monastic life should not be accepted without scrutiny

41 About those wishing to enter into enclosure

42 That those called hermits who have long hair on the head ought not to live in cities

43 That no one found guilty of any fault should be denied admittance into the monastic order

44 About a monk who commits fornication or takes a woman for marital intercourse

45 That those about to receive the monastic habit should not enter the monastery richly dressed

46 That women enrolled in a monastery should not go outside it without unavoidable necessity

47 That a man should not sleep in a women's monastery nor a woman in a men's monastery

48 That it is necessary for a wife of a consecrated bishop who has been separated from him by mutual consent to enter a monastery

49 That monasteries that have once been consecrated must not become secular residences

[Miscellaneous]

50 That those in priestly orders should not play at dice

51 A prohibition on watching mimes and hunting and dancing on the stage

78 That those being illuminated should learn the creed

79 About those who celebrate the childbirth after the appointed day of Christ's Nativity

80 On not tarrying without necessity without going to church

81 That 'who was crucified for us' should not be added to the Trisagion

82 That painters should not represent a lamb in the finger-pointing of the Precursor

83 That the eucharist is not to be given to the bodies of the dead

84 About those of whom it is not known for certain whether they were baptized

85 That those who are manumitted in the presence of three witnesses enjoy their freedom

86 About those who maintain prostitutes for the destruction of souls

87 About a woman who has left her husband or a man who has left his wife and married another person

88 That an animal is not to be brought inside a sacred building unless on a journey out of great necessity

89 About the hour at which the fast ends on the Great Saturday

90 That kneeling is not permitted on Sundays

91 About the penance for those who provide or receive abortifacient drugs

92 About those who abduct women on the pretext of marriage

93 That a woman who marries another before being convinced that her husband has died is an adulteress

94 About those who swear pagan oaths

95 About how converts from heresy are to be received

96 That men are not to braid their hair

97 About those who stay with their wives in churches without discrimination

98 About him who takes a betrothed woman while her fiancé is alive

99 About the Armenians offering pieces of cooked meat within the sacred sanctuary

100 About not painting on a panel things that incite to pleasure

101 That laymen are to receive communion in the mouth and not in a gold or silver receptacle
102 That it is necessary to take into account the disposition of the sinner and the character of the sin

LIST OF THE QUINISEXT CANONS
IN THEMATIC SEQUENCE

The Authoritative Sources of Doctrine and Canon Law and their Application

  1 Ordinance about preserving without innovation or impairment the faith handed down by the six holy ecumenical councils
  2 Confirmation of the apostolic canons, the traditions of the fathers, and the previous councils
102 That it is necessary to take into account the disposition of the sinner and the character of the sin

Church Hierarchy and Synods

36 About the ranking of the patriarchs
 8 That every year there should be a synod of the bishops in each province wherever the metropolitan decides

Dioceses

17 That a cleric should not be enrolled in another church without the consent of his own bishop
18 About clerics who on the pretext of an barbarian inroad or some other circumstance have emigrated, and that they should return to their own church after the departure of the [barbarian] nation
20 That a bishop should not teach publicly in a city not his own that has another bishop
25 That the rural and country parishes of each church remain under the bishops who possess them

35 That the property of a bishop should not be removed or appropriated after his death by the metropolitan

37 About bishops residing outside their own dioceses because of barbarian incursions

38 That in a newly founded city the ordering of the churches should be in accord

39 About the bishop of the island of Cyprus

Clerical Rank and Ordination

3 About the seating of presbyters who have entered into two marriages or contracted marriage after ordination or taken a widow or divorcee

7 That deacons should not take precedence over presbyters

14 That a presbyter should not be ordained before the age of 30 or a deacon before that of 25 or a deaconess before that of 40

15 That a subdeacon should not be ordained before the age of 20

16 That the number of seven deacons in Acts should not be applied to those in the church

21 About clerics who have incurred canonical charges and are repentant

26 That one who has entered into an unlawful marriage in ignorance should retain only his chair

Clerical Lifestyle and Behaviour

4 About penance for one who has had intercourse with a woman consecrated to God

5 That those of priestly rank should not live with a maidservant as companion

9 That a cleric is not allowed to keep an inn

10 That a priest should not take interest or a hundredth part

24 That one in priestly orders or a monk should not attend horse races

27 That no one enrolled in the clergy should wear inappropriate clothing

34 About bishops and clerics who conspire and band together

77 That clerics or ascetics are not to wash with women in a bathhouse

Simony

Monks and Nuns

Sacraments and Church Rituals

32 That it is necessary in the bloodless sacrifice to mix water with the wine

52 About celebrating the liturgy of the presanctified in holy Lent

57 That milk and honey should not be offered on the altar

59 That baptism is not to be celebrated in a chapel inside a house

83 That the eucharist is not to be given to the bodies of the dead

84 About those of whom it is not known for certain whether they were baptized

Lay Attendance and Behaviour in Church and Sacred Spaces

58 That a layman should not give himself communion at the divine mysteries

69 That a layman is not to enter the sacred sanctuary

70 That women are not to talk during the liturgy

74 That it is not permitted to eat in a sacred edifice

75 That chanting should not involve disorderly bellowing

76 That it is forbidden to have a bar within sacred precincts or to serve or sell varieties of food

80 On not tarrying without necessity without going to church

88 That an animal is not to be brought inside a sacred building unless on a journey out of great necessity

90 That kneeling is not permitted on Sundays

97 About those who stay with their wives in churches without discrimination

101 That laymen are to receive communion in the mouth and not in a gold or silver receptacle

Religious Observance outside Church

55 That one should not fast on Saturdays and Sundays

56 About the eating of cheese by the Armenians on the Saturdays and Sundays in holy Lent

66 About frequenting the churches throughout the week of the resurrection

87 About a woman who has left her husband or a man who has left his wife and married another person

92 About those who abduct women on the pretext of marriage

93 That a woman who marries another before being convinced that her husband has died is an adulteress

98 About him who takes a betrothed woman while her fiancé is alive

Moral Issues

4 About penance for one who has had intercourse with a woman consecrated to God

67 About abstaining from blood and from what is strangled

91 About the penance for those who provide or receive abortifacient drugs

86 About those who maintain prostitutes for the destruction of souls

Art Sacred and Profane

73 That figures of the cross should not be made on the floor

82 That painters should not represent a lamb in the finger-pointing of the Precursor

100 About not painting on a panel things that incite to pleasure

Against Certain Roman and Armenian Customs

3 About the seating of presbyters who have entered into two marriages or contracted marriage after ordination and [of those who have] taken a widow or divorcee

55 That one should not fast on Saturdays and Sundays

32 That it is necessary in the bloodless sacrifice to mix water with the wine

33 That it is a Jewish practice to enrol in the clergy only those of priestly descent

56 About the eating of cheese by the Armenians on the Saturdays and Sundays in holy Lent

THE CONCILIAR ACTS
TRANSLATION AND COMMENTARY

[17] The canons of the holy fathers who convened in Constantinople in the Trullos of the imperial place in the reign of our most pious and Christ-loving emperor Justinian.

I. THE ADDRESS TO THE EMPEROR

(*Logos prosphonetikos*)

The address of the same holy council to the most pious emperor Justinian, to which they have appended the canons they have issued.

To the most pious and Christ-loving emperor Justinian [from] the holy ecumenical council convoked by the divine will and the decree of your most pious authority in this God-protected and imperial city.

When the ineffable and divine grace of our redeemer and saviour Jesus Christ encompassed the whole earth and the life-giving message of the truth was disseminated in the hearing of all, the people who sat in the darkness of ignorance saw the great light of knowledge[1] and were freed from the bonds of error, receiving the kingdom of heaven in place of the ancient servitude. But the one who had been stripped of the beauty of his original brightness on account of his pride, the first dragon, the mighty intellect, the Assyrian, was taken captive by his former prisoners, and became stripped of all his strength by the power of the incarnate Word, as Scripture says: 'The swords of the enemy have failed utterly.'[2] For everywhere 'spiritual worship'[3] has

---

1 Cp. Is 9:1.
2 Ps 9:7.
3 Rom 12:1.

been laid down by law and a holocaust offered, and God, who is sacrificed and distributed for the salvation of both bodies and souls, deifies those who partake of him. By him demons are put to flight, and the sacred assembly of men, gathered in the churches, is sacramentally sanctified, while the 'paradise of delight'⁴ has been opened to all, and all things have at last been made new.⁵

But the devil, the murderer of men,⁶ who had once rebelled against the Lord and ruler of all and given birth with pangs to the pain of apostasy, could not bear to see us raised up from the fall of our transgression and ascending to heaven [18] through our first fruits,⁷ namely Christ who gave himself as a ransom for us; and so he did not cease from hurling the darts of evil⁸ and wounding the faithful with the passions, so that they might be separated from the operation of the Spirit, from his honour and grace, that had been given to them.⁹ Nor did God, our good champion and the 'pioneer of salvation',¹⁰ leave us without assistance, but he raised up in every generation those who in the contest of this life were arrayed against the devil with the weapons of piety and waged war with him. Those who drew 'the sword of the Spirit who is the speech of God'¹¹ to engage with the evil one stripped him of his tyranny over us; they became the guides of the flocks and made straight the ways of the Lord for the congregations, lest through ignorance of the better path they be pushed and tumble down the cliffs of lawlessness. For it was necessary for the one who had given us existence and with such greatness of condescension and abasement transformed our race, calling and raising us to himself, to reveal to us the path to wellbeing by means of the luminaries and teachers of the church, who guide our steps according to God and urge us on to follow the gospel, for 'our life is in heaven',¹² according to the divine apostle.

We at present are conducting our lives idly and dozing in the sloth of our thoughts, with the result that the highwayman who is our enemy has come upon us unawares, stolen our virtue little by little, and given us evil in its

---

4 Gen 3:24.
5 Cp. Rev 21:5.
6 Cp. Jn 8:44.
7 Cp. 1 Cor 15:20.
8 Cp. Eph 6:16.
9 Cp. Acts 2:38, 10:45.
10 Heb 2:10.
11 Eph 6:17.
12 Phil 3:20.

place. So Christ our God, who steers this greatest of vessels, the whole world, has raised you up as our wise helmsman, pious emperor and true champion, 'directing discourse with judgement',[13] 'protecting truth for ever, executing judgement and righteousness in the midst of the earth',[14] and 'travelling on a blameless road'.[15] Wisdom has carried you in her womb and given birth to you, nurtured and swaddled you well with the virtues, **[19]** and filled you with the divine Spirit. She has appointed you to be the eye of the world, as with the purity and lustre of your mind you give a clear light to those who are subject to you. To you she has entrusted her church and taught you to ponder her law day and night,[16] so as to equip and edify the peoples under your hand. In the fervour of your love of God you have surpassed the zeal of Phinehas,[17] piercing sin with the power of piety and understanding; you have set yourself to rescue the flock from evil and perdition. For it was right that the one who had taken the helm after the upward propulsion of the human race[18] should not only look to himself, how to direct his own life aright, but also rescue everything under his sway from the crashing waves and great turbulence of offences, while the spirits of wickedness pour in from every side and throw into turmoil 'the body of our lowliness'.[19]

The two holy ecumenical councils which were convened in this imperial and God-protected city, one in the time of Justinian of divine memory and the other in that of our emperor Constantine of pious memory, the father of your clemency, clarified the mystery of the faith in accord with the fathers, but they did not compose sacred canons, as the other four holy ecumenical councils had done, by which the congregations are led to forsake a worse and inferior pattern of life and converted to a better and superior one. In consequence the 'holy nation and royal priesthood'[20] 'for which Christ died'[21] has been rent asunder and dragged down by many disorderly passions, torn and sundered little by little from the divine sheepfold; in ignorance and forgetfulness it has fallen away from the feats of virtue, and, to use the

---

13 Ps 11:5.
14 Ps 145:6–7.
15 Ps 100:6.
16 Cp. Ps 1:2.
17 Cp. Num 25:7–13. For the significance of Phinehas in the present context see Humphreys (2015) 51–2.
18 Presumably with the advent of Christ.
19 Phil 3:21.
20 1 Pet 2:9.
21 Rom 14:15.

apostle's words, 'spurned the Son of God, treated as common the blood of the covenant by which it had been sanctified, and insulted the grace of the Spirit'.[22]

But your wish was to gather it together as a 'people for his possession',[23] in imitation of Christ the shepherd, who seeks on the mountain the sheep that has gone astray,[24] to restore it to his fold and to induce it to keep the commandments and divine ordinances, through which we forsake dead works and are made alive.[25] You reflected fully about salvation **[20]** and sought out God, according to the saying that runs, 'He who seeks the Lord will find knowledge with righteousness, and they who seek him rightly will find peace.'[26] You therefore decreed the convocation of this holy and divinely inspired ecumenical council, so that through the agreement and accord of the many there would be a due accomplishment of what you longed for, while, if any remnant of pagan or Jewish perversity had been mixed with the ripe grain of the truth, it would like a weed be pulled out at the roots and the crop of the church recover its purity.[27] 'For where two or three are gathered in my name, there am I in the midst of them,'[28] said the voice of the Lord. And he has cried out to us through Jeremiah: 'Seek me with your whole heart, and I shall appear to you.'[29]

It was for this reason therefore that at the command of your piety we convened in this God-protected and imperial city and composed sacred canons. We therefore make entreaty to your piety, as we address to you the words of the fathers who previously assembled in this God-protected city in the reign of our emperor Theodosius of pious memory, 'so that, just as you honoured the church with your letters of convocation, so too you may' with a pious communication 'put your concluding seal on what has been resolved. May the Lord confirm your rule in justice and peace, pass it down from generation to generation, and add to your authority on earth the enjoyment of the kingdom of heaven'.[30]

---

22 Heb 10:29.
23 Tit 2:14.
24 Cp. Mt 18:12, Jn 10:11.
25 Cp. Heb 9:14.
26 Prov 16:8.
27 Cp. Mt 13:24–30.
28 Mt 18:20.
29 Jer 36:13.
30 A citation from the *logos prosphonetikos* addressed to Theodosius the Great at the final session, on 9 July, of the Council of Constantinople of 381, reporting its decrees and

This address was delivered at the close of the council. The manuscripts always place it before the canons, however, and indeed it makes sense to place it in this position as providing a general introduction to the council and its purposes.

It begins by describing the unremitting battle between the agents of God, 'the luminaries and teachers of the church', and the devil. At present the people of God are living negligently, and the devil has 'stolen their virtue'. Mention is made in particular of the survival of 'pagan' and 'Jewish' practices. This had been compounded by the fact that the two previous ecumenical councils, Constantinople II (553) and Constantinople III (680–81), 'did not compose sacred canons, as the other four holy ecumenical councils had done, by which the congregations are led to forsake a worse and inferior pattern of life and converted to a better and superior one'. So Christ has now raised up a pious emperor 'in imitation of Christ the shepherd, who seeks on the mountain the sheep that has gone astray, to restore it to his fold and to induce it to keep the commandments and divine ordinances'.[31] He has appointed him 'to be the eye of the world ... giving light' to his subjects, and filled him with the Holy Spirit, so as to have both the power and the wisdom 'to rescue the flock from evil and perdition'. For this reason the emperor summoned an ecumenical council, which has now completed its work by the composition of 'sacred canons'. The bishops now request the emperor to confirm their work by his own subscription.

Such language is not to be dismissed as flattery to appease a despotic emperor. Lying behind Justinian II's religious policy was the belief, first enunciated centuries before by Constantine the Great, that the success of the empire against its enemies depended on the goodwill of God, and that this goodwill was conditional on the good estate of the church, its orthodoxy and good order. This meant that the emperor, as the one to whom God had entrusted the government of the 'world', had a responsibility to God and to his subjects to use his power to promote the good estate of the

asking the emperor to confirm them in writing – in Mansi 3, 557CD. 'With a pious communication' (κεραιῶν in the Greek) is an insertion, but it corresponds to a request in the preceding clause of the address of 381 that the emperor should confirm the decrees 'by a letter of your piety'. The evocation of Constantinople I has special relevance for the Quinisext Council, since it provided a precedent for a council in which Rome did not participate but which nevertheless was accounted ecumenical and subsequently received Roman approbation.

31 Note Humphreys (2015) 51: the passage 'is the first extant application of Christ the Shepherd imagery to any Roman or post-Roman ruler in legal literature'.

church.[32] It is not the pope against whom the emperor is measured in this address, but the kings of Israel and Judah, especially Josiah, described in the Books of the Kings as God's vicegerents on earth, entrusted with the task of purifying the cult, and promised, as their reward, victory over the common enemies of themselves and God. And yet, with its wealth of New Testament echoes, the emperor is represented as not the mere successor of the kings of Judah but rather their replacement, just as the gospel of Christ had supplanted the law of the Old Covenant.[33]

The unprecedented disasters of the seventh century, with the loss of the empire's richest provinces and a recent major siege of Constantinople (674–8) that had threatened the very survival of the empire, were therefore interpreted as a spur to ecclesiastical reform. This had been accomplished in part (as the address says) by the 'clarification of the mystery of the faith in accord with the fathers' at the two preceding councils, Constantinople II and Constantinople III, but more was manifestly required for the proper enactment and enforcement of the Christian law.

We have no information about the composition of this address. But the presumption must be that its content was determined by the emperor as the expression of his own policy and purposes. Otherwise the published acts of the council would have included further documentation, namely an address or letter of the emperor's, to give expression to this.[34]

---

32 See General Introduction, pp. 4–7.
33 Humphreys (2015) 56–7.
34 Cp. the edict that Constantine IV issued after Constantinople III, to give expression to his own intentions and convictions, in ACO² II.2, 832–56.

II. THE CANONS

CANON 1

Ordinance about preserving without innovation or impairment
the faith handed down by the six holy ecumenical councils[35]

[21] 'The best sequence for the beginning of every speech and matter is to begin with God and conclude with God,' according to the words of the theologian.[36] Consequently, since we are already preaching piety with urgency, and the church of which Christ is the foundation[37] is constantly growing and expanding so as top the cedars of Lebanon,[38] we now (as by divine grace we begin a sacred discourse) decree that the creed 'handed down to us by the eyewitnesses and ministers of the word',[39] the divinely appointed apostles, is to be preserved without innovation or impairment – and also that of the 318 holy and blessed fathers who assembled at Nicaea in the reign of our emperor Constantine against the impious Arius and the pagan assertion of another god or (to speak more properly) of many gods that he taught as doctrine. In unanimity of faith they revealed and expounded to us the consubstantiality of the three hypostases of the divine nature, not allowing this to be obscured by the bushel of ignorance, but giving clear teaching to the faithful that they are to worship with a single worship the Father and the Son and the Holy Spirit. They refuted and destroyed the doctrine of unequal degrees of Godhead and overturned and overthrew the childish sandcastles built by the heretics in opposition to orthodoxy.

We likewise confirm the confession of faith proclaimed in the reign of our emperor Theodosius the Great by the 150 holy fathers convened in this

---

35 This particular heading, unlike the others, occurs only in one twelfth-century manuscript (Florentinus Laurentianus). This and all the headings of the canons that follow are taken from what in the manuscripts that include them is a table of contents (πίναξ), separate from the text of the canons themselves, as also in the ACO edition, where they come on pp. 2–9. They are not an original part of the text and do not predate the twelfth century; see Ohme (2013) LII, summarized in the note to Canon 101 below (p. 174). Compare the headings to the Canons of Nicaea II, which likewise are not original (though much earlier) and not always apt; see Price (2018) II, 609.

36 Gregory Nazianzus, *or.* 2.1, SC 247, 84–6.

37 Cp. 1 Cor 3:11.

38 Cp. Ps 91:13, Sir 24:13.

39 Lk 1:2.

imperial city, as we embrace their theological statements about the Holy Spirit and expel together with the earlier enemies of the truth the profane Macedonius, who had the effrontery to consider the one who is Lord to be a servant and chose like a brigand to split the indivisible monad, leaving incomplete the mystery in which we hope. Together with this blackguard who raved against the truth they also condemned Apollinarius, that initiate in evil, who belched forth in his impiety that the Lord took a body that lacked a mind, whereby he too argued that our salvation was incomplete.

[22] We also validate as an unbreakable bulwark of piety the teaching issued by the 200 inspired fathers convened for the first time in the city of Ephesus in the reign of our emperor Theodosius the son of Arcadius, as we proclaim that the Son of God and the incarnate one are one Christ and hold that the one who bore him without seed is immaculate, ever-virgin and properly and truly Theotokos; and we reject the insane dividing by Nestorius as utterly alien to the divine destiny, for he taught that the one Christ is a divine individual and also a human individual, reviving thereby the impiety of the Jews.

In addition we confirm in orthodox fashion the confession of faith penned by the 630 inspired fathers in the metropolis of Chalcedon in the time of Marcian, who also was our emperor, which loudly proclaimed to the ends of the earth that the one Christ the Son of God is compounded from two natures and is to be acknowledged in the same two natures,[40] and also expelled from the sacred precincts of the church as a plague to be averted the feeble-minded Eutyches who asserted that the great mystery of the incarnation was accomplished only in appearance – and together with him Nestorius and Dioscorus, of whom the former was the champion and advocate of division and the latter the advocate of fusion, through which, though starting from diametrically opposite impiety, they fell into the same pit of perdition and godlessness.

We recognize no less as the work of the Spirit, and teach those under us, the pious statements of the 165 inspired fathers brought together in this imperial city in the reign of our emperor Justinian of pious memory, who by a conciliar decree anathematized and abominated Theodore of Mopsuestia the teacher of Nestorius, and Origen, Didymus and Evagrius, who in distraction and hallucination of mind revived the myths of the

---

40 Chalcedon deliberately adopted 'in two natures' rather than 'from two natures', but the two formulae were standardly conjoined and claimed to be the teaching of Chalcedon from the time of Justinian I. See Price (2009) I, 71–2, 126.

pagans and told us of journeys and transformations of certain souls and bodies and impiously besmirched the return to life of the dead, and also the writings of Theodoret against both the orthodox faith and the Twelve Chapters of the blessed Cyril, and the so-called Letter of Ibas.

[23] We also acknowledge as something to be kept inviolate the confession of faith of the holy sixth council convoked recently in this imperial city in the reign of our emperor Constantine of divine memory, which received powerful confirmation through the pious emperor's sealing its rolls in order to preserve it for all time.[41] It issued the devout clarification that we are to believe in two natural wills or volitions and two natural operations in the incarnate dispensation of our one Lord Jesus Christ true God. It condemned by a pious decree those who falsified the correct teaching of the truth and taught the congregations that there is one will and one operation in the one Lord our God Jesus Christ, namely Theodore of Pharan, Kyros of Alexandria, Honorius of Rome,[42] Sergios, Pyrrhos, Paul and Peter who presided in this God-protected city, Makarios bishop of Antioch, his disciple Stephen and the insane Polychronios. It thereby preserved intact the common body of Christ our God.[43]

To sum up, we decree that, as regards all the men who stood out in the church of God, as 'luminaries in the world, holding onto the word of life',[44] their faith and their God-given writings and doctrines are to be kept safe and remain unassailable until the end of the age, while we reject and anathematize those whom they rejected and anathematized as enemies of the truth who bellowed nonsense against God and reached a peak of unrighteousness.

41 See the epilogue to the Acts of this council composed by the protonotary Agatho: 'I wrote out in my own hand all the rolls of the proceedings at the council in a clean copy in ecclesiastical script; these rolls were sealed and placed securely in the imperial palace, where they were kept together with the signed definition of the faith that was published by the same holy council' (ACO² II.2, 898, 14–17). Agatho dates this to immediately after the council. Ohme (2013) LXI, however, takes this sentence to refer to the time of the confirmation of Constantinople III by Justinian II in 687, as recorded in his *keleusis* or instruction (ACO² II.2, 886–7).

42 The reaffirmation of the anathematization of Pope Honorius, because of his letter to Sergios of Constantinople of 634 that speaks of 'one will' in Christ, is not to be interpreted as an anti-Roman gesture, since the coupling of his name with those of the condemned monothelete bishops of the East was prominent in the Definition of Constantinople III (ACO² II.2, 772, 6–10), which Rome had fully accepted.

43 In other words, the doctrine of the full humanity that Christ shared with us.

44 Phil 2:15–16.

If anyone at all does not hold and embrace the aforesaid doctrines of piety and does not believe and teach accordingly but attempts to oppose them, he is to be anathematized according to the decree already issued by the aforesaid holy and blessed fathers, and is to be expelled and cast out from the list of Christians as alien. For we are utterly determined neither to add anything nor take away anything[45] from what has already been defined, nor could we do so on any ground whatsoever.

This summary of the work of the preceding five ecumenical councils, from Nicaea (325) to Constantinople III (680–81), follows the precedent of the similar summary in the Definition of the Sixth Council, Constantinople III, a definition that ends with decreeing penalties for those who fail to respect its authority – deposition for clerics and anathematization for monks or laymen.[46] This insistence on fidelity to the dogmatic decrees of earlier councils, without any addition or subtraction, goes back to Canon 7 (as it was numbered in later canonical collections) of Ephesus I, which deposed clerics and anathematized laymen who composed a creed different from that of Nicaea and imposed it on converts.[47] This canon was appealed to by bishops at Chalcedon who objected to the drawing up of a new and supplementary definition of the faith and interpreted the Ephesan canon as ruling out any new definition.[48] This canon was quoted verbatim at the end of the Chalcedonian Definition, which implied the reasonable interpretation that what was banned was not all and every supplementary definition of doctrine but anything that contradicted the Nicene faith, or (in other words) that a council could not *alter* the Nicene faith but could *clarify* it in response to new heresies.

This celebration of the work of the earlier ecumenical councils is more than simply a profession of orthodoxy: it implies a claim that the present council was their legitimate successor. Likewise, the mention of the previous emperors who had convened these councils implied a claim that Justinian II was their true successor, with the same authority and the same mission entrusted to him by God.[49]

45 Cp. Deut 13:1.
46 ACO² II.2, 768–70 and 776, 25–7. For the meaning of anathematization see my commentary on Canon 92, p. 165 below.
47 In ACO I.1.7, §77, 105–6.
48 See Acts of Chalcedon, II (III in the Greek Acts) 3. 5, 7, ACO II.1 [274]; Price and Gaddis (2005) II, 10–11.
49 Humphreys (2015) 57–9.

CANON 2

*Confirmation of the apostolic canons, the traditions
of the fathers, and the previous councils*

[24] This holy council has also adopted the excellent and weighty resolution that the eighty-five canons, received and confirmed by the holy and blessed fathers before us and handed down to us in the name of the holy and glorious apostles, are from now on to remain firm and secure for the cure of souls and the treatment of the passions. Now although in these canons we are directed to receive the Constitutions of the same holy apostles transmitted by Clement,[50] in which in time past heretics to the harm of the church made some bogus insertions alien to piety, obscuring for us the seemly beauty of the divine teaching, we have fittingly rejected these Constitutions, in order to build up and protect the most Christian flock, since we do not give our approval in any way to the concoctions of heretical falsity or include them in the authentic and perfect teaching of the apostles.

We set our seal on all the other sacred canons issued by our holy and blessed fathers, namely those of the 318 holy fathers convened at Nicaea, of those at Ancyra, also of those at Neocaesarea, likewise of those at Gangra, also of those at Antioch in Syria and those at Laodicea in Phrygia, and in addition those of the 150 gathered in this God-protected and imperial city, of the 200 assembled in the metropolis of Ephesus for the first time, and of the 630 holy and blessed fathers at Chalcedon, and also of those at Sardica and those at Carthage, and likewise of those also who assembled in this God-protected and imperial city in the time of Nectarius bishop of this imperial city and of Theophilus archbishop of Alexandria,[51] and in addition [the canons] of Dionysius archbishop of the great city of Alexandria, Peter archbishop of Alexandria and martyr, Gregory bishop of Neocaesarea and wonderworker, Athanasius archbishop of Alexandria, Basil archbishop of Caesarea in Cappadocia, Gregory bishop of Nyssa, Gregory the Theologian, Amphilochius of Iconium, Timothy I archbishop of Alexandria, Theophilus archbishop [25] of the same great city of Alexandria, Cyril archbishop of the same great city of Alexandria, and Gennadius patriarch of this God-protected and imperial city – and also the canon issued by Cyprian archbishop of the

---

50 For the so-called Apostolic Canons and their inclusion in the partly heretical *Apostolic Constitutions*, see p. 18 above.

51 These are the Canons of Constantinople dating to 394, Joannou (1962b) 438–44.

land of Africa and martyr and his synod, which was accorded authority solely in the regions of the aforementioned primates, according to the custom passed down by them.

No one is permitted to falsify or annul the aforementioned canons, or to receive in their place other canons concocted with false ascriptions by some who attempted to pervert the truth. If anyone is caught altering or trying to overturn one of the aforesaid canons, he will be liable, as this canon lays down, to receive a penance and so to be cured by the very canon he is violating.

This canon was the first official codification of which canons that had been issued previously, whether by councils or apostles or church fathers, possessed continuing and general authority.[52] Canon 1 of Chalcedon had decreed that 'the canons issued by the holy fathers of every council up till now remain in force', but did not provide a list.[53] After the Quinisext Council, Canon 1 of Nicaea II (787) summed up this canon and the list it provides by reaffirming the authority of 'those [canons] composed by the holy apostles, the celebrated trumpets of the Spirit, those published by the six holy ecumenical councils and by the councils convened locally to issue such injunctions, and those of our holy fathers'.[54]

Just as Canon 1 is concerned to enhance by implication the standing of the Quinisext Council itself, so this canon was clearly intended to imply that the council's own canons belonged to this venerable tradition, and that they were based on a thorough knowledge and appropriation of all the past documents of church law. This is not to say, however, that the council was either demanding or expecting that its own canons should and would immediately enjoy the same status as the canons inherited from the sixth-century collections. 'No one who drinks old wine wants the new, for he says, "The old is good"', in the words of Luke 5:39, and it took several centuries for the Quinisext Canons to attain classic status.[55]

The statement in Winkelmann (1980) 113 and others that this canon was anti-Roman in its ignoring of most western sources ignores the fact

---

52 See pp. 18–22 above for details of the compilation and contents of the Byzantine code of canon law, and p. 57 for a date list for the councils mentioned in this canon.

53 COGD 1, 138, trans. Price and Gaddis (2005) III, 94.

54 ACO² III.3, 17–19, trans. Price (2018) II, 610.

55 See pp. 46–50 above.

that this eastern list had been gradually built up through centuries and made no innovations.[56] Its inclusions and omissions have nothing to do with the ecclesiastical politics of the reign of Justinian II.

About priests and clerics[57]

CANON 3

About the seating[58] of presbyters who have entered into two marriages or contracted marriage after ordination or taken a widow or divorcee

[25] Our pious and Christ-loving emperor addressed this holy ecumenical council, telling it that it should make those who are enrolled in the clergy and transmit things divine to others into pure and irreproachable ministers, worthy of the rational sacrifice 'of the great God who is both high priest and victim',[59] and that it should purge the defilement incurred by them through unlawful marriages. In addition, those of the most holy Roman church hold that the rule of strictness should be observed, while those subject to the see of this God-protected and imperial city propose the observance of mercy and compassion. Therefore we ourselves – combining the two into one, according to both the fathers and the call of devotion, lest we let mildness be laxity or strictness be harshness, especially since a not inconsiderable number of men have fallen out of ignorance – resolve that those who entered into second marriages, becoming slaves to sin, and did not choose to mend their ways prior to 15 January last in the now past fourth indiction and the year 6199,[60] are to be subjected to canonical deposition.

[26] As for those who fell into this passion of a second marriage, but before our convening recognized what was beneficial, severed themselves from this evil and repudiated this alien and spurious union, or those whose

56 See the list of the contents of the Byzantine canon law collections from the fourth to the ninth centuries in Wagshaw (2015) 55–6.

57 This section heading, like the one 'about monks and nuns' that precedes Canon 40, is unlikely to be original, but occurs in a large number of MSS; both are apt. See Ohme (2013) LIII, and Wagschal (2015) 263, n. 114.

58 The place in the sanctuary for presbyters, even if they had been deposed from exercising ministry.

59 Gregory of Nazianzus, *or.* 2, 95, SC 247, 1–2.

60 15 January 691. The fourth indiction ran from 1 September 690 until 31 August 691.

wives in a second marriage have already died, or those who have themselves turned to repentance, learning continence and speedily abandoning their previous lawlessness, whether they are presbyters or deacons or subdeacons, it is resolved that they are to cease from all priestly ministry or activity and submit now to penance for a specified time. But they are to retain the honour of their seating and rank, 'being satisfied with their place of honour, and tearfully beseeching the Lord to forgive the offence they committed out of ignorance; for it is not appropriate for one who ought to be treating his own wounds to bless others.'[61]

As for those who have married only one wife but she a widow, and likewise those who have contracted a single marriage illegally after ordination, whether presbyters, deacons or subdeacons, they are now to be suspended from sacred ministry for a short time and subjected to penance, and then restored to their own rank, without ever progressing to a higher one, with their unlawful cohabitation having, of course, been dissolved.

All this we hereby lay down on the basis of our priestly authority in relation to those found to have committed the aforementioned offences up to 15 January of the fourth indiction, as stated above. From the present moment we re-enact and renew the canon that says that 'anyone who enters into two marriages after baptism or takes a concubine cannot be a bishop or presbyter or deacon or anything in the priestly list',[62] and likewise that 'he who marries a widow, divorcee, prostitute, slave or actress cannot be a bishop or presbyter or deacon or anything in the priestly list'.[63]

This canon begins by noting the contrast between the practice of the Roman church and that of Constantinople over those in major orders who enter into a second marriage (it is presumed after the death of the first wife) whether before or after ordination: the Roman Church treated this as an offence to be punished by deposition from the priesthood, the Church of Constantinople had come to treat it with leniency. The middle path laid down here allows clergy who had broken from their unlawful second marriages before the deadline of 15 January 691 to recover their rank, but not their ministry,

61   Canon 27 of Basil of Caesarea, in *ep.* 199, ed. Courtonne II, 159, §27, 4–5 and 10–11 (in reverse order).

62   Apostolic Canon 17, SC 336, p. 278.

63   Apostolic Canon 18, SC 336, p. 280. See too Lev 21:13–14: a priest is to marry a virgin and not a woman who has been divorced or defiled or a prostitute.

after performing due penance. Those who had not repented by the deadline are to lose their rank. Meanwhile, those in major orders who had married only once but either a widow or after their ordination and had also repented before the deadline were likewise to be suspended while they performed penance, but were then to return to ministry as well as recover their rank. In future, those who have married twice or married a widow are never to be ordained. This canon is to be compared to Canon 26, relating to future offences, which allows offenders 'out of ignorance' to retain clerical rank but never again exercise ministry, and Canon 6 which renews the specific prohibition of clerical marriage after ordination.

Why was the date of 15 January 691 chosen? Van Esbroeck has suggested it was to create a nine-month (or at least eight-month) interval before the close of the council, which he wishes to date to mid-September 691, adequate for the legitimization of children conceived before the deadline.[64] If this implies that the deadline was set retrospectively at the council itself, this would be bizarre in the extreme. We must rather presume that the deadline of 15 January 691 had originally been published before this date, which was itself at least eight months before the council and perhaps many more (for its date see pp. 7–8 above).

Out of earlier canonical legislation on this topic particular weight was placed on the Apostolic Canons 17 and 18, both of which are quoted here. Canon 12 of Basil of Caesarea forbade the ordination of those who had contracted a second marriage, while Basil's Canon 27 (which is cited in full in Canon 26 below) forbade those clergy who had entered into an unlawful marriage from ever exercising ministry again. Behind these canonical rules lie the relevant biblical passages, notably 1 Timothy 3:2,12 and Titus 1:6, which exclude those who enter, or have entered, into a second marriage from sacred ministry. This stigma against remarriage by clergy arose from the notion that remarriage, even after the death of the first wife, was a concession to human weakness, tolerable for the laity, but inapplicable to the clergy.

The ban re-enacted here had entered secular legislation in 535 in a law of Justinian's, which likewise forbids the ordination to major orders of those who are in second marriages, or have married a divorced woman, or who have taken a concubine, and the deposition from their rank of those who enter into such a union after ordination.[65] For the ban on clergy marrying after ordination see Canon 6 with annotation below.

---

64 Esbroeck (1995/6) 104.
65 Justinian, *nov.* 6.5 (Schöll–Kroll 42–3).

Both Balsamon and Zonaras (PG 137, 528–9) comment on this canon with extreme brevity, dismissing it (apart from its citation of the two Apostolic Canons) as an enactment applying only to a one-off amnesty and therefore without interest. But its contrast between Roman 'strictness' and Byzantine 'mercy' and respect for both make it for us one of the most significant of the canons.[66]

CANON 4

About penance for one who has had intercourse with a woman consecrated to God

[27] If any bishop, presbyter, deacon, subdeacon, lector, cantor or doorkeeper has had intercourse with a woman consecrated to God, he is to be deposed, as having corrupted the bride of Christ, and if he is a layman, he is to be excommunicated.

Those in major orders guilty of fornication after ordination were in any case subject to deposition, as stated in Canon 3 of Basil of Caesarea (in *ep.* 188) and Apostolic Canon 25 (SC 336, p. 280), but this canon covers an offence by laymen as well. There was related canonical legislation that treated the guilt of the offending woman consecrated to God; Canon 18 of Basil of Caesarea criticizes earlier practice that had imposed on her a mere one year of penance for ignoring the special gravity of breaking vows made to God. The present canon treats as obsolete legislation by Justinian I that had imposed the death penalty for the seduction of deaconesses or nuns on the grounds that it was a gross offence against God.[67]

The distinction between the treatment of offending clerics, who are to be deposed, and offending laymen who are to be excommunicated arose from the rule that no one could suffer a double penalty for a single offence, with the implication that a cleric could not be both deposed and excommunicated. Deposition was the more serious penalty in that it was permanent, while excommunication could subsequently be lifted. The rule that clerics should be deposed but not excommunicated had been stated in Canon 3 of

66 See p. 38 above: this canon is not to be classified as 'anti-Roman'.
67 *CJ* IX. 13 of 533 (Krüger 378).

Basil of Caesarea (in his *ep.* 188) and Apostolic Canon 25 (SC 336, p. 280), both of which cite Nahum 1:9, 'You shall not punish with affliction twice for the same offence.'[68] That for a given offence clerics are to be deposed and laymen excommunicated appears explicitly as a formula already in the Apostolic Canons, e.g. 63–64 and Canons 2, 8 and 27 of Chalcedon.[69]

CANON 5

That those of priestly rank[70] should not live
with a maidservant as companion[71]

[27] Let no one of those enrolled in the priestly order acquire a woman or servant, apart from living with those persons mentioned in the canon as beyond suspicion; this will protect him from criticism. If anyone violates our decree, he is to be deposed. Eunuchs also must observe this, keeping themselves free from blame. Those who violate this, if they are clerics, are to be deposed, and if they are laymen, excommunicated.

This cites and renews Canon 3 of Nicaea (COGD I, 21), which bans all clergy, whether in major or minor orders, from 'having a female companion (συνείσακτον)', unless she be a close relative 'or other woman beyond any suspicion'. Canonical collections also included as Canon 88 of Basil of Caesarea his *ep.* 55 (Courtonne I, 141–2), in which he orders an elderly priest who was living with a virgin to separate from her to avoid scandal. The rule had been confirmed by Justinian I with reference to unmarried clerics of any grade.[72]

68 Despite this, Apostolic Canons 29 and 65 (SC 336, pp. 282, 298) decree both deposition and excommunication for clerics who, respectively, commit simony or pray in a synagogue or heretical conventicle.
69 SC 336, p. 298 and COGD 1, 138–50, trans. Price and Gaddis (2005) III, 94–103, respectively.
70 Meaning those in major orders, down to that of subdeacon.
71 'Companion' translates ἐπεισάκτῳ, 'brought in from outside'.
72 Justinian, *nov.* 123.29 of 546 (Schöll–Kroll 615–16).

CANON 6

That presbyters or deacons are not permitted
to contract marriage after ordination

[27] Since the Apostolic Canons state that 'of those admitted unmarried into the clergy only lectors and cantors may marry'[73] and we maintain this, we decree that from now on a subdeacon, deacon or presbyter is totally without any licence after ordination has been conferred on him to set up for himself marital cohabitation. If he has the presumption to do this, he is to be deposed. If anyone admitted into the clergy wishes to be conjoined to a woman in lawful matrimony, he must do this before ordination to the subdiaconate, diaconate or priesthood.

Apostolic Canon 26 (SC 336, p. 280) allowed lectors and cantors to marry after ordination but none of the higher clergy to do the same. Canon 16 of Carthage laid down that 'when lectors reach early manhood they are either to take a wife or make a vow of continence', while Canon 14 of Chalcedon forbade lectors and cantors from marrying heretics. Canon 1 of Neocaesarea condemned to deposition presbyters who married after ordination. Canon 10 of Ancyra imposed the same rule on deacons, with the significant modification that, if they declared their intention to marry at ordination and this was accepted by the ordaining bishop, they were free to do so; this concession was withdrawn by Justinian I in 546.[74] See too an earlier law of Justinian's: 'If it happens therefore that a priest, a deacon or a subdeacon should take a wife or concubine, he is to be immediately removed from his rank and treated thereafter as a layman.'[75] An explanation for this ban was provided by the Third Novel of Leo VI (886–912), which argued that it would be improper for a man already ordained to plan to marry and thereby descend from the spiritual heights to fleshly depths; it was clearly felt that, while a man who proceeds from marriage to ordination is making spiritual progress, marriage for one already ordained would be a retrograde step that would constitute infidelity to his calling.

73 Apostolic Canon 26 (SC 336, p. 280).
74 Justinian, *nov.* 123.14.1 (Schöll–Kroll 605).
75 Justinian, *nov.* 6.5 of 535 (Schöll–Kroll 43, 5–9).

CANON 7

That deacons should not take precedence over presbyters

[27] Since we have learnt that in some churches there are deacons holding ecclesiastical offices of whom some in consequence, out of insolence and self-will, assume precedence over the presbyters, we decree that a deacon, even if he holds a dignity, that is, an ecclesiastical office of any kind, is not to take precedence over a presbyter – the one exception being when he visits another city on some matter of business as the representative of his patriarch or metropolitan, for then he should be honoured as filling his place. If anyone presumes to do this with insolent usurpation, he is to be degraded from his rank and take the lowest place of all [28] in whatever order he is enrolled in his church.[76] For our Lord exhorts us not to take pleasure in the first seats, according to the teaching in the holy Gospel of Luke, as coming from our Lord and God himself: 'For he told to those invited a parable, noting how they chose the first seats, saying to them: "When you are invited by someone to a wedding, do not recline in the first seat, lest someone of greater honour than you has been invited by him, and he who invited both you and him come and say to you, 'Give this man your place.' And then you will begin with shame to take the lowest place. But when you are invited, go and recline in the lowest place, so that, when the host comes, he will say to you, 'Friend, come up higher.' Then you will win glory in the presence of those seated with you. For everyone who exalts himself will be humbled, and whoever humbles himself will be exalted."'[77] The same is to be observed in the case of the other sacred orders, since we know that spiritual dignities are greater than secular ones.

Comparable is Canon 18 of Nicaea (COGD I, 29), which condemned the practices current in some cities of deacons at the eucharist giving communion, on occasion, to presbyters and even receiving communion before bishops, and of deacons sitting among the presbyters; it reminded

---

76 The distinction between 'rank' (βαθμός) and 'order' (τάγμα) is not obvious, but the meaning must be that the offending deacon is to lose his prestigious office and descend to the lowest position among the deacons of his church. This implies that, quite apart from particular posts, there was a ranking among deacons according to seniority.

77 Lk 14:7–11.

deacons that 'they are servants of the bishop and inferior to the presbyters'. There was a natural tendency for a more exalted rank to be assumed by those deacons who were the immediate assistants and executants of patriarchs or bishops, for example as *synkelloi* (chief assistants of a patriarch) or *skeuophylakes* (in charge of the sacred vessels and other church property); such senior deacons were often elected bishops, popes or patriarchs without an intermediate period as presbyters.

CANON 8

*That every year there should be a synod of the bishops in
each province wherever the metropolitan decides*

[28] Since we too wish that the decrees of our holy fathers should be in force as regards all matters, we renew the canon that says that every year there are to be synods of bishops in each province, wherever the bishop of the metropolis decides.[78] But since because of barbarian inroads and other accidental causes it is impossible for those who preside over the churches[79] to hold synods twice a year, it is resolved that once a year in any event, because of the ecclesiastical business that is likely to arise, there is to be a synod of the aforesaid bishops in each province, between the holy feast of Easter and the end of the month of October in each year, in the place (as said above) which the bishop of the metropolis chooses. 'The bishops who do not assemble but stay in their own cities, even though they are in good health and are not impeded by any essential and unavoidable business, are to receive a fraternal rebuke.'[80]

Canon 5 of Nicaea (COGD I, 22) had laid down that provincial synods should be held twice yearly, especially in order to review excommunications imposed by bishops; this was reaffirmed in Canon 20 of Antioch and Apostolic Canon 37 (SC 336, p. 286). Canon 19 of Chalcedon, noting that this was often not observed, reiterated the rule. This Quinisext

---

78 This echoes Canon 19 of Chalcedon (COGD 1, 146), trans. Price and Gaddis (2005) III, 100.

79 Meaning all the bishops, not just the metropolitans.

80 Canon 19 of Chalcedon, last sentence.

reduction of the requirement to a single annual synod was repeated in Canon 6 of Nicaea II,[81] which specifies as its justification the inconvenience and expense that the earlier rule had imposed on bishops. Secular law, however, had already made the change: Justinian I in 546 had laid down that such synods should be held 'once or twice a year'.[82] In 565 he laid down an annual synod, while recommending more frequent assemblies (in accordance with Canon 5 of Nicaea) when accusations against clerics or monks needed to be heard, doubtless when they appealed against verdicts delivered by their bishops.[83]

As for the time of year of these synods, while Nicaea had laid down that the meetings were to be in Eastertide[84] and in the autumn, both the Apostolic Canons and Antioch specified the fourth week of Pentecost and October, as is pointed out in Justinian's law of 565 already cited. In the case, however, of a single annual synod, this same law laid down that it should be in either June or September. The Quinisext canon allows any date between Easter and the end of October.

CANON 9

That a cleric is not allowed to keep an inn

[29] [It is laid down that] no cleric is allowed to keep an inn. For if he is not allowed to enter an inn,[85] it is all the more forbidden for him to serve others in one and to undertake what is forbidden to him. If someone were to do this, he is either to discontinue or be deposed.

The Greek word translated here as 'inn' is καπηλεῖον, which strictly meant an eating-place in a city, as contrasted to a πανδοχεῖον or a public house on a highway. Canon 24 of Laodicea forbade clerics from entering a καπηλεῖον, while Apostolic Canon 54 (SC 336, p. 296) excommunicated clerics who ate

81 COGD 1, 316, trans. Price (2018) II, 614–15.
82 Justinian, *nov.* 123.10 (Schöll–Kroll 602).
83 Justinian, *nov.* 137.4–5 (Schöll–Kroll 698).
84 The phrase in the canon is 'before the fortieth day', which in both medieval and modern times has often been misunderstood to mean 'before Lent', but this clashes with both probability and the later fourth-century canons. See L'Huillier (1996) 42–3.
85 This had been banned in Canon 24 of Laodicea, Joannou (1962b) 140.

in a καπηλεῖον, unless it were a πανδοχεῖον where they needed to eat when travelling; this special exemption to meet the needs of a cleric or monk on a journey was repeated in Canon 22 of Nicaea II.[86] Canon 16 of Carthage forbade those in major orders from earning their livelihood 'from any shameful or dishonourable occupation', which would have included inn-keeping.

CANON 10

That a priest should not take interest or a hundredth part

[29] A bishop, presbyter or deacon who takes interest or the so-called hundredth part must either discontinue or be deposed.

Canon 17 of Nicaea (COGD I, 29) had similarly prohibited clerics from practising usury, as had Apostolic Canon 44 (SC 336, p. 288) and Canon 4 of Laodicea.[87] The canon repeats the wording of the Apostolic Canon, with the addition of the reference to 'the so-called hundredth part'.

CANON 11

About not associating or conversing with Jews or
receiving medical treatment from them

[29] No one of those enrolled in the priestly order nor a layman is to eat the unleavened bread of the Jews or associate with them, or to call them in case of illness and receive medical treatment from them, or to wash in their company in any way in bathhouses. If anyone chooses to do so, if he is a cleric, he is to be deposed, and if a layman, excommunicated.

Compare Canon 38 of Laodicea, which forbids Christians from 'accepting unleavened bread (ἄζυμα) from Jews or sharing in their impieties'. Apostolic Canon 70 (SC 336, 300) links this to a Jewish custom of giving

---

86 COGD 1, 342–3, trans. Price (2018) II, 623–4.
87 Joannou (1962b) 30 and 132 respectively.

unleavened bread to all who joined them in celebrating one of their feasts. John Chrysostom had famously inveighed against Christians who took part in Jewish festivals or visited Jewish doctors.[88] The present canon restricts contact between Christians and Jews in certain purely secular contexts. It incidentally reveals that friendly and close relations between many Christians and Jews had continued down into the late seventh century. The disapproval of this expressed in this canon reflects the worsening relations between the two faiths from the time of Justinian I and with further deterioration in the first half of the seventh century, when the loss of half the empire to the Persians and then the Arabs produced an acute sense of insecurity in Byzantium, and Jews in Palestine were widely accused (it is hard to know with what justice) of having actively supported first the Persian and then the Arab invaders. This resulted in an intensification of repressive measures against dissident minorities and especially the Jews, seen as both God's enemies and natural allies with the empire's enemies.[89]

CANON 12

That a bishop should not live with his wife after consecration

[29] This too has come to our notice that in Africa, Libya and elsewhere as well, the most God-beloved bishops of those there do not decline to live with their wives even after their consecration, thereby causing offence and scandal to their congregations. Therefore, because we are extremely keen that everything should be done for the good of the flocks in our charge, we hereby resolve that from now on this is not to occur at all. This we say not to annul or overturn the apostolic regulations,[90] but with forethought for the salvation and moral improvement of the congregations and to leave no ground for censure of the priestly state. For the divine apostle says, 'Do everything for the glory of God. Give no offence to Jews or Greeks or the church of God, [30] just as I too please everyone in everything, seeking not

---

88 See Kelly (1995) 63–6.

89 See Haldon (1990) 345–8, and Cameron (2002).

90 Apostolic Canon 5 (SC 336, p. 276) forbade bishops (and all in major orders) to repudiate their wives 'with the pretext of piety'. See my commentary on Canon 48 on p. 129 below.

my own advantage but that of the many, so that they may be saved. Be imitators of me, as I am of Christ."[91] If anyone is caught doing this, he is to be deposed.

'Africa' means the two provinces of Africa and (lying to the south) Byzacena, most of which had been lost to the Arabs shortly before the council, though Carthage did not fall until 711. 'Libya' must mean Tripolitania, since Cyrenaica was under the patriarchate of Alexandria. So these were regions under Roman jurisdiction; and the western rule, as we find it in Canons 3, 4 and 25 of Carthage, while imposing permanent sexual continence on all in major orders and their wives, did not demand separation. The different eastern discipline finds clear expression in the Quinisext Canon 48, which lays down that the wife of a married man who becomes a bishop must enter a monastery. The council was acting *ultra vires* in condemning a Roman practice as followed in regions under Roman jurisdiction, though the phrase 'elsewhere as well' may refer to regions in the east.

CANON 13

That presbyters, deacons and subdeacons should keep their wives

[30] We have learnt that in the Roman church it is handed down as a canonical rule that those about to be ordained deacon or presbyter must promise that they will no longer have sexual relations with their wives. We, however, in accordance with the ancient canon of apostolic strictness and discipline, wish to confirm henceforth the lawful marriages of sacred men. We in no way dissolve their union with their wives or deprive them of intercourse with each other at the appropriate time.[92] Consequently, if anyone be found worthy of ordination to the subdiaconate, diaconate or presbyterate, he is in no way to be prevented from entering into this rank because he is living together with a lawful wife, nor at the time of his ordination is he to be required to promise that he will abstain from lawful intercourse with his own wife, for otherwise we shall find ourselves impelled

91 1 Cor 10:31–11:1.
92 Inappropriate times would be during fasting periods and the night before celebrating the eucharist, as is mentioned below through citation from the Council of Carthage.

in consequence to insult marriage, even though it was ordained and blessed by God through his presence.[93] For the gospel saying declares, 'What God had joined together, let not man put asunder,'[94] and the apostle teaches, 'Marriage is honourable and the bed undefiled,' and 'Are you bound to a wife? Do not seek a dissolution.'[95]

We are aware, however, as was declared by those who convened at Carthage and took thought for the sacred character of the life of ministers, that 'subdeacons who touch the sacred mysteries and deacons and presbyters according to their particular statutes should abstain from their wives',[96] 'so that we too may preserve the tradition of the apostles that has been in force since ancient times',[97] in our awareness that there is a time for everything and especially for fasting and prayer.[98] For those who serve at the altar at the time of the handling of the holy gifts 'must be self-controlled in everything, so that they may be able to receive what they ask from God in all simplicity'.

Therefore, if anyone in opposition to the Apostolic Canons presumes to deprive anyone of those in sacred orders, we mean presbyters or deacons or subdeacons, of union and fellowship with his lawful wife, he is to be deposed. Likewise, [31] if any presbyter or deacon or subdeacon repudiates his wife on the pretext of piety, he is to be excommunicated and, if he persists, deposed.

It is a familiar fact that over the question of marriage for those in priestly orders West and East diverged in the latter part of the fourth century. In the East, for example, Apostolic Canon 5 (SC 336, p. 276) laid down that anyone in priestly orders who repudiated his wife 'on the pretext of piety' was to be excommunicated and, if he persevered, deposed. A rule requiring bishops to separate from their wives became generally accepted (see below on Canon 48), but presbyters were normally married.[99] In the West, in

---

93 Cp. Gen 2:24, Mt 19:5, Jn 2:1–11.
94 Mt 19:6.
95 Heb 13:4, 1 Cor 7:27.
96 Canon of Carthage 25.
97 Canon of Carthage 3.
98 Cp. Rom 7:5.
99 Gradually it became an actual requirement in the Orthodox East that candidates for the presbyterate were married, unless they were, or became, monks. In modern Greek 'married priest' is the standard expression for a secular priest.

contrast, a rule that bishops, presbyters and deacons must abstain from marital relations was forcefully enunciated in a series of papal decrees that begin in the 380s, with letters from Pope Siricius to Bishop Himerius of Tarragona (385) and to the bishops of Africa (386) and an anonymous *Letter to the Gallic Bishops* sometimes attributed to Pope Damasus (d. 384) but now generally assigned to Siricius or to a compiler at the papal court.[100] The Roman rule had no legal force in the Byzantine East. Around 400 there was some demand in the eastern provinces for the adoption of the Roman practice, but it was countered by a legend that now entered circulation to the effect that the matter had been discussed at Nicaea and the Roman rule rejected.[101]

Of the canonical legislation within the Byzantine canonical corpus the only canons that impose permanent sexual continence on all in major orders were Canons 3, 4, 25 and 70 of Carthage, which entered the Byzantine corpus in the sixth century. There was reluctance to contradict or annul earlier canons,[102] but they could be reinterpreted. So in the present canon these canons of Carthage are not rejected but reinterpreted as imposing continence only as a temporary preparation for participation in the eucharist, meaning in practice abstinence during the night before, which is still the discipline in the Orthodox churches, and equally applies to laypeople who wish to receive holy communion.

It would be a mistake to seek an explanation for this divergence in practice between East and West in supposed differences between western and eastern Christianity. The demand for clerical continence existed within both; if it prevailed in the West, this may be attributed to the accident that Siricius and his successors adopted it and had the authority (which no bishop in Byzantium possessed) to enforce their will.

In contrast, Canon 30 below accepts the Roman celibacy rule in 'barbarian lands', probably where predominantly Slavic parts of the Balkans were under western influence, but with the derogatory comment, 'We have conceded this to them on no other ground than their timorousness of mind and their bizarre and irresolute behaviour.'

---

100 These three letters appear as, respectively, *epp.* 1, 5, 10 in PL 13, 1131–93. For the western adoption of a rule of clerical continence and its later supplementation by a rule of clerical celibacy see Price (2004).

101 Socrates, *HE* I. 11, SC 477, 142–6.

102 For an exception see, however, Canon 16 below, which rejects a canon of Neocaesarea.

CANON 14

*That a presbyter should not be ordained before the age of 30 or
a deacon before that of 25 or a deaconess before that of 40*

[31] The canon[103] of our holy and inspired fathers is to remain in force in this respect too, that 'a presbyter is not to be ordained before the age of thirty but made to wait, even if the man is worthy. For the Lord Jesus Christ was baptized and began to teach in his thirtieth year'.[104] Likewise a deacon is not to be ordained before the age of twenty-five nor a deaconess before the age of forty.

This is all traditional. Canon 11 of Neocaesarea had laid down thirty as the earliest age for presbyteral ordination, Canon 16 of Carthage twenty-five for diaconal ordination, and Canon 15 of Chalcedon forty for ordination as a deaconess; these three ages reappear in a law of Justinian's of 546.[105] The rule for deaconesses was itself a compromise between the practice in some regions of allowing diaconal ordination to young unmarried women and the edict issued by Theodosius I in 390 which restricted the office to those aged 60 or over.[106] This Quinisext canon says nothing about the earliest age for episcopal ordination; the same law of Justinian I had laid down a minimum age of 35.[107]

CANON 15

That a subdeacon should not be ordained before the age of 20

[31] A subdeacon is not to be ordained before the age of twenty. If anyone in any priestly order has been ordained contrary to the age laid down, he is to be deposed.

---

103 'The canon' means here 'canon law'.
104 Canon 11 of Neocaesarea. That Christ was 'around thirty' at the start of his ministry is stated by Lk 3:23.
105 Justinian, *nov.* 123.13 (Schöll–Kroll 604).
106 *CTh* 16.2.27.
107 Justinian, *nov.* 123.1 (Schöll–Kroll, 594).

Contrast Justinian's novel of 546, cited above, which had laid down 25 as the minimum age for subdiaconal as of diaconal ordination.[108] Eastern canon law counted the subdiaconate among the 'priestly' or major orders, while the West did not at this date.

CANON 16

That the number of seven deacons in Acts should not be applied to those in the church

[31] The book of the Acts hands down that seven deacons were appointed by the apostles, and those at the Council of Neocaesarea in the canons they issued explicitly concluded, 'That there ought to be seven deacons according to the canon, even if the city is a very big one, is something you will be convinced about by the book of the Acts.'[109] But we, harmonizing the mind of the fathers to the apostolic statement, have found that they were not speaking about the men who serve the mysteries, but about the provision of table service, for the book of the Acts says the following: 'In those days as the disciples multiplied there was a complaint by the Hellenists against the Hebrews, that their widows were being overlooked in the daily distribution. The twelve summoned the multitude of the disciples and said, "It is not right that we should leave the word of God to serve at tables. Therefore, brothers, pick out from among you seven men of good repute, full of the Holy Spirit and wisdom, whom we shall appoint for this need, while we shall persevere in prayer and the service of the word." [32] And these words pleased the whole multitude, and they chose Stephen, a man full of faith and the Holy Spirit, and Philip, Prochoros, Nicanor, Timon, Parmenas and Nikolaos, a proselyte of Antioch, whom they brought before the apostles.'[110]

The teacher of the church John Chrysostom interprets this passage as follows: 'It is worthy of wonder how the multitude was not divided in its choice of men and how the apostles were not criticized by them. But we need to discover what rank they had and what ordination they received. Was it that of deacons? But this did not yet exist in the churches. Did the

---

108   Justinian, *nov.* 123.13 (Schöll–Kroll 604).
109   Canon 15 of Neocaesarea.
110   Acts 6:1–6.

management fall to the presbyters? But no one was yet a bishop, but there were only apostles. And therefore I think that it is clear and plain that it is neither deacons nor presbyters who are being referred to.'

Therefore on this matter we too declare, in accordance with the teaching just cited, that the afore-mentioned seven deacons are not to be understood as serving the mysteries, but that they were those entrusted with the management of the ordinary needs of those who had then assembled. This makes them a model for us in this respect – of zeal and charity towards those in need.

In the pre-Nicene church even the major sees considered themselves bound by the precedent in the apostolic church of Jerusalem. We know from a letter of Pope Cornelius that in 251 there were still only seven deacons in the church of Rome.[111] In Constantinople Justinian I raised the number to a hundred and Heraclius (in 612) to 150.[112] The present canon regularizes the situation canonically by abrogating Canon 15 of Neocaesarea – an unusual step in view of the heavy emphasis in the Byzantine church on preserving all authentic early traditions, even if sometimes reinterpreting them. What made this step possible was the support provided by John Chrysostom, as quoted here, the most read and cited of all the Greek Fathers.

CANON 17

That a cleric should not be enrolled in another church
without the consent of his own bishop

[32] Clerics of various churches, leaving their own churches in which they were ordained, have gone off to other bishops and without the consent of their own bishop have been enrolled in the churches of others. The result has been that they have shed all discipline. We therefore decree that from the month of January in the fourth indiction now past no one of all the clergy, whatever his rank, has the freedom without a letter of release from his own bishop to be enrolled in another church. Whoever in future does not observe this but brings disgrace (in so far as he is able) on the one who

---

111 Letter to Bishop Fabius of Antioch, preserved in Eusebius, *HE* VI.43.11.
112 Justinian, *nov.* 3.1 of 535 (Schöll–Kroll 21) and Konidaris (1982) 62–4.

conferred ordination on him is to be deposed, both he and also the one who received him for no good reason.

This was a perennial problem, involving not just clergy who found life in another city (generally, of course, a large and richer one, notably Constantinople) more agreeable – Canon 15 of Nicaea (COGD I, 27–8) ordered such clergy to return to their original city – but also bishops who accepted such clergy into their own church without the express approval of their original bishop. Canon 16 of Nicaea (COGD I, 28) declared the ordination of such a cleric (that is, to a higher rank) by his adopting bishop to be invalid. Canon 3 of Antioch (Joannou 1962b, 106–7) decreed that such a bishop was to be tried and punished by the synod of the province (no particular penalty is laid down). Canon 20 of Chalcedon decreed that such a bishop and the cleric he received were to be excommunicate until the cleric returned to his own church. The present canon increases the penalty for the bishop and the cleric alike. The qualification made in the Chalcedonian canon, to the effect that it does not apply to 'those who have left their own homelands out of necessity and so moved to another church', is omitted here, since this case is addressed in the following canon.

Canon 15 of Nicaea (COGD 1, 27–28) banned all such transfers *tout court*. But later practice allowed them when the original ordinary of the cleric involved gave his permission. There was still concern lest such clerics would hold benefices in both their original and their adoptive churches; this was banned by Canon 10 of Chalcedon (COGD 1, 142–3).

CANON 18

About clerics who on the pretext of a barbarian inroad or some
other circumstance have emigrated, and that they should return to
their own church after the departure of the [barbarian] nation

[33] We order those clerics who on the pretext of a barbarian inroad or some other circumstance have emigrated to return again to their own churches, once the situation has come to an end, whether it be the barbarian inroads or whatever was the reason for their withdrawal, and not to abandon their churches for a long time on no good ground. If any of them does not obey

the present canon, he is to be excommunicated until he returns to his own church. The same is to happen to the bishop who retains him.

In the disturbed conditions of the seventh and eighth centuries a particular problem arose from clergy who moved to a more secure or wealthier city whether for safety or because their original church could not support them. A law issued by Heraclius in 617 had prohibited this.[113] Canon 20 of Chalcedon had allowed transfers by clerics 'who had left their own homelands out of necessity'.[114] The implication of the present canon is that this permission had been overused, and needed restriction. Canon 15 of Nicaea II was more generous: it forbade such clergy from seeking clerical employment in Constantinople, but permitted it in other cities.[115]

Unexpected in the present canon is the penalty of excommunication rather than deposition for offending clergy – the latter being the standard penalty for clerics, while a simultaneous excommunication was excluded by the tradition that ruled out two penalties for the same offence.[116] The implication is that such a cleric by deserting his church had already ceased to hold clerical office. Canon 6 of Chalcedon had forbidden ordination without assignment to a particular church and a particular pastoral charge.[117] The implication was that abandonment of such a charge without permission from higher authority suspended the original ordination.

CANON 19

That those who preside in the churches should instruct
the clergy and people with words of piety according to
the tradition of the holy and inspired fathers

[33] [We lay down] that those who preside in the churches[118] ought every day and especially on Sundays to instruct the whole clergy and people

---

113 Heraclius, *nov.* 2, Konidaris (1982) 72–8.
114 COGD 1, 147, trans. Price and Gaddis (2005) III, 101.
115 ACO² III.2, 196, 12–13, trans. Price (2018) 619–20.
116 See pp. 86–7 above.
117 COGD 1, 141, trans Price and Gaddis (2005) III, 96.
118 The bishops.

with the words of piety, gathering out of sacred Scripture the ideas and judgements of the truth, and not transgressing the limits already laid down or the tradition of the inspired fathers. But even when the topic is a passage of Scripture, they are not to interpret it differently from what the luminaries and teachers of the church have expounded in their writings; let them seek a reputation for this rather than for composing their own sermons, since sometimes they lose their way in this and depart from what is appropriate. For it is through the teaching of the aforesaid fathers that the congregations, learning what is good and to be chosen and what is harmful and to be shunned, change the character of their lives for the better and do not fall victim to the defect of ignorance, but, cleaving to the teaching, brace themselves against evil impulses and through fear of the punishments that hang over them work out their salvation.

Canon 19 of Laodicea had laid down that prayers in the liturgy for catechumens, then penitents and finally the faithful should regularly follow the bishop's homily, with the implication that bishops preached at every eucharist. Apostolic Canon 58 (SC 336, p. 296) had threatened bishops and presbyters who neglected their duty to instruct the laity in the faith with (temporary) excommunication, and permanent deposition if they continued to do so. But there are several new points in the present canon – the strong recommendation for daily preaching (and not only during Lent) and the insistence that sermons should stick closely to the scriptural exegesis of the Church Fathers. Indeed, the wording of the canon encourages bishops simply to read out patristic homilies; collections of homilies to serve this purpose had begun to appear in the fifth century.[119] When in mid-seventeenth-century Russia Patriarch Nikon of Moscow ordered his clergy to deliver their own sermons, it was a novelty and excited a charge of 'heresy'.

---

119 For a bibliography of Greek collections of homilies see Sachot (1994) 165.

CANON 20

That a bishop should not teach publicly in a city
not his own that has another bishop

[33] A bishop is not allowed to teach publicly in another city that does not belong to him. If anyone is apprehended doing this, he is to cease from episcopal functions, and do the work of a presbyter.

Earlier canons – Canons 13 and 22 of Antioch and Apostolic Canon 35 (SC 336, p. 284) – had forbidden bishops from carrying out ordinations outside their own diocese, but the present canon goes beyond this in forbidding bishops from preaching in cities outside their jurisdiction, except of course if they were specially invited by the bishop of the city in question. There was a precedent for this enactment in Canon 11 of Sardica, which castigated any bishop who preached frequently in the church of a less educated bishop, in the hope of being installed in his place.

CANON 21

About clerics who have incurred canonical charges
and are repentant

[34] Regarding those who have incurred canonical charges and have therefore been subjected to total and permanent deposition and relegated to the lay state, if they look to amendment of their own free will, cancel the sin through which they fell from grace, and make themselves complete strangers to it, they are to be tonsured in the manner of clerics. But if they do not choose this voluntarily, they are to wear their hair like laymen, for having preferred the ways of the world to the heavenly life.

The issue here is whether clerics who because of offences have been relegated to the lay state preserve sufficient vestige of their clerical dignity to be allowed to preserve their clerical tonsure – a mark of clerical dignity that had been adopted, imitating monastic practice, in the sixth century. A distinction is made between clerics who have fully repented of their sin and demonstrated this in their mode of life and those who have not. The former may continue to exhibit the clerical tonsure, the latter may not. There was no precedent for this canon in earlier canonical legislation.

CANON 22

About those who are ordained for money

[34] We order that those, whether bishop or clerics of any kind, who are ordained for money, and not after scrutiny and according to the mode of life they have chosen, are to be deposed, as are also those who ordained them.

This canon forbids the sin of simony, so called after Simon Magus of Acts 8. This obviously grave offence had already been condemned in several canons, notably Apostolic Canon 29 (SC 336, p. 282) and Canon 2 of Chalcedon.[120] The canon of Chalcedon imposes the penalty of deposition on both the one ordaining and the one ordained. Apostolic Canon 29, however, imposes excommunication as well as deposition on both. This imposition of a double penalty was contrary to a standard canonical rule (see pp. 86–87 above), perhaps under the influence of the sinister reputation of Simon Magus, less in canonical Acts than in the legendary Acts of Peter.[121]

A problem is revealed, however, by Justinian, *nov.* 123.2–3 of 546 (Schöll/Kroll 595–8), which forbids simony in the case of bishops (596 §1), but proceeds immediately to allow and indeed commend a bishop who presents some or all his property to the diocese either after or even before his ordination, 'since this is not a purchase but an offering' (597. 7–8). Such permission and indeed encouragement of voluntary gifts surely muddied the waters. In the eighth century simony was so widespread that after Nicaea II (787) a number of formerly iconoclast bishops who had been ordained for money – chosen as representative cases rather than exceptional ones – were, as a special concession, made to do penance for only one year and then restored to their episcopal functions.[122]

---

120   COGD 1, 138, trans. Price and Gaddis (2005) III, 94.
121   For state legislation against simony see, applying to bishops, *CJ* I.3.30(31) of 472 (Krüger 22) and, applying to all clerics, I.3.41(42).19 of 528 (Krüger 27).
122   See Price (2018) I, 54–9.

CANON 23

*That those who give out communion should
not make charges of any kind*

[34] On the subject that none of the bishops, presbyters or deacons who give out the spotless communion should exact from the one who receives it either cash or anything else in return for this communion. For grace is not sold, nor do we bestow sanctification by the Spirit for money, but it is to be given in all simplicity to those worthy of the gift. If any of those enrolled in the clergy is found demanding anything from one to whom he gives the spotless communion, he is to be deposed as an emulator of the deviation and wickedness of Simon.[123]

This canon treats as equivalent to simony (ordaining for money) the giving out of holy communion on payment of money. This latter offence had not been mentioned in any previous canonical legislation.

CANON 24

That one in priestly orders or a monk should not attend horse races

[34] No one of those enrolled in the priestly order or a monk is to be allowed to go to horse races or attend theatrical plays. But if any cleric is invited to a wedding, whenever the deceitful mummers make their appearance, he is to 'get up and leave at once',[124] as the teaching of the fathers directs us. If anyone is caught doing this, he is either to cease or be deposed.

This canon cites Canon 54 of Laodicea, which forbade clerics of all grades from attending theatrical performances put on as an entertainment at banquets or weddings. It expands this to cover attendance in the hippodrome or theatres. It had been typical of the more earnest church fathers to deplore attendance at these games even by laymen: this includes Tertullian,

123 Simon Magus, Acts 8:9–20.
124 Canon 54 of Laodicea.

Augustine, John Chrysostom and Severos of Antioch.[125] For those in major orders or monks to attend them would generally have been regarded as scandalous, and so this legislation simply formalized a longstanding restriction.

CANON 25

That the rural and country parishes of each church
remain under the bishops who possess them

[35] In addition to all the other canons we also renew the one that says that 'the rural or country parishes of each church are to remain undisturbed under the bishops who possess them, especially if they have held and administered them for a thirty-year period without recourse to force. If, however, within the thirty years there has occurred or shall occur dispute over them, those who claim to have been wronged have the right to raise the matter with the synod of the province.'[126]

Canon 17 of Chalcedon[127] proceeded after the passage quoted here to lay down that in the event of the foundation of a new city the ecclesiastical arrangements were to imitate the secular ones (this is cited in Canon 38 below), but this is not the issue in the present canon. In the context of the seventh century the problem will have been the virtual disappearance of some dioceses, due to barbarian inroads and a scattering of populations. Even in more peaceful times disputes over boundaries could arise. Nor could the matter always be decided by respecting the boundaries between cities in the secular sphere, since the ecclesiastical and secular boundaries did not always coincide.[128] The rule issued at Chalcedon and repeated here concedes that, if a bishop had controlled a parish, even if not obviously his own, for thirty years or more, it would be vain to try and prove that he did

---

125 Tertullian, *De spectaculis* (CCSL 1, 227–53), Augustine, *Sermon* 51.2 (CCSL 41 Aa, 10–12), John Chrysostom, *Homily against those who desert the church and hasten to horse races and theatrical shows* (PG 56, 263–70), Severus of Antioch, *Cathedral Homily* 26 (PO 36.4, 540–57).

126 From Canon 17 of Chalcedon, COGD I, 145, trans. Price and Gaddis (2005) III, 100.

127 COGD 1, 145, trans. Price and Gaddis (2005), III, 100.

128 Jones (1964) 878–9.

so improperly. Thirty years would be within living memory; this canon presumes that documentary proof of precise diocesan boundaries before that was not to be expected.

CANON 26

That one who has entered into an unlawful marriage
out of ignorance should retain only his chair

[35] 'A presbyter who has entered into an unlawful marriage out of ignorance is to retain his chair', as the sacred canon lays down for us, 'but to abstain from all other activities. For forgiveness is all he deserves, and it is not appropriate for one who ought to be attending to his own wounds to bless others; for a blessing is an imparting of sanctification, and how can one who does not possess the latter as a result of his offence out of ignorance impart it to another? He is not to give blessings either in public or in private, he is not to distribute the body of Christ to others, nor perform any other liturgical action, but to be satisfied with his place of honour and tearfully beseech the Lord to forgive the offence he committed out of ignorance.'[129] It is obvious that such an unlawful marriage will be dissolved and that the man will no longer have intercourse with the one because of whom he has been banned from sacred ministry.

This canon may be compared to Canon 3, which addresses clergy who have married twice or married a widow and cites the final lines of the canon of Basil of Caesarea quoted here. But the 'ignorance' referred to in the present canon (which must surely be ignorance of the facts rather than ignorance of the law) covers a broader range of improper marriages, and it would be most unusual for a bridegroom not to know whether his bride was a widow or not. And so this canon, both here and in its original context in St Basil, must relate to other disqualifications – forbidden degrees of kinship, or marriage to a woman with a shameful past, such as a prostitute or actress. It takes for granted that a presbyter who had knowingly entered into such a relationship is to be deposed, but enacts that, when the presbyter had so acted in ignorance, he is to keep his rank but is excluded from ministry. As

---

129 Canon 27 of Basil of Caesarea, in *ep.* 199, ed. Courtonne II, 159.

a presbyter he was, of course, not free to enter into a new marriage, even though his first marriage was now deemed null and void.[130]

CANON 27

That no one enrolled in the clergy should wear inappropriate clothing

[35] None of those enrolled in the clergy is to wear inappropriate clothing, neither when staying in a city nor when going on a journey, but he is to wear the dress that has already been appointed for those enrolled in the clergy. If anyone violates this, he is to be excommunicated for one week.

Clerics were distinguished from the laity by a distinctive dress and a clerical tonsure (for the latter see Canon 21 above). This is the earliest eastern canon that insists that clergy are always to be distinctively dressed, but there had been earlier canonical legislation on the subject in the West: for example, synods of Mâcon (*c*. 582) and Bordeaux (*c*. 670) had forbidden clergy from appearing in lay dress.[131] We may note the later Canon 16 of Nicaea II, which forbade clergy from using expensive materials for their clothes.[132]

CANON 28

That the offering of grapes should not be combined
with the bloodless sacrifice of the offering

[35] Since we have learnt that in various churches according to a prevailing practice a bunch of grapes is offered at the altar, while the ministers combine this with the bloodless sacrifice of the offering and so distribute both together to the congregation, we hereby decree that none of the sacred ministers is to do this in future, but instead for the bestowal of life and the forgiveness of sins he is give the congregation the offering alone. As

---

130   Pitzakis (1995) 296–9.
131   *Concilia Gallica a. 511–695*, CCSL 148A, 224 and 312.
132   COGD 1, 336, trans. Price (2018) II, 620–21.

for those who consider the grapes to be an offering of first-fruits, the priests should bless and distribute them separately to those who request it [36] as a thanksgiving to the giver of the fruits through which our bodies grow and are nourished according to the divine decree. Therefore, if any cleric violates what we have laid down, he is to be deposed.

The Apostolic Canons had allowed the offering in the sanctuary 'in due season'(τῷ καιρῷ δέοντι) of new wheaten groats and grapes (Canon 3; SC 336, p. 274) and of 'oil for the lamp and incense for the time of the holy offering' (Canon 4; p. 276). The phrase 'in due season' is vague, but the contrast in the wording of these two canons implies distinction between such offerings and the eucharistic sacrifice itself. More explicitly, Canon 37 of Carthage had insisted that such first-fruits as milk and honey, grapes and corn 'are to receive a special blessing to distinguish them from the sacrifice of the body and blood of the Lord'. Likewise the present canon does not prohibit the offering of grapes, but insists that they must be kept clearly distinct from the eucharistic offerings.

Compare Canon 57, which makes a similar prohibition as regards milk and honey, and Canon 99, which forbids an Armenian practice of offering meat in the sanctuary.

CANON 29

*That the holy [mysteries] of the altar are to be
celebrated by men who are fasting*

[36] A canon of Carthage lays down that 'the holy [mysteries] of the altar are not to be performed except by men who are fasting, with the exception of the one day in the year when the Lord's Supper is celebrated'.[133] Perhaps it was for certain local reasons relating to the convenience of the church that those divine fathers made use of this dispensation.[134] But since nothing compels us to abandon strictness, we decree, in accordance with the traditions of the apostles and the fathers, 'that it is not permitted to abolish

---

133 Canon 41 of Carthage.
134 'Dispensation' translates οἰκονομία – the waving of strictness (ἀκρίβεια) on the grounds of pastoral benefit.

[the fast on] the Thursday in the final week of Lent and thereby dishonour the whole of Lent'.[135]

The date of the introduction of a strict eucharistic fast is uncertain, but evidence of this practice begins to accumulate in the late fourth century.[136] For example, a canon attributed to Timothy of Alexandria gives special permission to someone who has accidentally swallowed some water to take communion.[137] Canon 41 of Carthage, cited here, relaxed the eucharistic fast on Maundy Thursday, doubtless in memory of the Last Supper. This practice must also have been prevalent in the East, where it had already been condemned in Canon 50 of Laodicea, also cited here. It offended against the rules requiring a strict Lenten fast: Apostolic Canon 69 (SC 336, p. 300) decreed deposition for a cleric who failed to fast throughout Lent.

CANON 30

That those who have promised continence by
agreement should not live with their wives

[36] In our wish to do everything for the building up of the church, we have decided to make regulations for the priests in barbarian churches. Therefore, if they think that they ought to surpass the Apostolic Canon which forbids repudiating one's wife with the pretext of devotion[138] and to go beyond what is laid down and in consequence come to an agreement with their wives to abstain from intercourse with each other, we decree that they are no longer to live with them in any way, so that they may thereby give us a perfect demonstration of their promise. We have conceded this to them on no other ground than their timorousness of mind and their bizarre and irresolute behaviour.

135 Canon 50 of Laodicea.
136 See Jungmann (1955) II, 366 with n. 35.
137 Canon 16 of Timothy of Alexandria, Joannou (1963) 251. Joannou (pp. 238–9) questions the attribution of this canon to Timothy (for the majority of MSS lack it) but dates it to the same period – the late fourth century.
138 Apostolic Canon 5 (SC 336, p. 276).

A prime concern of the Quinisext Council was to insist that marital continence was not to be imposed on clergy living with a wife; see Canon 13 above. The present canon agrees, however, though with strongly expressed reluctance, that 'priests in barbarian lands' may practise marital continence. In the twelfth century Balsamon (PG 137, 608CD) was puzzled by this rule, since clerical celibacy was unheard of in Russia (for him the barbarian country *par excellence*), but the present canon probably relates to parts of the Balkans where recently converted Slavs were under the influence of the western rule of clerical celibacy. For this there is evidence specifically relating to the Balkans in the *Church History* of Socrates (dating to the mid-fifth century): 'I myself have knowledge of another custom in Thessaly. There a cleric who has slept with the wife he married lawfully before his ordination is excommunicated, for all the clerics in the West voluntarily abstain and the bishops too.'[139] The Apostolic Canon cited here forbade bishops and presbyters from repudiating their wives 'on the pretext of piety'. So it is strange that this canon insists that clergy who wish to practice marital continence must separate from their wives. This arose from extending to presbyters the rule imposed on bishops by Canons 12 and 48, which lay down that bishops must not live with their wives, even if they practice continence, for fear of scandalizing the faithful.

CANON 31

That the liturgy should not be performed in domestic
chapels without the permission of the bishop

[36] We decree that clerics who perform the liturgy in domestic chapels must have the permission of the local bishop. If a cleric does not observe this accordingly, he is to be deposed.

Compare Canon 59, which forbids baptisms in private houses, and also Canon 58 of Laodicea: 'Offerings [of the eucharist] should not be made in houses by bishops or presbyters'.[140] Other fourth-century canons which condemned private liturgical celebrations, such as Canon 6 of Gangra,

139 Socrates, *HE* V.22.50, SC 505, p. 230, 169–73.
140 Joannou (1962b) 153.

Canon 5 of Antioch and Apostolic Canon 31 (SC 336, p. 282), were concerned to prevent heretical and schismatic sacraments. This canon was cited and renewed in Canon 12 of the 'Prima Secunda' Council of Constantinople of 861, in the context of condemning unauthorized celebrations in private houses by those 'living in anarchy and indiscipline' for giving rise to 'confusion and scandal' in the church.[141]

In 537 Justinian I had issued a general ban on the celebration of the eucharist in private houses; but a subsequent law of 545 prohibited such celebrations when the clergy involved were not of the local diocese, which is equivalent to this canon in permitting such celebrations with the approval of the local bishop.[142] This restriction was lifted, however, by Leo VI the Wise (886–912), who decreed that priests have the right to celebrate the eucharist and even to baptize in any domestic chapel. Balsamon, when mentioning this decree, points out that in virtue of the present canon a bishop could choose to prohibit this (PG 137, 613AB).

These laws, taken together, suggest that the concern was over the celebration of the eucharist by ministers who were not under the control of the local bishop, rather than stressing the unique status of the parish church.[143]

CANON 32

That it is necessary in the bloodless sacrifice to mix water with the wine

[37] It has come to our notice that in the land of Armenia those who perform the bloodless sacrifice offer only wine at the sacred table without mixing water with it, citing the doctor of the church John Chrysostom, who speaks as follows in his commentary on the Gospel according to Matthew: 'When he rose again, why did he drink not water but wine? In order to pull out by the roots another evil heresy! For since there are some who use water in the mysteries, he showed that when he handed down the mysteries he handed down wine, and when after the resurrection he set out a simple table without the mysteries, he used wine from the fruit of the vine, as he said,[144] and a

---

141   Joannou (1962b) 469.
142   Justinian, *nov.* 58 of 537 (Schöll–Kroll 314–16) and 131.8 of 545 (Schöll–Kroll 657–8).
143   Ohme (2006a) judges otherwise.
144   Cp. Mt 26:29.

vine produces wine and not water.'[145] On the basis of this they think that the teacher rejected the addition of water at the sacred sacrifice. But so that they may not from now on be kept in ignorance, we shall reveal in an orthodox manner the father's meaning.

Since there existed the wicked and ancient heresy of the Hydroparastatae,[146] who used water only instead of wine in their own sacrifices, this inspired man composed this text in order to refute the lawless teaching of this heresy and to show that they set themselves in opposition to the apostolic tradition. In his own church, where he had been entrusted with pastoral leadership, he handed down that water is to be mixed with wine when the bloodless sacrifice is to be performed, thereby pointing to the mixture out of the honourable side of our redeemer and saviour Christ God of blood and water,[147] which flowed forth to give life to the whole world and redemption from sin. And this God-given ordinance is in force in every church where the spiritual luminaries have shone their light. For James too, the brother in the flesh of Christ our God, who was the first to be entrusted with the see of the church of Jerusalem, and Basil archbishop of Caesarea, whose fame has spread throughout the world, both of whom handed down to us in writing the holy and mystic ritual, taught that at the divine liturgy the holy cup is to be consecrated from water and wine.[148] And the sacred fathers who convened at Carthage made explicit mention that 'in the holy [mysteries] nothing more than the body and blood of the Lord is to be offered, as the Lord himself handed down, that is, bread and wine [38] mixed with water.'[149] Therefore, if any bishop or presbyter does not follow the ordinance handed down by the apostles and does not when offering the spotless sacrifice mix water with wine, he is to be deposed for an incomplete proclamation of the mystery and for distorting the tradition through innovation.

The mixing of water with the wine of the eucharist was a longstanding practice, which we find already in the mid-second century in Justin

---

145 John Chrysostom, *Homilies on Matthew* 82.2, PG 58, 740.

146 A sect which celebrated the eucharist with water in place of wine. Basil, Canon 1 (ed, Courtonne II, 122, 47–50) says they had been condemned in the third century by Cyprian and Firmilian of Caesarea in Cappadocia. See *PGL* 1423 for further references.

147 Cp. Jn 19:34.

148 See the Anaphoras of St James and St Basil.

149 Canon 37 of Carthage.

Martyr.[150] This practice was adopted by all the Christian churches, including the anti-Chalcedonian ones, with the sole exception of the Armenian Church.

The Armenian catholikos Sahak III (678–703) in his *Discourse*, a substantial controversial text principally directed against Chalcedonian Christology, had condemned the Byzantine mixing of water in the wine, citing precisely the same passage of John Chrysostom that is cited here.[151] The fact that Sahak's argument shows no knowledge of the argument advanced in the Quinisext canon, while the canon reads as a direct response to *his* argument, enables us to date his discourse to shortly before the Quinisext council. It is the council and not Sahak who understood Chrysostom's argument correctly, namely that Chrysostom was attacking those who celebrated with water instead of wine. For Sahak and his involvement in Armenian and ecclesiastical politics in the early years of the reign of Justinian II see pp. 30–32 above.

CANON 33

That it is a Jewish practice to enrol in the
clergy only those of priestly descent

[38] We have learnt that in the land of the Armenians only those of priestly descent are enrolled in the clergy – those who perpetrate this are following Jewish customs – and that some of them are made cantors and lectors of the divine law without being tonsured.[152] We therefore resolve that henceforth it is not allowed for those wishing to admit anyone into the clergy to consider the descent of the candidate. But it is after examination whether they are worthy to be enrolled in the clergy according to the requirements set out in the sacred canons that they are to be appointed to ecclesiastical office, whether they have priestly forebears or not. But no one at all is allowed to read from the ambo the divine words to the congregation, according to the office of those enrolled in the clergy, unless he has the priestly tonsure and

---

150   Justin Martyr, 1 *Apology* 65.3 and 67.5, SC 507, pp. 304, 9–10 and 310, 14.

151   In Esbroeck (1995) 434–5, §88, with comment at 325–6. In the same section Sahak cites Chrysostom on the wine and water that flowed from Christ's side on the cross (Jn 19:34), where Chrysostom takes the water to refer not to the presence of water in the chalice but to baptism (*Commentary on John*, PG 59, 463). For the context of the *Discourse* see p. 31 above.

152   See Canon 21 above for the clerical tonsure.

has received from his pastor the blessing laid down by the canons. If anyone is caught acting contrary to what is written above, he is to be excommunicated.

The priesthood of the Old Covenant was indeed restricted to those in the tribe of Levi or indeed to certain families within that tribe.[153] When Armenia was Christianized early in the fourth century, Gregory the Illuminator transformed the formerly pagan Armenian priesthood, which was hereditary, into a new Christian priesthood, in order to place this new priesthood in the hands of the most educated and respected part of the Armenian population. This practice seemed as alien to the other Christian churches then as it does today.

The abuse of the office of lector being exercised by those who had not been properly ordained was condemned again in Canon 14 of Nicaea II: 'Some who received the clerical tonsure in childhood without ordination, and have not yet received ordination from a bishop, can be seen reading at the ambo in the synaxis.'[154] Presumably these lectors were the children of clerical families, and were as such regarded as quasi-clerical even without ordination.

CANON 34

About bishops and clerics who conspire and band together

[38] Since the priestly canon states clearly that 'since the crime of conspiracy or banding together is utterly forbidden even by the civil laws, it should all the more be prohibited in the church of God', and we are keen to ensure that 'if any clerics or monks are found conspiring together or banding together or plotting intrigues against bishops or fellow clerics, they are to be completely stripped of their rank.'[155]

This canon repeats verbatim Canon 18 of Chalcedon, whose purpose was to strengthen the authority of the bishop of Constantinople over clerics or

---

153 See *Encyclopaedia Judaica* 13, 1070–73.
154 COGD 1, 334, trans. Price (2018) II, 619. In the light of this, 'his pastor' in the Quinisext canon must mean the bishop.
155 Canon 18 of Chalcedon (COGD I, 146), trans. Price and Gaddis (2005) III, 100.

monks who banded together and used support at court in opposition to him, something that the then bishop, Anatolius, had experienced and which had led earlier to the fall of both John Chrysostom and Nestorius. We do not know any particular circumstances that prompted the renewal of this canon, but such circumstances there could well have been, and the opportunities for clerics or monks, or laymen, living in the capital or visiting it to seek lay patronage and protection as a counterweight to the authority of their patriarch will have remained a constant threat to his authority.

CANON 35

That the property of a bishop should not be removed or appropriated after his death by the metropolitan

[39] None of all the metropolitans when a bishop under his see dies is to be permitted to remove or appropriate his property or that of his church, but it is to be in the safekeeping of the clergy of the church over which the deceased presided, until another bishop is appointed. There is an exception if no clerics are left in this church, for then the metropolitan will keep these things safe, and hand over everything undiminished to the bishop who will be ordained.

Canon 24 of Antioch and Apostolic Canon 40 (SC 336, pp. 286–8) had forbidden clergy on the death of their bishop from purloining any of the church's property or of the deceased bishop's personal property, which should go to his designated heirs. The present canon reflects the very different circumstances of the seventh century, when the administration of a see could be completely disrupted by barbarian incursions and the bishop and many of his clergy might no longer be residing in it (see Canon 37), leaving matters in the hands of the metropolitan.

CANON 36

About the ranking of the patriarchs

[39] Renewing the legislation of the 150 holy fathers who convened in this God-protected and imperial city and of the 630 who assembled at

Chalcedon, we decree that the see of Constantinople 'enjoys the same privileges as the see of Elder Rome and is exalted like her in ecclesiastical matters, being second after her'.[156] The see of the great city of Alexandria is be numbered next, and then that of the great city of Antioch, and finally that of the city of Jerusalem.

Canon 3 of Constantinople I had accorded the see of Constantinople 'the privileges of honour after the bishop of Rome'.[157] Alexandria continued to contest this until Chalcedon confirmed it in what came to be called its Canon 28, which is cited here. The purpose of Canon 28 in its original context, however, was less to bestow on Constantinople primacy throughout the East than to justify assigning it jurisdiction over the dioceses (groups of provinces) of Pontica, Asiana and Thrace. The listing of the four eastern patriarchates in order of precedence occurs first in the legislation of Justinian I (*nov.* 123.3 of 546, Schöll/Kroll 597, 12–14), though without an explicit statement that the order of listing corresponds to a gradation in standing and authority. However, in the attendance and subscription lists in the Acts of Chalcedon and of subsequent ecumenical councils the five great sees are invariably listed in the same order, with a clear implication of relative status.

The primacy of Constantinople in the East depended on its status as the imperial residence and capital. This was not altered by the loss of Egypt, Syria and Palestine to the Arabs, partly because the sees of Alexandria, Antioch and Jerusalem were now much weakened, but also because their patriarchs continued to regard and address the emperor at Constantinople as their rightful overlord.

After Chalcedon Pope Leo the Great had rejected the council's Canon 28, not as a challenge to Roman primacy, which indeed it reasserted, but as demoting Alexandria and Antioch; perhaps he foresaw that it would lead to Constantinople replacing Rome as the see with most influence in the Orient. It was not accepted in the West until Canon 5 of the Fourth Lateran Council (1215), at a time when the authority of the new Latin patriarch of Constantinople needed boosting. Like others of the canons that have been interpreted as anti-Roman, its reaffirmation in this Quinisext canon is evidence not of hostility to Rome, nor of a claim by Constantinople to equal status, but, at the worst, of an indifference to Roman sensibilities.

---

156 Canon 28 of Chalcedon, ACO II.1 [448] 5–9, trans. Price and Gaddis (2005) III, 76.
157 COGD 1, 66.

CANON 37

About bishops residing outside their own dioceses
because of barbarian incursions

[39] Since at various times there have been barbarian inroads and a great number of cities in consequence fell under the control of the lawless ones, with the result that the bishop of such a city was unable after his ordination to take up his see, be installed in it by priestly investiture and so perform and conduct ordinations and everything that falls to the bishop in the established way, we, to preserve the honour and venerability of the priesthood and not wishing that heathen outrage should harm the rights of the church, have resolved that those so ordained and not installed in their sees for the reason just given are to preserve without detriment their right to carry out canonical ordinations of the various [grades of] clerics, exercise their episcopal authority according to its norms, and [40] that all the administrative measures they take are valid and legitimate. For when strictness is hampered by the constraints of the time, the scope for dispensation will not be limited.

For the problems caused by the flight of bishops or their clergy or their congregations from their diocese under the pressure of barbarian inroads (whether by Slavs in the Balkans or Arabs in Asia Minor) compare Canons 18 and 39. This canon treats the case of bishops who even on their election could not reside in their sees, and insists that they still possess the right to ordain clergy and settle matters relating to their sees, doubtless in the hope that they or their successors would at some date be able to return to their sees. This had not been a problem in earlier centuries, but note Canon 18 of Antioch, which had decreed that a bishop unable to take up residence in his diocese, whether because of local opposition or some other cause, still preserved his episcopal rights. The final sentence of the present canon, however, with its reference to 'strictness', implies that in normal circumstances a bishop was not permitted to exercise his authority when outside his own see.

   This canon had a particular relevance for the bishops at the council who were themselves not resident in their sees, such as all the oriental patriarchs who attended (see pp. 9–11 above). Contrast, however, the bishop of Stoboi, previously the metropolis of Macedonia II. The fact that in the subscription list of this council he comes among the suffragans (as sixtieth in the list) shows that his metropolitan rights had lapsed.

CANON 38

That in a newly founded city the ordering of
the churches should be in accord

[40] We also observe the canon issued by our fathers which runs as follows: 'If any city has been newly founded by imperial authority or is in future so founded, the ordering of ecclesiastical matters is to accord with the civic and public regulations.'[158]

This canon simply cites the last sentence of Canon 17 of Chalcedon, even though the late seventh century was a period of retrenchment when foundations of new cities were exceptional. It had long been a standard principle that the status of ecclesiastical sees corresponded to the secular status of the city in question, ensuring that the bishop would enjoy comparable status and sphere of authority to the secular official he would have most dealings with. How is this canon in accord with the following Canon 39, which transferred the authority of the bishop of Kyzikos over the province of Hellespontus to the bishop of the newly founded Nea Iustinianupolis? See our commentary on this canon for how this was treated as a special and unique case.

CANON 39

About the bishop of the island of Cyprus

[40] Our brother and fellow minister John, bishop of the island of Cyprus, together with his people left the same island for the province of Hellespontus because of barbarian incursions and in order to be freed from

---

158 Canon 17 of Chalcedon (COGD 1, 145, trans. Price and Gaddis, III, 100) with one small change of wording, the phrase 'ecclesiastical matters' replacing 'ecclesiastical dioceses (παροικιῶν)'.

slavery to pagans and be wholly subject to the rule of the most Christian state, through the forethought of God in his mercy and the exertion of our Christ-loving and pious emperor. We resolve that the privileges granted to the see of the aforesaid man by the inspired fathers who convened at Ephesus for the first time are to be preserved without alteration,[159] in such a way that Nea Iustinianupolis is to enjoy the rights of the city of Konstanteia and its most God-beloved bishop is to have precedence over all the bishops in the province of Hellespontus and is to be consecrated by his own bishops according to ancient custom. For our inspired fathers decided that the customs in each church are to be preserved. The bishop of the city of Kyzikos is to be subordinate to the one presiding in the said Iustinianupolis, after the manner of all the other bishops under the said most God-beloved bishop John, by whom, when need calls, the bishop of this city of Kyzikos is to be ordained.

Kyzikos on the Sea of Marmara, the metropolis of Hellespontus, was held by the Arabs throughout the 670s, when it was used as a base for attacks on Constantinople. A treaty of 680 restored this city to the empire. A generation before, in 647–8, the Arabs had seized Cyprus; Konstanteia (formerly Salamis), its metropolis, was destroyed; war between the two powers continued on the island, whose Christian population was greatly reduced by massacre and deportation as slaves. A treaty agreed early in Justinian II's reign assigned the island to a Byzantine–Arab condominium with an equal division of the revenues.[160] Immediately before the Quinisext Council Justinian II forced the remnants of this population (or at least some to them) to emigrate to the doubtless depopulated province of Hellespontus, where a city named Nea Iustinianupolis was founded near Kyzikos.[161] The bishop of Kyzikos, doubtless severely ravaged after being the base of the

---

159 The Council of Ephesus, or rather the Cyrillian faction of it, accorded Cyprus autonomy, separating it from the patriarchate of Antioch, in 431. See ACO I.1.7, 118–22. The matter remained contentious, however, even after universal recognition of the ecumenical status of the Cyrillian council, since the see of Antioch had not been consulted over the matter. But when in 488 the supposed relics of St Barnabas were discovered on the island, 'proving' that it had not been evangelized from Antioch, the emperor Zeno decreed Cypriot autonomy, and this was later confirmed by Justinian. See *DHGE* 12, 795.

160 Theophanes, *Chronicle* 363, trans. Mango and Scott 506.

161 Theophanes, *Chronicle* 365, trans. Mango and Scott 509, records with relish that a 'multitude' of the Cypriots were drowned or expired of disease during the crossing.

Arab siege of Constantinople (674–8), may have remained officially the metropolitan of Hellespontus, but he was placed under the authority of the metropolitan of Cyprus, now bishop of Nea Iustinianupolis, to whom were delegated the rights of Constantinople, as the patriarchal see, over the province.[162] It is this arrangement that the present canon enshrines in canon law. In fact the arrangement proved extremely short-lived, for a new treaty between the empire and the caliphate enabled the Cypriots to return to their island within a decade.[163]

About monks and nuns[164]

CANON 40

About monks and monasteries and that those who choose monastic life should not be accepted without scrutiny

[40] Since it is most salutary to cleave to God through withdrawal from the turmoil of life, it is incumbent on us [41] not to admit those choosing the monastic life at the wrong time and without scrutiny, but to observe the decree handed down to us by the fathers as regards these persons as well. Consequently 'it is necessary to accept a profession of the life according to God at the time when it is now firm and the result of personal will and judgement after the attainment of the use of reason'.[165]

Therefore the one intending to take on the monastic yoke must be not less than ten years old, and it is incumbent on the presider[166] to examine

---

162 This is the interpretation of this canon in the later Byzantine canonists Balsamon, Zonaras and Aristenos (PG 137, 648–52). Hellespontus was not divided into two ecclesiastical provinces, thereby respecting the letter of Canon 12 of Chalcedon, which forbade such a division in the case of the bestowal of metropolitan status on a second city within a province. This canon was intended to protect the rights of the original metropolitan, which the present canon singularly fails to do.

163 *DHGE* 12, 'Chypre', 796.

164 See n. 51 above for this useful, but probably not original, indication of the subject matter of the following group of Canons (40–49).

165 Basil of Caesarea, *Longer Rules* 15.4, PG 31, 956B, with 'of the life according to God' replacing 'of virginity'.

166 The word is πρόεδρος. Balsamon took it to mean the bishop and Aristenos the monastic superior (PG 137, 656A and 657B). Konidaris (1992) 275 comments that it is the monastic superior who will have been the competent person to make this decision.

if he thinks it more advantageous to lengthen the time before entry and settlement into monastic life. For even if the great Basil in his sacred canons lays down that she who presents herself voluntarily to the Lord and embraces virginity is to be numbered in the order of virgins on reaching the age of seventeen,[167] we have followed the example of widows and deaconesses and laid down the specified time for those choosing the monastic life analogously; for it is written in the divine apostle that a widow is to be enrolled in the church at the age of sixty,[168] and yet the sacred canons have handed down that a deaconess is to be ordained at the age of forty,[169] after having seen 'the church grow in strength through divine grace'[170] and make progress and also the firmness and reliability of the faithful in observing the divine commandments. We ourselves, who are also fully conscious of this, have now decided to impress rapidly like a seal the blessing of grace on the one intending to embark on the contest according to God. We therefore prompt him not to delay and hesitate for a long time, but urge him instead to choose the good and settle into it.

Basil of Caesarea in his *Longer Rules* 15 (PG 31, 952–7) had encouraged monasteries to take in and bring up children of either sex – that is, to run orphanages and schools – but this was quite distinct from accepting them as monks and nuns, and in his canonical letters he laid down (in his Canon 18, cited here) that seventeen was the youngest age at which a nun could be clothed. The present canon is most interesting as an example of how a canon could be modified. The fact that a canon of Chalcedon gave forty as the age at which a deaconess could be ordained, despite the Pauline rule that widows could not be enrolled before the age of sixty, is taken as evidence that rules of this kind could be modified. Basil's own argument that the

---

167   Canon 18 of Basil of Caesarea, in *ep.* 199, ed. Courtonne II, 156–7, §18, 35–48. Basil insists that girls, despite the tendency of families to present them much earlier, are not to be admitted as virgins until they have fully attained the age of reason, have been thoroughly tested, and are firmly resolved on adopting the monastic life.

168   Cp. 1 Tim 5:9.

169   See Canon 15 of Chalcedon (trans. Price and Gaddis, 2005, III, 99), which reduced the age of ordination for deaconesses from 60 (as laid down in *CTh* 16.2.27, analogously to the age for widows) to 40.

170   Basil of Caesarea, Canon 18, in *ep.* 199, ed. Courtonne II, 155, §18, 7–9. But Basil adduces progress in the church not as a ground for admitting children to monasteries but as a reason for treating virgins who break their vows with greater severity.

spiritual advance of the church justified modifications in church discipline – even though Basil used this as an argument for greater strictness – is now employed against him, as an argument for allowing children as young as ten years old to take monastic vows.

As Ohme observes,[171] the turmoil of the seventh century will have made many children orphans and many parents unable to look after their children. This will have led to an influx of children into monasteries. In this situation the rule that they could never take vows before the age of ten, and that it was the responsibility of the superior to decide (presumably in each case) whether a later age should not be required, represents an attempt to impose a measure of discipline rather than simply abandon it.

CANON 41

About those wishing to enter into enclosure

[41] Those in cities or villages who wish to withdraw into enclosure and attend to themselves in solitude must first enter a monastery and be trained in the eremitical life. In fear of God they are to be subject to the superior of the monastery for three years and, as is proper, exercise obedience in all things. When they profess their choice of this life accordingly and that they are embracing it freely from their whole heart, [42] they are to be examined by the local bishop. They are then to persevere for another year outside enclosure, so that their intention may become all the more clear; for then they will inspire conviction that they are pursuing this life of solitude in quest not of empty glory but of what is really good. After they have completed this period, if they continue in the same resolution, they are to enter enclosure and no longer be allowed to withdraw from this state when they wish, except if they be impelled to this by the common good and advantage or by some other pressure that is life-threatening, and even so only with the blessing of the local bishop. If apart from these reasons they try to leave their quarters, they are first to be confined in the said enclosure even against their will, and then subjected to a regime of fasts and other austerities, since they know, as Scripture says, that 'no one who puts his hand to the plough and turns backwards is fit for the kingdom of heaven'.[172]

171 Ohme (2006a) 149.
172 Lk 9:62.

This is apparently the only canon in the Byzantine corpus treating life in 'enclosure' (ἐν ἐγκλείστραις), by which is meant withdrawing to a cell and never leaving it – a stage of withdrawal going well beyond permanent residence in a monastic community. This new canon requires that the person enclosed must first have completed a monastic noviciate,[173] and also that he is not to abandon enclosure without a compelling reason and without the permission of the local bishop. The canon's insistence that those enclosed should remain enclosed even against their will and the reference to 'seeking empty glory' shows that its concern is with those who practise enclosure for a while and then return to the world, basking in the veneration shown them by the devout while respecting the authority of no one.

CANON 42

That those called hermits who have long hair
on the head ought not to live in cities

[42] Regarding those called hermits who wear black and go round the cities with long hair on their heads, living among laymen and women and demeaning their own calling, we decree that, if they are ready to be tonsured and to accept the dress of other monks, they are to settle in a monastery and be counted with the brothers. If they do not choose this, they are to be totally banned from the cities and live in the desert, from which their name derives.[174]

Like the preceding canon, this canon is concerned to subject freewheeling ascetics to proper monastic discipline. Canon 4 of Chalcedon had condemned monks who 'move around the cities indiscriminately' and 'cause trouble in ecclesiastical or secular affairs',[175] with reference to monks who depended on lay patronage and either ignored the local bishop or even campaigned against him, which was currently a problem in Constantinople for the patriarch. Canon 34 above shows that this was a continuing cause

---

173   The canon lays down a three-year period of preparation, in line with the three-year noviciate laid down for monks by Justinian I, *nov.* 5,2 (Schöll–Kroll 28–30).
174   ἐρημίτης ('hermit') derives from ἔρημος ('desert').
175   ACO II.1 [355] 11–12.

of anxiety. But the context of the present canon, which had no precise precedent, is the very different one of parasites who wandered around cities and depended on the alms of naïve laymen. The freewheeling ascetics in question here, who looked like monks without living like monks, are less reminiscent of the monks of Constantinople in the mid-fifth century who had caused trouble to church and state by standing up to Nestorius and later Anatolius than of the illiterate and bibulous wandering monks in Pushkin's *Boris Godunov*. They are ordered to enter a proper monastery or leave the cities. For the insistence that being a monk must involve wearing the monastic habit and displaying the monastic tonsure compare canons 43 and 45. Balsamon paraphrases this canon in the present tense (PG 137, 665A): clearly the problem had continued into his own time.

CANON 43

That no one found guilty of any fault should be denied admittance into the monastic order

[42] Every Christian is allowed to choose the ascetical life, renounce the tumultuous surge of the affairs of life, enter a monastery and receive a monastic tonsure, even if he has been found guilty of whatever fault. For God our Saviour said, 'Whoever comes to me I shall never cast out.'[176] Since the monastic mode of life impresses on us a life of repentance, we give our approval to whoever adopts it sincerely, and no impediment should prevent him from fulfilling his intention.

This canon is also a novelty. It may be evidence of a shortage of monastic vocations and a need to be less discriminating in accepting recruits. It also has the implication that those wishing to adopt the monastic life without accepting the discipline of community life (compare Canons 41–42) could no longer use as an excuse that monasteries were closed to them. Compare John Climacus, *The Spiritual Ladder* 1.19 (PG 88, 640A), 'Let no one, appealing to the weight and multitude of his sins, say that he is unworthy of the monastic vow, concocting excuses for his sins.' The purpose of this canon will have been to encourage monasteries to take novices who had

---

176 Jn 6:37.

committed grave sins but were truly repentant, but not to encourage them to admit novices without proper scrutiny, which would have been flatly contrary to Canon 40.

CANON 44

About a monk who commits fornication or takes a woman for marital intercourse

[43] A monk who is found guilty of fornication or who takes a woman for marital intercourse and life together is to be subjected to the canonical penance for fornicators.

Canon of Ancyra 19 had imposed the penalty for bigamy on those who had taken a vow of virginity and later got married. Canon 19 of Basil of Caesarea laid down that those who had taken such a vow should, if they broke it, be subjected to the penalty for fornication, which his Canon 59 defines as seven years of excommunication.[177] Konidaris supposes that it was intended to keep fornicating monks within their monasteries, rather than letting them loose on the world.[178] But the brevity of the canon leaves its purpose unclear.

CANON 45

That those about to receive the monastic habit should not enter the monastery richly dressed

[43] We have learnt that those about to receive the sacred habit in certain women's monasteries are first dressed in silk and other clothing of all kinds and even in jewellery encrusted with gold and precious stones by those presenting them, and then when they go up to the sanctuary they take off this material attire, their habits are immediately blessed, and they are

---

177 Canon 19 of Basil of Caesarea, in *ep.* 199, ed. Courtonne II, 157. Canon 59 in *ep.* 217, Courtonne II, 211.
178 Konidaris (1992) 280.

clothed in the black garment. We decree that from now on this is not to happen. For it is utterly improper for one who has already renounced all the delights of this life through her own choice, embraced the life according to God, confirmed this with the constancy of her thoughts, and so entered the monastery, to be reminded through this perishable and transient adornment of the things she has already consigned to oblivion, causing her to be thrown into doubt and troubled in soul, as if by waves overflowing in a flood in this direction and in that. The result is that sometimes she does not display with her body the compunction in her heart by shedding a tear, while even if a little tear does fall, as indeed it might, those who witness it will attribute it not to a disposition arising from ascetical combat but to leaving the world and the things of the world.

This is a new rule, like Canons 41–43, that forbids a striking piece of theatre, whereby the new nun was decked up in worldly finery so as to cast it off dramatically immediately before being clothed in the sober black of religious life. Considering the many dramatic and visually striking moments in the sacred liturgy (performed uniquely, of course, by men), it is hard not to see in this an element of misogyny. Despite this prohibition, the custom deplored here continued for centuries. Balsamon (PG 137, 673B) attributes this to the fact that this canon failed to impose any punishment on those who ignored it, and makes a recommendation that the local bishop should impose one.

CANON 46

That women enrolled in a monastery should not go
outside it without unavoidable necessity

[43] Women who choose the ascetical life and are enrolled in a monastery are never to go outside at all. But if some unavoidable necessity forces them to do so, they are to do so only with the permission and blessing of their superior, and even then they are to go out not alone by themselves, but with some elderly and senior nuns in the monastery and at the bidding of the superior, and certainly they are never allowed to sleep outside the monastery. Likewise men who practise the solitary life are only to go out, if need impels, with the blessing of the one entrusted with the office of

hegumen. In consequence, those who violate this decree that we now issue, whether they are men or women, are to be subjected to appropriate penances.

A novel (new law) of Justinian addresses the situation where a monastery did not have its own church and the monks (or nuns) had to go outside the enclosure to attend the liturgy.[179] This canon insists that they are to be led and supervised by their superior(s) on these occasions and prevented from using the opportunity for unsuitable encounters.

CANON 47

That a man should not sleep in a women's monastery
nor a woman in a men's monastery

[44] A woman is never to sleep in a men's monastery nor a man in a women's monastery. For the faithful must avoid all offence and scandal and direct their lives 'according to what is seemly and to constant attendance on the Lord'.[180] Anyone who does this, whether a cleric or a layman, is to be excommunicated.

A novel of Justinian's forbade women from ever entering a men's monastery and vice versa.[181] No mention is made either there or in this canon of 'double monasteries', containing both monks and nuns; these were banned by Justinian, but continued to exist.[182] As for the penalty the canon imposes, the standard one for a serious offence in the Quinisext (and other) canons is deposition for a cleric and excommunication for a layman. Since deposition was permanent while an excommunication could be lifted, the specification of excommunication for a cleric in the present canon was actually a lesser penalty.

179 Justinian, *nov.* 132.2 of 539 (Schöll–Kroll 669).
180 1 Cor 7:35.
181 Justinian, *nov.* 133.3 of 539 (Schöll–Kroll 669–71).
182 Justinian, *nov.* 123.36 of 546, (Schöll–Kroll 619–20). For their continued existence see Canon 20 of Nicaea II, translated and annotated in Price (2018) II, 622–3.

CANON 48

*That it is necessary for a wife of a consecrated bishop who has been
separated from him by mutual consent to enter a monastery*

[44] The wife of one who is promoted to the presiding role of a bishop,
after being separated from her husband by mutual consent, is, after his
episcopal consecration, to enter a monastery built far from the residence of
the bishop, and is to enjoy the bishop's financial support. If she is seen to be
worthy, she is to be promoted to the dignity of deaconess.

Canon 12 insists that bishops must separate from their wives, and this canon
ensures that such separation would be permanent. This canon would seem
to infringe Apostolic Canon 5 (SC 336, p. 276), which forbade clergy from
repudiating their wives 'with the pretext of piety', but a distinction could
be made between the repudiation forbade by this canon and the separation
(without divorce) that the present canon lays down. It is also to be noted that
bishops' wives could not be simply discarded but had to give their consent.

The canon states that the wife of a bishop must enter a monastery, but
not that she must become a nun. Balsamon (PG 137, 685C–688A) argued
that she should, since otherwise she could choose to leave it, but notes
that others disagreed, appealing to the fact that the dignity of deaconess
(specially mentioned here) was sometimes bestowed on lay women.

This canon presupposes an older rule, or rather a presumption, that
bishops were forbidden to have marital relations with their wives, with at
a later date separation being imposed as a way of ensuring that this rule
was followed and of making clear to everyone that this was the case. The
odd episode related in non-canonical texts gives support to the existence
of such a rule: one of the charges brought against Bishop Antoninus of
Ephesus in 400 was that he had resumed marital relations with his wife and
had children by her.[183]

It is also to be noted that the legislation of Justinian I had laid down
that men who had children or grandchildren should not be made bishops,
since this would distract them from their episcopal duties and lead them
to spend money on their own children rather than the poor; a slightly

---

183 Palladius, *Dialogue on the Life of John Chrysostom*, SC 341, XIII.171–2. For further
evidence see L'Huillier (1991) 278–9 and Pitsakis (1995) 276–8.

later law extended this to all married men.[184] This was to ignore the fact that a bishop without children might still have grasping relatives.[185] The present canon presupposes that this Justinianic rule was no longer in force. Subsequent practice in the Orthodox churches has continued to allow in theory the consecration of married bishops, on condition that their wives enter a monastery, although in practice monastic candidates are standardly preferred.

CANON 49

That monasteries that have once been consecrated must not become secular residences

[44] Renewing another sacred canon,[186] we decree that 'monasteries that have once been consecrated with the approval of the bishop are to remain monasteries perpetually; the property belonging to them is to be kept for the monastery, and they may not thereafter become secular residences', nor can they be handed over to laymen by anyone at all. If this has happened before now, we decree that it has no validity. From now on 'those who attempt to do this are to be subjected to the penalties laid down in the canons'.[187]

The possibility of monastic buildings being misappropriated by laymen, whether through forcible dispossession or desertion by their monks, was a constant one, particularly in times of disruption caused by continual barbarian raids. The canon of Chalcedon renewed here can scarcely have

---

184   *CJ* I.3.41(42).2–4 of 528 (Krüger 528) and I.3.47(48) of 531 (Krüger 34). For *novellae* of Justinian on this subject see Ohme (2006a) 145, n. 586.

185   Note the plaint presented against Dioscorus at Chalcedon (Acts III.57, ACO II.1 [216–18]), where the natural explanation of his confiscation of property owned by the relatives of his predecessor Cyril is that Cyril has enriched his family out of ecclesiastical property. See Price and Gaddis (2005) II, 58–9, nn. 77 and 83.

186   Canon 24 of Chalcedon (COGD I, 148), made up of the two passages that are quoted in the text that follows.

187   Which canons is Chalcedon referring to here? Possibly, by an extension of their application, to Apostolic Canons 72 and 73 (SC 336, p. 302), which subject the misappropriation of holy oil or consecrated vessels to the penalty of excommunication.

prevented it, though it would help the church to recover misappropriated monastic buildings subsequently. The ban reissued here needed to be repeated in Canon 13 of Nicaea II, which imposed deposition on clergy guilty in this matter and excommunication on monks and laymen.[188]

Ohme (2006a) 154 adduces estimates that by this date as much as a third of usable land may have become the property of monasteries; land that monastic communities could not make use of was often granted to landed gentry who would put a lay administrator in charge of them. This canon could at best hope to put a curb on this, but scarcely to abolish it.

[*Other canons*][189]

CANON 50

That those in priestly orders should not play at dice

[44] [We lay down that] no one at all, whether a layman or a cleric, is henceforth to play at dice. If anyone is caught doing this, if he is a cleric, he is to be deposed, and if a layman, excommunicated.

This canon renews Apostolic Canons 42 and 43 (SC 336, p. 288), which condemn those repeatedly guilty of this offence, which was a form of gambling – those in major orders to deposition and lower clergy and laymen to excommunication. This in our eyes harmless recreation was perceived by stricter churchmen as involving a pagan belief in the power of Tyche, the goddess of chance. However, the prohibition of this game in the Code of Justinian has the more mundane justification of protecting inexperienced players from heavy financial loss, and lays down as the sole penalty that the winner should return his winnings to the loser.[190] Balsamon notes that, while the Apostolic Canons say that one committing this offence must

---

188 COGD I, 333–4, trans. Price (2018) II, 618–19.

189 A mere four MSS (Ohme 2013, LIII) head this last and longest section as 'about the laity', which it is not in any exclusive sense; contrast the vastly more common insertion in our manuscripts of section headings before Canons 3 and 40. The title I have chosen reflects the fact that it is a miscellaneous section after two sections with a specific focus.

190 *CJ* III.43 (Krüger 147).

either 'cease' or be subjected to deposition or excommunication (according to his status), the present canon gives the offender no second chance, and argues that in this matter the more lenient provisions of the Apostolic Canons should be followed.[191] The omission of the mention of the laity in the heading (the headings are of late date, see below under Canon 101) represents a different attempt to mollify the severity of this canon.

CANON 51

A prohibition on watching mimes and hunting and dancing on the stage

[45] This sacred and ecumenical council totally forbids those called mimes and their displays, and in addition the performances of shows with hunting and of dancing on the stage. If anyone ignores the present canon and indulges in something forbidden, if he is cleric, he is to be deposed, and if a layman, excommunicated.

Similar is Canon 66, which bans dancing on the Kalends of January and certain other days. Disapproval of stage and similar shows had found expression in the church in the exclusion from the catechumenate of actors, musicians, charioteers and athletes.[192] Compare also the ban on dancing at weddings in Canon 53 of Laodicea. Before Christianization, shows of a wide variety of kinds had been linked to pagan ritual or celebration. The existence of survivals *from* paganism do not prove, however, a survival *of* paganism. See p. 26 above.

CANON 52

About celebrating the liturgy of the presanctified in holy Lent

[45] Throughout the fast days of holy Lent, apart from Saturdays and Sundays and the holy day of the Annunciation, the sacred liturgy of the presanctified is to be celebrated.

---

191 PG 137, 692AB.
192 See *Apostolic Constitutions* VIII.32.9, SC 336, 236–8, dating to the late fourth century.

The only earlier mention of this liturgy of the presanctified – that is, a communion service, attached to Vespers, using bread previously consecrated – is the *Chronicon Paschale* under the year 615.[193] For the exclusion of Saturdays and Sundays as not fast days see Canon 55. The canon presupposes that the Lenten fast lasted until sunset and from each Monday until Friday inclusive (as already implied by Canon 49 of Laodicea). Note that Canon 51 of Laodicea banned the commemoration of martyrs on fast days during Lent, while Canon 50 of Laodicea banned the 'offering of bread' (i.e. the eucharist) on these days. Apostolic Canon 69 (SC 336, p. 300) condemned to deposition clergy who failed to perform the full Lenten fast.

CANON 53

That godfathers should not contract marriage with the widowed mothers of their godchildren

[45] Since spiritual kinship is more important than a bodily relationship, and we have learnt that in some places some who have received children [as their godchildren] at the holy and salvific rite of baptism subsequently enter into marital cohabitation with the mothers of these children when widowed, we decree that from now on nothing of this kind is to be done. If after the present canon any are caught doing this, they are first to discontinue this unlawful cohabitation, and are then to be subjected to the penances for fornicators.

This is the first treatment of this topic in canon law. The Code of Justinian forbade marriage between godfather and goddaughter.[194] The present canon extends the ban, not by formally extending the range of invalid marriage (which only the civil law could do) but by imposing continence and penance. It takes the civil prohibition for granted and as part of canon law, and feels no need to repeat it.

---

193 *Chronicon Paschale*, trans. Whitby and Whitby, p. 158.
194 *CJ* 5.4.26 §2 (Krüger 197).

CANON 54

About marriages prohibited because of kinship

[45] While the divine Scripture teaches us explicitly that 'you shall not go in to any blood relation to uncover their shame', the inspired Basil enumerated in his canons some of the prohibited marriages, while passing most of them over in silence and thereby securing for us a double benefit: on the one hand he avoided a quantity of shameful terms, so as not to defile his discourse with the words, and yet he indicated the varieties of impurity with generic terms with which [46] he defined the unlawful marriages for us comprehensively. But since because of his silence and the lack of definition in the prohibition of illegitimate marriages nature was confused, we have decided to set out the matter in more explicit terms. We decree that from now on he who contracts marital union with his own cousin, or father and son with mother and daughter, or father and son with two sisters, or mother and daughter with two brothers, or two brothers with two sisters, incur the canonical penalty of seven years, after, obviously, they terminate the unlawful cohabitation.

Apposite in the New Testament is the prohibition of πορνεία at the Council of Jerusalem mentioned in the Acts of the Apostles 15:28–9, where the probable meaning is not sexual immorality in a broad sense but specifically incestuous marriage. Note too John the Baptist's protest at Herod's marriage to his sister-in-law (Mk 6:18) and Paul's insistence in 1 Cor 5:1–5 on the 'delivery to Satan' of man who had married his mother-in-law. Roman law likewise prohibited marriage by a man with his mother-in-law or sister-in-law and between close cousins. In canon law this matter had been treated only in the Canons of St Basil 67, 68, 75, 76, 78, 79, 87,[195] which set out the prohibited degrees of kinship, condemning attempted marriages by a man with his half-sister, his daughter-in-law, sister-in-law, mother-in-law or stepmother. Note how here the conciliar canon takes for granted the full authority of Basil's rules and does not repeat them but extends them. The ban on marriage with the relatives of one's spouse ('affinity') is now extended to include marriage between the relatives of one spouse and the

195 Canons 67–79 are in Basil *ep.* 217, ed. Courtonne II, 213–14. Canon 87 (as it is called in the Byzantine collections) is his *ep.* 160, ed. Courtonne II, 88–92.

relatives of the other ('quasi-affinity'). The claim is made, however, that this does not represent a new degree of strictness but simply a readiness to mention explicitly cases that Basil had thought best to leave in decent obscurity. The Quinisext Canons are consistently keen to claim continuity with the tradition. As for the penalty imposed, the illicit marriage is not condemned as invalid (a matter which lay in the competence of the civil law) but as requiring a canonical penalty of excommunication for seven years.[196]

CANON 55

That one should not fast on Saturdays and Sundays

[46] Since we have learnt that those in the city of Rome, contrary to the traditional practice of the church, fast on the Saturdays during the holy fast of Lent, it is the resolution of the holy council that even in the case of the church of Rome the canon is to be immutably in force that says, 'If any cleric is found fasting on Sunday or Saturday, save for the one single Saturday, he is to be deposed, and if a layman, excommunicated.'[197]

This canon cites Apostolic Canon 64, which had been included in the Byzantine canon law collections since the time of Justinian I but, like all the Apostolic Canons after no. 50, was not accepted in the West, and directs it explicitly against a contrary practice in the city of Rome, where all Saturdays (and not simply the Saturday immediately before Easter, as in the East) were fast days. This difference became a serious matter of dispute between Rome and Byzantium in the ninth century, when Photios cited this canon against the Roman practice of fasting on Saturdays, even outside Lent.[198]

196 See Pitsakis (1992) 168–78.
197 Apostolic Canon 64 (SC 336, p. 298).
198 See Ohme (2010b) 277–8.

CANON 56

*About the eating of cheese by the Armenians on
the Saturdays and Sundays in holy Lent*

[46] We have similarly learnt that in the land of Armenia and in other places some people eat eggs and cheese on the Saturdays and Sundays of the fast of holy Lent. We therefore resolve that the church of God throughout the world is to follow a single rule in observing the fast, and is to abstain, as from every kind of meat, so also from eggs and cheese, which are the fruit and produce of what we abstain from. If they do not observe this, if they are clerics, they are to be deposed, and if they are laymen, excommunicated.

Saturdays and Sundays in Lent were not fast days in the Byzantine practice (see the previous canon), but days of abstinence from meat and also from dairy products, since these likewise come from animals.[199]

CANON 57

That milk and honey should not be offered on the altar

[46] [We decree] that it is wrong to offer milk and honey on the altars.

Compare Canon 28, which makes a similar prohibition in regard to grapes. From the early centuries down to around 600 the Roman church administered milk and honey to the newly baptized at their first communion, as symbolic of their admittance to 'the land flowing with milk and honey', an expression repeatedly used in Exodus and Deuteronomy with reference to 'the promised land', meaning Canaan in the Pentateuch but allegorized in Christianity as heaven. This was also the practice in the Egyptian church, and remains so even today. This custom is enjoined in Ps.-Hippolytus, *The Apostolic Tradition* 21, a work of uncertain origin that entered both Latin and Coptic canon law but does not survive in Greek. And indeed

---

199 For further details on the history and varieties of Lenten practice see Ohme (2006a) 82–5.

this practice was never followed in the Greek or Syrian churches. Canon 37 of Carthage prescribes the offering of milk and honey 'on the one day determined for the sacrament of infants', but insists that these must receive a particular blessing of their own, in order to distinguish them from the offering of the bread and wine.

CANON 58

That a layman should not give himself
communion at the divine mysteries

[46] No one enrolled in the laity is to administer the divine mysteries to himself if a bishop or presbyter or deacon is present. Whoever presumes to do this contrary to the ordinance is to be excommunicated for one week, in order to be taught thereby not to have ideas that he ought not to entertain.

Canon 94 of St Basil (in *ep.* 93, Courtonne I, 203–4) recommends frequent communion, including communion taken at home in the absence of a sacred minister, when necessarily the layman or monk would give himself communion – from a store of hosts taken from a church and kept in the home. The present canon refers implicitly to this practice, but insists that, when a sacred minister is present, only he can administer communion. This serves to express the unique priestly status of an ordained minister.

The implication of the canon is that in the absence of major clerics it was normal for laymen to communicate themselves, and that this practice has seeped into occasions when major clerics *were* present.

CANON 59

That baptism is not to be celebrated in a chapel inside a house

[47] Baptism is never to be celebrated in a chapel inside a house. But those who wish to receive the spotless illumination should go to the public[200]

---

200 'Public' translates καθολικαῖς (catholic). *PGL* 690 misunderstands the reference to be to the principal church of the diocese or province.

churches and there enjoy this gift. If anyone is caught violating our decree, if a cleric, he is to be deposed, and if he is layman, excommunicated.

Compare Canon 31 and my commentary on concern to rein in liturgical celebrations in private chapels by unauthorized persons. The desirability of public celebration had a special raison d'être in the case of baptism, which admits a new member into the church. Even so, Leo VI (886–912) gave permission for baptism to be celebrated in domestic chapels, even though, as Balsamon points out, a bishop could prohibit this (PG 137, 613AB).

CANON 60

About those who pretend to be demonically possessed

[47] Since the apostle declares that 'he who cleaves to the Lord is one spirit',[201] it is clear that he who makes friends with the adversary becomes one in union with him. It is therefore our resolution that those who pretend to be demonically possessed and imitate those possessed in depravity of behaviour are to be subjected to every kind of punishment, and that they are to be subjected to the harsh treatment and afflictions to which those who are truly possessed are rightly subjected in order to free them from the activity of the demon.

What was the motive for 'pretending to be demonically possessed'? Balsamon in his commentary on this canon (PG 137, 717A) refers to such people going round the cities and being regarded by some as holy – doubtless as 'holy fools' like St Symeon Salos a century before.[202] People might simulate holy folly in order to have their outrageous behaviour not only tolerated but rewarded with alms. Why was this minor nuisance thought to deserve a conciliar canon? The final sentence suggests anxiety over the difficulty in identifying the possessed and a desire to be on the safe side by punishing all who behave as if they are. As for the 'harsh treatment

201 1 Cor 6:17.
202 For a translation of Leontios of Neapolis, *Life of Symeon Salos*, with a long introduction see Krueger (1996).

and afflictions' imposed on the possessed, it was doubtless believed that the demon itself would feel them and thereby be driven out.[203]

CANON 61

About soothsayers, sorcerers and bear-trainers

[47] Those who entrust themselves to soothsayers or those called 'Hekatontarchs',[204] or others of this kind, in order to learn from them whatever they wish to be revealed to them, are to fall under the canon that lays down six years [of penance] according to the previous decrees of the fathers concerning them. This same penance is to be incurred by those who drag around bears or animals of this kind for play and to harm the more simple, and talk about chance and fate and genealogy and a quantity of such terms of deceitful nonsense, and also those who are called cloud-gazers, fortune-tellers, sellers of amulets and soothsayers. If they persist in these things without repenting of them and do not shun these destructive and pagan practices, we decree that they are to be totally expelled from the church, as the sacred canons state. 'For what fellowship has light with darkness,' says the apostle, 'or what agreement has the church of God with idols, or what portion does a believer share with an unbeliever, or what accord has Christ with Belial?'[205]

Soothsaying (μαντεία) was understood to involve traffic with demons. Canon 24 of Ancyra imposed five years of penance on those who had recourse to soothsayers, while Canon 72 of St Basil imposes on them the same penance as for murder: compare his Canon 56, which imposes twenty years of penance on a murderer who repents. Canon 3 of Gregory of Nyssa ruled more compassionately that those who, while remaining faithful Christians, have recourse to soothsayers in order to escape from

---

203 Wortley (1984) 256 refers to a passage of Michael Psellos (PG 122, 872C–873A) which argues that demons, although disembodied, can experience bodily pain.

204 In the context the meaning must be 'fortune-teller' or the like, but the etymology is unclear. Ohme (2006a) 50, n. 118 suggests a connection with the goddess Hekate, as the patroness of magicians.

205 1 Cor 6:14–16.

afflictions brought about by sorcery should be treated like those who commit apostasy under torture. The Code of Justinian includes a law of Diocletian's decreeing that soothsayers (*haruspices*) are to be burnt and those who solicit them are to be exiled to an island.[206]

Foretelling the future could, however, be practised by monks believed to have recourse to holy and unimpeachable sources of information. Justinian II himself, on recovering the throne in 705, rewarded with the patriarchal throne of Constantinople a monk, Cyrus, who had predicted his restoration.[207] Likewise amulets could represent saints as well as demons.

CANON 62

About the Kalends, Vota and Brumalia

[48] It is our will that the so-called Kalends, the so-called *Vota* and the so-called *Brumalia* and the festival celebrated on 1 March be abolished once and for all from the way of life of the faithful. We also reject the public dances of women, which can cause much harm and damage, and also the dances and rites performed by men and women according to an ancient custom alien to the life of Christians in the name of those falsely called gods by the pagans. We decree that no man is to dress in female attire or a woman in that suitable for men, nor are they to put on the masks of comedies, tragedies or satirical plays, nor to shout the abominable name of Dionysus when they are crushing grapes in wine-presses; neither when they pour wine into jars are they to provoke laughter and so through ignorance or frivolity activate demonic deceit. We lay down that henceforth those who set themselves to perform any of the aforesaid, although aware of these [prohibitions], if they are clerics, are to be deposed, and if they are laymen, excommunicated.

The Kalends was 1 January, a day (extending to four days) of carnival, involving feasting, cross-dressing and semi-magical practices. In 742 St Boniface wrote to Pope Zaccharias to say that he had heard that the Kalends was still celebrated annually in Rome with dancing in the streets,

206 *CJ* IX.18.3 (Krüger 379).
207 PmbZ 1, §4215.

pagan acclamations and sacrilegious songs and pressed the pope to forbid it; Zaccharias replied admitting the truth of the report, but claiming that he had prohibited it only a year before – one wonders with what degree of success.[208] The *Vota* were vows (or prayers) traditionally made for the emperor on 3 January and accompanied by banqueting and (originally) pagan sacrifice; Tertullian, *De corona* 12.3 had deplored any Christian participation in it. The *Brumalia*[209] was celebrated from 24 November until 17 December with dancing and feasting. It included a celebration of the end of the cycle of wine production, and therefore the invoking of Dionysus that is mentioned in this canon. In 743 Pope Zaccharias got a Roman synod to condemn it.[210] Ignatios the Deacon in his *Life of Stephen the Younger* castigates Constantine V for celebrating the *Brumalia* in the 760s.[211] The feast of 1 March remains mysterious; Balsamon refers to 'improper dances' by both men and women on this day.[212]

The banning of these celebrations in this canon proved ineffectual. The Kalends continued to be celebrated in Constantinople at least into the twelfth century, while the *Vota* and the *Brumalia* continued to be celebrated at court at least into the tenth.[213] By the time of the twelfth-century, however, these feasts had gone into sharp decline, for Balsamon and Zonaras (PG 137, 728–32) treat them in the main as no more than an historical memory, though it is notable that Balsamon mentions that some country folk still celebrated the Kalends in the belief that if they started the year with festivities the whole year would go well, which had been the purpose of the feast in pagan times.

See p. 26 above on the dubiousness of viewing these feasts as survivals of paganism, for there is no reason to suppose that they were the expression of pagan *beliefs*. By the late seventh century Byzantine Christians are no more likely to have believed in Dionysus than we today in Santa Claus.[214] This accounts for the survival of these celebrations and the ineffectiveness of this canon.

---

208 PL 89, 747A and 921AB.
209 The etymology is from Latin *bruma*. But in the Greek East the name became linked to *broumos*, an epithet of Dionysus.
210 Mansi XII, 384.
211 *Life of Stephen the Younger* 63. See Auzépy (1997) 262–3, nn. 393–9, and *ODB* I, 327.
212 PG 137, 729A.
213 See references in Ohme (2006a) 55.
214 Contrast Trombley (1978) 8–9, who opines that in some rural areas paganism may have survived under a veneer of Christianization.

CANON 63

That false and fabricated accounts of martyrs should not be read

[48] We order that the accounts of martyrs fraudulently compiled by the enemies of the truth, in order to dishonour the martyrs of Christ and drive their hearers to disbelief, are not to be read out in churches but consigned to fire. Those who adopt them or accept them as true we anathematize.

The cult of the saints, and in particular of martyrs, had been growing in intensity since the fourth century, although at the time of this council the catastrophes of the seventh century were calling into question the effectiveness of the saints' patronage.[215] On the feast-days of saints their lives would often be read out in church. For the meaning of anathematization see p. 165 below. The whole canon is remarkable for its intemperateness, which suggests that it was composed with a particular case in mind.

What were the bogus martyr accounts that this canon shows concern over? Possibly extravagant fictions that discredited the genre. More probably perhaps, martyrology coming from heretical groups, notably the Monophysites. Within the empire only Armenia was monophysite, so this canon can perhaps be added to the canons specially affecting Armenia.[216]

CANON 64

That a layman should not seek the status of a teacher

[48] [We lay down] that a layman is not to deliver a public address on doctrine or teach, thereby claiming for himself the status of a teacher, but should yield to the order handed down by the Lord and open his ears to those who have received the grace of speaking as teachers, and should accept instruction in divine things from them. For God has made a variety of limbs in the one church according to the statement by the apostle.[217] When interpreting this,

---

215 See Dagron (1992) and Krausmüller (2015).
216 Esbroeck (1992) 78.
217 Cp. 1 Cor 12:12–21.

Gregory the Theologian gives a lucid presentation of the order that pertains here in the following words: 'Let us respect this order, brothers. Let one of us be the ear, another the tongue, another a hand, another something else; let one teach and another learn,'[218] and a little further down, [49] 'Let also the learner be docile, the giver cheerful, and the server be eager. Let us not all be the tongue, which is always the most ready of all [the members]. Let us not all be apostles, not all be prophets, and not all interpret,'[219] and further down, 'Why do you make yourself a shepherd, when you are a sheep? Why do you become head, when you are a foot? Why do you try to be a general, when your rank is that of a soldier?',[220] and in another place, 'Wisdom charges us, "Be not hasty with words, do not emulate the rich when you are poor, and do not seek to be wiser than the wise."'[221] If anyone is caught violating the present canon, he is to be excommunicated for forty days.

A 'public address' (δημοσία ... λόγον): presumably in church. This rule was new in canon law. The development of a rule that preachers in church had to be ordained ministers may be illustrated from the life of Origen in the early third century. Theoctistus of Caesarea (Palestine) allowed him to preach, despite his being a layman; when Origen's own bishop, Demetrius of Alexandria, protested vehemently, Theoctistus put up a defence but soon thought it prudent to have Origen ordained as a presbyter.[222] This canon cites a sermon of Gregory Nazianzen's, delivered in Constantinople in 379, which insists that doctrine should only be taught by those who are members of the ecclesiastical hierarchy. The Council of Constantinople of 869–70 criticized the elevation to the patriarchate of laymen such as Photius on the grounds (echoing Gregory Nazianzen's citation of St Paul) that a recent layman was no more qualified to teach than a man to be made a general before having been a recruit.[223] The implication is that the learning that a layman might acquire was no substitute for the discipline of rising gradually through the clerical and priestly grades.

---

218 Gregory Nazianzen, *or.* 32, *c.* 12, SC 318, 110, 2–3.
219 Ibid., *c.* 12, p. 110, 9–13. Cp. 1 Cor 12:29.
220 Ibid., *c.* 13, p. 112, 2–4.
221 Ibid., *c.* 21, p. 130, 21–3, echoing Prov 29:20, 23:4, 30:24.
222 Eusebius, *HE* VI.19.16–18 and 23.4.
223 Acts of Constantinople IV, ed. Leonardi, 207, 593–8.

CANON 65

About the fires that some people light in front of
their houses on the days of a new moon

[49] The fires that some people light in front of their workshops and houses when there is a new moon, while some commit the folly of jumping over them according to an ancient custom, we order are to cease from now on. Therefore, whoever does such a thing, if he is a cleric, is to be deposed, and if a layman, excommunicated. For it is written in the fourth book of Kings, 'And Manasseh built an altar to the whole host of heaven in the two courts of the house of the Lord, and he made his children pass through fire, practised divination and augury, appointed ventriloquists and multiplied mediums, and multiplied doing evil before the Lord and angering him.'[224]

The passage cited from 4 Kings (21:5–6) might seem less relevant than the later 23:5, which tells of King Josiah suppressing sacrifices to the moon, but Manasseh was a particularly notorious example of a king who fell into paganism. As a continuing Jewish practice, celebration of the new moon had been criticized in St Paul, Colossians 2:16. But this is the first appearance of this ban in canon law.

CANON 66

About frequenting the churches throughout the week
of the resurrection

[49] From the holy day of the resurrection of Christ our God until the following Sunday the faithful should spend the whole week in the holy churches without intermission, rejoicing in Christ and holding festival with psalms, hymns and spiritual canticles, paying attention to the reading of the divine Scriptures and delighting in the holy mysteries. For in this way we shall rise with Christ and be exalted with him. On these days no horse races or other public shows are to be performed.

---

224   4 (2) Kgs 21:5–6.

Canon 24 forbade clergy from ever attending horse races. High-minded pleas that the laity should also shun them had fallen on deaf ears; here the demand is made that they should at least not be held in Easter Week. Canon 61 of Carthage laments that during this week Christians frequented the hippodrome more than churches and urges that races and theatrical shows be held only at other times of the year. Imperial law forbade public shows in the Easter season.[225] As Ohme notes, the issuing of such a general prohibition would seem a matter outside the church's competence: the implication is that the whole population, as God's people, was subject to church law.[226]

CANON 67

About abstaining from blood and from
what is strangled

[50] Divine Scripture commands us 'to abstain from blood and from what is strangled and from unchastity.'[227] We therefore impose an appropriate penance on those who for the sake of their greedy stomach use skill to make the blood of any animal edible and so eat it. Therefore, if from now on anyone sets himself to eat the blood of an animal in any way, if he is a cleric, he is to be deposed, and if a layman, excommunicated.

Canon 2 of Gangra testifies to a continuing Christian prohibition of eating blood and what is strangled, in accordance with the apostolic decree of Acts 15:29. Its origin lay in a sense of the unique status of blood in the body – Deut 12:23, 'The blood is the life.' Apostolic Canon 63 (SC 336, p. 298), which was not recognized in the West, also bans the eating of blood, as also of animals who had died or been killed by wild beasts. The ban on blood was later taken into secular law by Leo VI (886–912), *nov.* 58. It was not adhered to in the West.

225 *CJ* 3.12.6 (of 389) and 9 (of 469).
226 Ohme (2006a) 98.
227 Acts 21:25.

CANON 68

*That a volume of the Old and New Testament should
not be destroyed or cut up for scent-makers*

[50] On the subject that no one at all is allowed to destroy or cut up a volume
of the Old and New Testament or of our holy and approved preachers and
teachers, or to hand it over for destruction to bookdealers or those called
scent-makers or anyone else at all, unless it has been made utterly unusable
by worms, water or something else. For now on anyone caught doing this is
to be excommunicated for one year. Likewise the purchaser of such books,
if he is neither keeping them for his own edification nor out of generosity
giving them to another to preserve, but were to attempt to destroy them,
is to be excommunicated.

This canon was new in church law. Before the invention of paper writing
materials were expensive, particularly parchment; so it was usual practice to
reuse them after scraping off the old text. This canon forbids the subjection
of sacred texts to this indignity. It is striking that the ban is here extended
from biblical to patristic texts.

CANON 69

That a layman is not to enter the sacred sanctuary

[50] No one at all among the laity is to be allowed to enter the sacred
sanctuary, save that the emperor's power and authority is in no way to be
hampered in this respect, whenever he wishes to present gifts to the Creator
according to a most ancient tradition.

The only related canon in earlier legislation appears to be Canon 44 of
Laodicea, which forbade women from entering the sanctuary. Commenting
on this Quinisext canon, Balsamon mentions that some interpreted the
special permission for emperors to enter the sanctuary to relate only to
the presentation of the gifts, but insists that they can do so whenever they
please, since they are 'the anointed of the Lord' and themselves 'invoke the

holy Trinity when they appoint patriarchs', and 'cense [the altar] as bishops do'.[228] This unique imperial privilege arose from Old Testament notions of the priest–king, even if in the church strictly priestly roles were restricted to those so ordained.[229]

CANON 70

That women are not to talk during the liturgy

[50] At the time of the divine liturgy women are not allowed to talk, but, as Paul the Apostle said, 'They are to keep silent, for they are not permitted to talk but to be submissive, as the law says. If they wish to learn something, let them ask their husbands at home'.[230]

A comparable Pauline text is 1 Tim 2:11, 'Let woman learn in silence in all subjection.' Compare Canon 44 of Laodicea which specifically prohibits women from entering the sanctuary; the comment on this by the Byzantine canonist Zonaras is that, since laymen were prohibited from entering the sanctuary, women were so also *a fortiori*, because of their (supposedly) greater bodily impurity.[231] Yet deaconesses still had a particular status (Canon 14). What form or forms of talking or speaking (the verb used here, λαλέω, could mean either)[232] are being referred to in the present canon? Balsamon says that the canon forbids women to speak during the divine liturgy but not during the other services, and that its aim is to correct women who wish to indulge in discussion about the Scripture readings.[233] In support of this interpretation is the fact that the passage of St Paul that is cited relates specifically to women putting questions. It is not credible that this canon forbids women from joining in the liturgical responses.[234]

---

228 PG 137, 752C–753A.
229 See Dagron (2003).
230 1 Cor 14:34–5, citing Gen 3:16.
231 PG 137, 1400BC.
232 In classical Greek λαλέω meant 'chat' or 'chatter', while λέγω was the word for 'speak'. But in later writers the distinction was lost, and λαλέω could be used even of the words of Christ. See *PGL* 790–91.
233 PG 137, 753C–756A.
234 The opposite is assumed by Herrin (2013) 120, who takes this canon as a prime

This rule was novel, and the most interesting thing about it is that it was thought to be needed.

CANON 71

That those studying civil law should not follow pagan customs

[51] Those studying civil law ought not to follow pagan customs, and should not frequent theatres or practise the so-called *kulistrai*,[235] or wear clothing contrary to what is usual, neither at the time they embark on their studies, nor when they near their end, nor, to speak comprehensively, during the whole course of their education. If anyone from now on has the effrontery to do this, he is to be excommunicated.

This canon is without parallel. Other canons, of course, condemn pagan customs, and the clergy were forbidden from attending theatrical shows (Canon 24) or wearing inappropriate clothing (Canon 27). But this remains a strange intrusion into the education of civil lawyers. Though little is known of law schools in this period (see *ODB* II, 1196), the implication of the present canon is that there was a prominent law school in Constantinople at this time, seen by the church as a potential rival to the church as an intellectual centre. This canon attempts to place law students under a degree of clerical oversight.

CANON 72

That an orthodox man is not to marry a woman who is a heretic

[51] An orthodox man is not to be allowed to marry a woman who is a heretic, nor an orthodox woman to be joined to a man who is a heretic; and if it transpires that anything of this kind is done by anyone at all, the marriage

example of a concern supposedly manifest in the Quinisext Canons 'to keep women under control' (127). See pp. 25–6 above.

235 *Kulistrai* were urns for drawing out the names of horses and charioteers in the hippodrome (Rochow 1978, 495).

is to be considered invalid and the unlawful cohabitation is to be dissolved. For it is wrong to mix what should not be mixed, for a wolf to be joined to a sheep, and for the lot of sinners to be joined to the portion of Christ. If anyone violates what we have decreed, he is to be excommunicated.

If some have been joined to each other in lawful marriage when they were in unbelief and not yet enrolled in the flock of the orthodox, and then one of them has chosen what is good and come over to the light of the truth, while the other partner has been held back by the bond of error and does not choose to contemplate the divine rays, and yet the unbelieving wife wishes to live together with the believing husband or conversely the unbelieving husband with the believing wife, they are not to be separated, according to the divine apostle: 'For the unbelieving husband has been made holy through his wife, and the unbelieving wife through her husband.'[236]

Canon 21 of Carthage forbade the children of clerics to marry heretics. Canon 14 of Chalcedon (COGD I, 144) extended this, in prohibiting lectors and cantors from themselves marrying or marrying their children to heretics, unless the latter converted to the true faith. This echoed Canon 31 of Laodicea, which imposed the same restriction on all Christians; but the introduction at Chalcedon of a special rule for lectors and their children implies that this general prohibition was no longer in force. So the present canon represents a significant tightening of the discipline. There was no such prohibition in civil law.

CANON 73

That figures of the cross should not be made on the floor

[51] Since the life-giving cross has shown us salvation, we must employ all our zeal in paying due honour to that through which we have been saved from the ancient transgression. Because, therefore, we venerate it in thought and word and sight, we order that the figures of the cross that some have had made on the floor should be completely obliterated, so that [52] what is for us a trophy of victory should not be insulted by being trampled on by

---

236 1 Cor 7:14.

those walking over it. We decree that from now on those who make a figure of the cross on the floor are to be excommunicated.

Another novel canon. Such floor crosses are found from the fourth century, but Theodosius II forbade them.[237] Here the ban is reinforced by the imposition of a severe canonical penalty. The loss and then recovery of the True Cross had led to an intensified reverence towards the Cross; note the introduction of the Feast of the Exaltation of the Cross that followed hard on the loss of Jerusalem to the Arabs in 638. Compare the obliteration of religious images on the floors of Palestinian churches in the eighth century, discussed in Reynolds (2017): figurative art came to be rejected in floor mosaics, not through any anticipation of iconoclasm, but because of the danger of the profanation of sacred symbols.

CANON 74

That it is not permitted to eat in a sacred edifice

[52] We lay down 'that it is not permitted to hold a so-called *agape* on Sundays or in churches, to eat inside the church building and to set out dining couches.'[238] Those who dare to do this are either to cease or be excommunicated.

For the agape a few centuries before see Ps.-Hippolytus, *The Apostolic Tradition* 28: it was supposed to be a solemn communal meal, presided over by a bishop, presbyter or deacon, involving instruction or edification by the clergyman present and with the eating of blessed bread. This text finds it necessary to insist that the proceedings must be orderly and restrained. We do not know the character of the agape as celebrated in the seventh century, but this canon implies that it was thought to desecrate sacred space. This canon was without precedent in canon law. It is related to Canons 76 and 97 below, which are also concerned to prevent such desecration.

237 Law of 427 in *CJ* 1.8 (Krüger 2, 61).
238 Canon 28 of Laodicea.

CANON 75

That chanting should not involve disorderly bellowing

[52] It is our will that those who go to the churches in order to chant should not indulge in disorderly bellowing or force shrieking on nature, nor should they choose anything that is neither appropriate nor proper to the church, but with great care and compunction they should address their psalmody to God who sees what is secret. For the sacred saying has taught us that 'the sons of Israel will be devout'.[239]

Disorderly chanting and the use of non-canonical texts had also been treated in Canons 15 and 59 of Laodicea, which laid down that only properly appointed cantors could chant in church and only biblical psalms could be used. The concern here is with the use of unauthorized texts as well as the mode of performance. The expansion of suitable texts outside biblical confines was already well under way, notably in the *kontakia* of Romanos the Melodist.

CANON 76

That it is forbidden to have a bar within sacred
precincts or to serve or sell varieties of food

[52] [We lay down] that it is not permitted within sacred precincts to have a bar, offer varieties of food or to have other things on sale, since we respect the sacredness of churches. For our God and Saviour, in teaching us by his mode of life on earth, ordered us 'not to make his Father's house a house of trade', when he overturned the coins of the money-changers and drove out those who were profaning the sacred place.[240] Therefore, if anyone is caught committing the aforementioned offence, he is to be excommunicated.

See Canon 74 with my annotation. 'Precincts' (περιβόλων) in the plural seems to cover the area immediately outside the church as well as the

239 Lev 15:31.
240 Jn 2:15–16.

building itself. The concern again is to preserve the sacred character of land dedicated to divine service.

CANON 77

That clerics or ascetics are not to wash with women in a bathhouse

[52] '[We lay down] that those in priestly orders or clerics or ascetics are not to wash in a bathhouse together with women, nor is any Christian, for this is the first charge made by pagans.'[241] If anyone is caught doing this, if he is a cleric, he is to be deposed, and if a layman, excommunicated.

The reference in the canon of Laodicea cited here to a 'charge made by pagans' is understood by Zonaras to refer to even pagans criticizing for depravity any man who bathes with women, and by Aristenos less plausibly to refer to a specifically Christian practice of men bathing with women (PG 137, 1380A). Balsamon (PG 137, 777BC), commenting on this canon, says that some laymen denied that it had reference to married couples bathing together. Ohme in this context cites texts on the Roman and Byzantine habit of the sexes bathing together, and identifies Slavs and Arabs as the critical pagans in question.[242]

CANON 78

That those being illuminated should learn the creed

[52] '[We lay down] that those being illuminated[243] should learn the creed and recite it to the bishop or the presbyters on the Thursday.'[244]

---

241 Canon 30 of Laodicea.
242 Ohme (2006a) 95–7.
243 That is, candidates for baptism.
244 Meaning the Thursday in Holy Week, before baptism at the Easter vigil.

This canon is no more than a verbatim repetition of Canon 46 of Laodicea, which applied to a context where baptism was largely restricted to the Easter Vigil and where it was normal for Christians to be baptized in adulthood. Since these practices had long passed away, superseded by infant baptism at any time of year, this canon, if taken literally, was simply defunct. Its intention was presumably to insist that all the baptized should be taught the creed by heart at some stage. If this was the point intended, it should have been clearly stated, with reference to the older canon, but not by merely repeating it.

CANON 79

About those who celebrate the childbirth after
the appointed day of Christ's Nativity

[53] Since we profess that the divine birth from the Virgin was without travail, just as it did not involve seed, and preach this to the whole flock, we subject to correction those who out of ignorance do something they should not. Therefore, since some after the day of the holy Nativity of Christ our God are seen to cook fine wheat flour and serve it to each other, supposedly in honour of the travail of the immaculate Virgin Mother, we decree that nothing of the kind is to be performed by the faithful. For it is no honour for the Virgin who incomprehensibly and inexpressibly gave fleshly birth to the infinite Word to delimit and describe her ineffable birth with reference to things that are common and on our level. Therefore, if anyone from now on is caught doing anything of the kind, if he is a cleric, he is to be deposed, and if he is a layman, excommunicated.

Another novel prescription. It would appear to be the application to the Mother of God of a rite involving wheat flour to celebrate ordinary childbirth. That there was no travail or labour-pains in the case of Christ's birth was standard doctrine. The curse on Eve in Gen 3:16 runs: 'Multiplying, I shall multiply your pain and your distress; in pain you will bring forth children.' It was natural to exempt the Mother of God from this penalty.

CANON 80

On not tarrying without necessity without going to church

[53] If any bishop or presbyter or deacon or anyone enrolled in the clergy or a layman, 'without any grave necessity or practical difficulty that keeps him away from his church for a long period, does not attend for three Sundays in three weeks, despite staying in the city', if he is a cleric, he is to be deposed, and if a layman, he is to be 'excluded from communion'.

This canon quotes part of Canon 11 of Sardica that runs: 'Remember that in past time our fathers laid down that, if a layman staying in a city does not attend for three Sundays in three weeks, he is to be excluded from communion. If, therefore, this was laid down in the case of laymen, it is wrong, improper and also inexpedient for a bishop, without any grave necessity or practical difficulty, to keep away from his church for a long period and sadden the flock entrusted to him.' This was the first time that this traditional rule was expressed in an extant text. Even here the reference to the laity must be to their practice in their own cities, since laymen staying in other cities could not be monitored. Nor is the new specification that the rule extends to all the clergy significant, since the Sardican canon surely takes this for granted. More interesting is the fact that both canons accept the required norm for church attendance to be one Sunday in three. The extension of the clause referring to practical impediments from the bishop to the laity shows awareness that the rule had to be waived for the laity as well in such cases as infirmity or domestic duties that allow no respite. Excommunication would be meaningless in the case of those who never came to communion, and the purpose of the canon is surely not to dragoon the whole population but to make infrequent attendance less infrequent.

CANON 81

That 'who was crucified for us' should not be added to the Trisagion

[53] Since we have learnt that in some places as an addition in the Trisagion hymn there is chanted after 'Holy immortal' the words 'who was crucified for

us, have mercy on us', although this was banished from this hymn by the holy
fathers of old as alien to piety,[245] together with the lawless heretic who had
introduced this innovation, we too confirm the previous pious legislation
of our holy fathers and anathematize those who after the present decree
still accept this expression and add it to the Trisagion hymn in churches or
elsewhere. If the transgressor of our decree is of priestly rank, we lay down
that he is to be stripped of priestly dignity; if he is a layman or monk, he is
to be excommunicated.

The Trisagion hymn in its original form (still used in the Orthodox
churches) runs, 'Holy God, holy strong, holy immortal, have mercy on
us.' This is understood to be an address to the whole Trinity. In 471 the
non-Chalcedonians (or Monophysites) at Antioch inserted the words 'who
was crucified for us' after 'holy immortal', interpreting the whole hymn to
be addressed specifically to the second person of the Trinity, Christ God,
and expressing thereby their conviction that it was Christ God, and not just
some human person conjoined with him, who was crucified on the cross,
and this at a time when theopaschite expressions (attributing the passion to
Christ God) were looked on askance by the official church; they had been
avoided in the Chalcedonian Definition of 451. Theopaschite expressions
were adopted in the Byzantine Church, however, under Justinian I, for
example in Canon 3 of the Fifth Ecumenical Council (551),[246] and this
should have resolved the controversy. But the Chalcedonians continued
to insist that the theopaschite addition was improper, on the grounds that
the hymn is addressed to the whole Trinity, and if the three acclamations
it contains are attributed to the three divine persons in turn, then 'holy
immortal, have mercy on us' attributes the suffering to the Holy Spirit.

The Armenian Church, as non-Chalcedonian, used the monophysite
version of the Trisagion, and so its condemnation here may be linked to
the other canons (32, 33, 56, 99) that single out Armenian practices for
reprobation. The Armenian catholikos Sahak III, in the context of insisting
that the divine Word is the subject of the human sufferings, had recently in
his *Discourse* made much of this version of the Trisagion;[247] and this may

---

245 Here, as often, 'piety' (εὐσεβεία) means orthodoxy.
246 ACO IV.1, 240, trans. in Price (2009) II, 120.
247 *Discourse* 67–9, in Esbroeck (1995) 422–3. For the context of Sahak's *Discourse* see
pp. 30–31 above.

well have stimulated this canon, just as his attack on mixing water with the wine of the eucharist was doubtless the stimulus for Canon 32.

CANON 82

That painters should not represent a lamb in
the finger-pointing of the Precursor

[54] On some of the depictions of the venerable images a lamb is represented, with the finger of the Precursor pointing to it, which was adopted as a type of grace, indicating to us in advance by means of the law the true lamb, Christ our God.[248] Although we embrace the ancient types and shadows handed down to the church as symbols and prefigurations of the truth, we give greater honour to grace and truth,[249] since we received it as the fulfilment of the law.[250] So that the perfect may be portrayed before the eyes of all even in painting, we decree that the lamb who takes away the sin of the world, Christ our God, is from now on to be represented, even in images, in human form in place of the lamb of old. Through this we grasp the sublimity of the abasement of God the Word and are led to the memory of his life in the flesh, of his passion and salvific death, and the redemption that resulted for the world.[251]

The words of John the Baptist referring to Christ – 'Behold the lamb of God' (Jn 1:36) – had inspired representations of Christ as a lamb. The present canon insists that, while the passover lamb of Old Testament sacrifice was a type or prefiguration of Christ, in the present age, now that the incarnation

248 The lamb of 'the law' is the Passover lamb (Exod 12:1–28) and is here contrasted to 'the true lamb', who takes away the sins of the world (Jn 1:29).

249 Cp. Jn 1:18, 'The law was given through Moses, [but] grace and truth came through Jesus Christ.'

250 See Vogt (1988) 143 for the expression in this canon both of anti-Judaism and of an insistence on the theological seriousness of art.

251 This insistence on a realistic portrayal of the incarnate Christ, in place of a representation inspired by Old Testament prophecy or even pagan myth, marks a final turning away from the earliest representations of Christ (those of the third century), which generally shunned direct portrayals of Christ; see Spieser (2015) 27–98. For late antique images which combine Christ in human form with Christ the lamb of God see ibid., 268–77.

has taken place, Christ must be represented as a human being, as the shadow is superseded by the reality.[252] The canon takes it for granted that images of Christ in his humanity are unproblematic. The canon does not ban *all* symbolical representations of Christ: after all, the cross was and remained an ubiquitous symbol, not only of the passion but of Christ as victor and saviour.

After the iconoclasts of the eighth century condemned images of Christ in his humanity, notably at the Council of Hiereia of 754, this canon was a favourite text for iconophiles to appeal to, and is cited frequently in the Acts of Nicaea II (787). For it goes beyond saying that Christ should be represented in human form (which the iconoclasts criticized for obscuring his Godhead), for it describes images of Christ as σεπτῶν, that is, holy and therefore requiring veneration. The same adjective was used in the key sentence of the Definition of the Second Council of Nicaea: 'We therefore decree with all care and precision that venerable (σεπτὰς) and holy images are to be dedicated ... in the holy churches of God'.[253]

CANON 83

That the eucharist is not to be given to the bodies of the dead

[54] No one 'is to give the eucharist to the bodies of those who have died. For Scripture says, "Take, eat," but the bodies of the dead can neither take nor eat.'[254]

It was an ancient Christian custom to give viaticum ('food for the journey') to the dying. There would naturally be distress if someone died suddenly without viaticum. Either in the hope that the deceased was not quite dead, or without that hope but to comfort the relatives, it was easy for this to develop into giving communion to the dead. This canon shows that this practice was as alive in the seventh as it had been in the fifth, when the canon of Carthage cited here was enacted.

---

252 See further pp. 27–8 above, and also p. 42 for a fresco commissioned by Pope John VII (705–7) in S. Maria Antiqua, where the expected Lamb of God is replaced by a Christ figure, presumably in response to this canon.
253 ACO² III.3, 826, 5–7, trans. Price (2018) II, 564.
254 From Canon 18 of Carthage.

CANON 84

About those of whom it is not known for
certain whether they were baptized

[54] Following the canonical regulations of the fathers, we decree about infants, 'whenever there are not found reliable witnesses testifying that they were certainly baptized, and when because of their age they themselves are unable to answer this question about the sacramental initiation they received, they are to be baptized without any hindrance, lest hesitation over this should deprive them of this sacramental cleansing.'[255]

Evidence for the baptism of infants begins to appear in the second century. Irenaeus (*Adv. Haer.* 2.22.4) refers to the baptism of 'infants and children and boys and young men and old men'. Despite objections, as by Tertullian (*De baptismo* 18) that innocent infants have no need of baptism, and some anxiety as to whether it was safe to give baptism, with the obligations it entailed, to the very young (see Augustine, *Confessions* I.11), it had become the normal practice by the fifth century. Theodoret wrote: 'If the only meaning of baptism were the forgiveness of sins, why would we baptize the newborn children who have not yet tasted of sin? But the sacrament is not limited to this; it is a promise of greater and more perfect gifts. In it are the promises of future delights; it is a type of the future resurrection, a communion with the Master's passion, a participation in his resurrection, a mantle of salvation, a tunic of gladness, a garment of light, or rather, it is light itself.'[256]

CANON 85

That those who are manumitted in the presence
of three witnesses enjoy their freedom

[55] We have received from Scripture that 'by two or three witnesses every word is confirmed'.[257] We therefore decree that slaves who are freed by their

---

255 Canon 72 of Carthage.
256 Theodoret, *Haeret. fabul. compend.* 5.18 (PG 83, 512).
257 Dt 19:15, Mt 18:16, 2 Cor 13:1, with slightly variant vocabulary.

masters are to obtain this honour when there are three witnesses, who confer validity on this manumission by their presence and will themselves provide assurance of what took place.

That manumission of slaves was appropriately performed in churches had been recognized by both Constantine the Great and Justinian I, and indeed it became the most common form of manumission. Canon of Carthage 64 mentions that manumission in church was standard practice in Italy, and extends this to Africa; Canon of Carthage 82 records a decision to seek imperial approval for this. The present canon lays down the need for a minimum of two or three witnesses, in accordance with biblical precedent (e.g. Dt 17:6, Mt 18:16, Heb 10:28), in contrast to the civil requirement of five. In practice, the ceremony is likely to have been carried out before an assembled congregation.

CANON 86

About those who maintain prostitutes for the destruction of souls

[55] We decree that those who for the destruction of souls collect prostitutes and maintain them, if they are clerics, are to be deposed, and if laymen, excommunicated.

Justinian I had tried to outlaw prostitution altogether.[258] The civil law did not penalize the prostitutes themselves, but dealt with pimping severely.[259]

258 Justinian, *nov.* 14 of 535 (Schöll–Kroll 195–7).
259 See Irmscher (1969).

CANON 87

About a woman who has left her husband or a man
who has left his wife and married another person

[55] 'She who has left her husband is an adulteress, if she has gone to another,'[260] according to the sacred and divine Basil, who took most aptly from the prophet Jeremiah that 'if a woman becomes another man's, she is not to return to her husband, but polluted, she will be polluted,' and again, 'He who possesses an adulteress is insane and impious.'[261] Therefore, 'if it transpires that she has left her husband for no good reason, he deserves forgiveness while she deserves a penance; this forgiveness will entitle him to receive communion.'[262] 'But he who abandons his lawfully wedded wife and takes another, is liable to condemnation for adultery according to the statement of the Lord. It has been canonically decreed by our fathers that such men are to lament for a year, be among the hearers for two years and among those who prostrate themselves for three years, and stand with the faithful in the seventh year, and then be admitted to the offering, if they repent with tears.'[263]

Basil of Caesarea left a number of canons on the penalties for infidelity by a married man or woman, several of which are cited here. In Canon 9 he extends the Matthaean commandment that a man should not divorce his wife save for adultery to the wife as well, but then proceeds to argue that even in the case of her husband's adultery a wife should not leave him; if she does, he allows a forsaken husband to take another woman, while condemning a husband who himself initiates a divorce. In Canon 35 he restricts this permission to cases where the wife has no adequate reason for leaving her husband, which implies that in some cases a wife does have a right to leave her husband. In Canon 77 he allows a husband who has left his wife for another to return after communion after doing penance for seven years, in line with Canon 20 of Ancyra, but in his Canon 58 Basil

260 Canon 9 of Basil of Caesarea, in *ep.* 188, ed. Courtonne II, 129, §9, 23–4.
261 Canon 9, in *ep.* 188, ed. Courtonne II, 128, §9, 7–10, citing Jer 3:1 and Prov 18:22a (LXX).
262 Canon 35 of Basil of Caesarea, in *ep.* 199, ed. Courtonne II, 161, §35, 2–4.
263 Canon 77 of Basil of Caesarea, in *ep.* 217, ed. Courtonne II, 214, §77, 1–8.

imposes on an adulterer a penance of fifteen years. In Canon 21 he accepts the custom by which a husband was not considered an adulterer if he fornicated with an unmarried woman.

This Quinisext canon sticks together various sentences of Basil, avoiding contradiction, but too much is left unsaid. It prohibits a wife who has left her husband for another from returning to him, but fails to say that she can return to her husband if he is willing to take her back, as Balsamon points out (PG 137, 809C): what is denied is that such a wife has the right to actually require her husband to take her back. When forgiveness and readmittance to communion is promised to a husband deserted by his wife, it needs to be said, as Aristenus does when commenting on Basil's original text (PG 138, 701C), that this relates to a deserted husband who marries another wife.

It is to be noted that the church's concern, as expressed in this canon, is specifically with canonical penance. The actual law of marriage remained in secular hands, even when the church was involved. See, for instance, the rule laid down in Justinian, that a wife who leaves her husband without a legally recognized ground for divorce is to be handed over to the bishop and incarcerated lifelong in a monastery.[264]

CANON 88

That an animal is not to be brought inside a sacred
building unless on a journey out of great necessity

[55] No one is to bring an animal of any kind inside a sacred edifice, except if, when on a journey and under the pressure of great necessity and in the absence of any house or accommodation, he lodges in such a church; for as a result of his not bringing the animal indoors it would sometimes perish, while he, through the loss of his beast of burden and the resultant impossibility of continuing his journey, would be in danger of death. For [56] we are taught that 'the sabbath was made for man',[265] and therefore that in all circumstances priority is to be given to keeping a man safe and unharmed. But if anyone is caught bringing an animal into a sacred edifice without

---

264 Justinian, *nov.* 117.13 of 542 (Schöll–Kroll 563).
265 Mk 2:27.

necessity, as stated above, if he is a cleric, he is to be deposed, and if a layman, excommunicated.

Compare Canons 74, 76 and 97, all of which are concerned to protect the sacred character of a religious building from desecration. What is striking in the present canon is that, despite this, priority is given to 'keeping a man safe and unharmed'.

CANON 89

About the hour at which the fast ends on the Great Saturday

[56] Observing the days of the saving passion in fasting, prayer and compunction of heart, it is necessary for the faithful to end the fast at midnight on the Saturday, since the divine evangelists Matthew and Luke, the former with the expression 'after the Sabbath' and the latter 'at early dawn',[266] indicate the lateness of the night.

The intention was to end the fast at the time of the resurrection, but when exactly had this taken place? The canon cites two gospel passages, while omitting Jn 20:1, which specifies that Mary Magdalene came to the tomb and found it empty 'while it was still dark'. The matter had been treated at length by Dionysius of Alexandria in a text included in Byzantine canonical collections.[267] Acknowledging the lack of precision in the gospel accounts, Dionysius criticized equally those who ended the fast before Saturday midnight and those who ended it at the fourth watch of the night, on the grounds that this was the hour when on an earlier occasion Christ had appeared walking on the water (Mt 14:25), but did not attempt to define the precise time between these two extremes. The present canon is concerned to end this ambiguity.

266 Mt 28:1, Lk 24:1.
267 Joannou (1963) 4–11.

CANON 90

That kneeling is not permitted on Sundays

[56] We have been taught canonically by our inspired fathers that in honour of Christ's resurrection we should not kneel on Sundays. Therefore, to provide clear knowledge of how this practice is to be observed, we inform the faithful that, according to the custom in force, after the entry into the sanctuary of the sacred ministers on Saturday evening no one is to genuflect until the following evening on the Sunday, when after the entry for the lighting of the lamps we again bend the knee and so offer the prayers to the Lord. For we consider Saturday night to be a forerunner of the resurrection of our Saviour and begin our spiritual hymnody then, while we complete the festival from darkness into light in such a way that we celebrate the resurrection for a whole night and day.

Canon 20 of Nicaea (COGD I, 30) had forbidden kneeling on Sundays. The present canon is concerned to define exactly when Sunday begins and ends. Tertullian and later Basil of Caesarea had linked kneeling with fasting, and forbidden both of them on Sundays and throughout the Easter season.[268] Note that according to this canon late evening on Saturday is counted as part of Sunday, in contrast to the preceding canon where Easter day is said to begin at midnight.

CANON 91

About the penance for those who provide or receive abortifacient drugs

[56] 'Women who provide abortifacient drugs and those who receive poisons that kill embryos'[269] we subject to the penance for murder.

---

268 Tertullian, *de corona* 3.4 (CCSL 2, 1043). Basil, *On the Holy Spirit* 27, 66 (SC 17², 484).
269 Canon 8 of Basil of Caesarea, in *ep.* 188, ed. Courtonne II, 128, 46–8, which prescribes the same penance.

Abortion became illegal in Roman law only at the beginning of the third century. The church had always been less tolerant. Canon 21 of Ancyra says that the penalty had been lifelong (presumably allowing reconciliation on the deathbed) and reduces it to ten years of penance.[270] Since the penalty for murder was lifelong excommunication according to Canon 22 of Ancyra, this implies treating abortion as less serious. But the length of the penance laid down continued to be variable. Canon 2 of Basil of Caesarea confirms that lifelong excommunication is inappropriate and like Ancyra assigns a penance of ten years, adding that Christians make no difference between the abortion of formed and unformed foetuses.[271] But his Canon 8, cited here, equates abortion with murder, for which according to his Canon 56 the penalty was twenty years of excommunication.

CANON 92

About those who abduct women on the pretext of marriage

[57] 'The holy council decrees that those who abduct women on the pretext of marriage or aid and assist those so doing, if they are clerics, are to lose their rank, and if laymen, be anathematized.'[272]

Abduction was clearly a common phenomenon, normally in cases where a young couple could not obtain the consent of the girl's parents. This denial of parental authority shocked society, or at least imperial legislators. A notorious law of Constantine the Great imposed the death penalty, apparently in the cruellest possible form, on both the abductor and his accomplices.[273] A law of Justinian's of 528 confirmed the death penalty, ruling out any attempt to cover up the crime by the abductor marrying the girl with the parents' consent.[274]

In contrast to this, church law had for a time been surprisingly lenient. Canon 22 of Basil of Caesarea had laid down that the girl was to be

---

270   Joannou (1962b) 71.
271   In Basil, *ep.* 188, ed. Courtonne II, 124.
272   Canon 27 of Chalcedon (COGD I, 150).
273   *CTh* 9.24.1 of 320 (to be corrected to 326), for which see Evans-Grubbs (1989).
274   *CJ* ix.13.1 (Krüger 378). For further legislation see Karlin-Hayter (1992) 36–44.

returned to her parents, who could decide to let her abductor marry her; if the abductor did not return her, he was to be subjected as a fornicator to four years of penance.[275] Meanwhile, his Canon 30 recommended a penalty of three years' exclusion of both the abductor and his assistants from participation in the prayer of the church, save where the abduction was not forcible, in which case no penalty at all is incurred.[276] Likewise Apostolic Canon 67 (SC 336, p. 300) had imposed excommunication for an unspecified period in cases of *forcible* abduction. Canon 27 of Chalcedon, which the present canon repeats, treats this offence with greater severity. The purpose of repeating the canon of Chalcedon was to imply that it had replaced the canon of Basil on the same subject.

This canon is revealing about the relations between law and practice and between civil and church law.[277] The implication of all these canons is that the death penalty laid down by emperors was not in fact enforced, and very possibly that their enactments were not widely known. It is also to be noted that the concern of the canons is specifically and narrowly with the question of the ecclesiastical status of the abductor.

As regards the canonical penalty, it was a regular conciliar formula for offenders against a particular canon to be 'deposed' if they were clerics and 'excommunicated' if they were laymen. When, as here, anathematization is spoken of instead of excommunication, what does this mean? Excommunication was temporary, in that, once the offender had performed penance and given evidence of contrition, he would be readmitted to communion. Was anathematization different in that it excluded the possibility of reconciliation? Compare Canon 81, which 'anathematizes' those who use the Monophysite version of the Trisagion, but then proceeds to impose the standard penalties of deposition for clergy and excommunication for laymen: clearly the 'anathematization' was lifted if the offender repented. We may presume the same in the present case. Why then is 'anathematization' spoken of at all? Doubtless to express the particular gravity of the offence, which will have required forgiveness to be earned by longer penance and indisputable evidence of real repentance. Balsamon argued that no one could be permanently excluded from salvation until the Last Judgement.[278]

---

275 In Basil, *ep.* 199, ed. Courtonne, II, 158.
276 In Basil, *ep.* 199, ed. Courtonne II, 160–61.
277 Clark (1993) 11–12 and 36–8.
278 Balsamon, PG 137, 1236C–1237C.

CANON 93

That a woman who marries another before being
convinced that her husband has died is an adulteress

[57] 'A woman whose husband has departed and disappeared and who marries another before being convinced of his death commits adultery.'[279] Similarly, 'the wives of soldiers who have remarried when their husbands have disappeared are to be treated in the same way as those whose husband has gone on a journey and who do not wait for his return, except that the affair has some excuse because of the greater supposition that he has died.'[280] 'A woman who has married in ignorance a man who has been left by his wife for a time and has then been dismissed because the earlier wife has come back to him has committed fornication, but in ignorance; therefore she is not to be excluded from marriage, although it is better if she remains as she is.'[281] If a soldier returns after a time whose wife because of his long absence has married another man, he, if he so chooses, is to recover his wife again, after forgiving her for her ignorance and also the man who cohabited with her in a second marriage.

This canon cobbles together what Basil of Caesarea had written on the subject, instead of thinking through the whole matter and producing clear and coherent rules. In civil law Justinian had legislated on this matter, allowing a man or woman to remarry after five years, if his/her first spouse fell into enemy hands and no information has since been forthcoming.[282] The problem will have become more widespread as a result of the chaos resulting from constant Slav and Arab raids.

---

279 Canon 31 of Basil of Caesarea, in *ep.* 199, ed. Courtonne II, 161.
280 Canon 36 of Basil of Caesarea, in *ep.* 199, ed. Courtonne II, 161.
281 Canon 46 of Basil of Caesarea, in *ep.* 199, ed. Courtonne II, 163.
282 Justinian, *nov.* 22.7 of 535 (Schöll–Kroll 151).

CANON 94

About those who swear pagan oaths

[57] The canon[283] subjects to penances those who swear pagan oaths. Accordingly, we decree that they are to be excommunicated.

Canon 81 of Basil of Caesarea had treated the problem of those who had taken pagan oaths and eaten unclean foods under pressure from barbarians making incursions.[284] It imposed eight years of excommunication on those who did so under torture and eleven on those who did so under less than serious constraint. To swear by pagan gods was to recognize their authority and power, and therefore constituted apostasy, though the guilt was reduced by the element of compulsion involved. Compare Canon 11 of Nicaea (COGD I, 25–6), which treats those who had apostatized 'without compulsion or distraint of property or danger of anything of the kind', and decrees that, 'even though they do not deserve kindness', they are to be excommunicated for only twelve years. It says nothing about those who apostatized under compulsion, and the implication is that they could be readmitted to communion without penance.

CANON 95

About how converts from heresy are to be received

[57] 'Those who come over from heresy to orthodoxy and the lot of those saved we accept according to the following sequence and custom. Arians, Macedonians, Novatianists, who call themselves Cathars and Aristeroi, Quartodecimans or Tetradites and Apollinarians we accept when they present petitions[285] and anathematize every heresy that does not share the faith of God's holy, catholic and apostolic church, after they have first been sealed or anointed with holy oil on the forehead, **[58]** the eyes, the nostrils,

---

283 The meaning is not 'this canon' but the current rule in force.
284 In Basil, *ep.* 217, ed. Courtonne II, 215.
285 λιβέλλοι, requesting admission to the church and taking the form of an orthodox profession of faith.

the mouth and the ears; and when we seal them, we say, "The seal of the gift of the Holy Spirit."'[286]

'Concerning the Paulianists who seek refuge in the catholic church, the regulation requires them to be completely rebaptized.'[287]

'Eunomians, however, who are baptized with a single immersion, Montanists, who are here called Phrygians, and Sabellians, who teach Son-Fatherhood[288] and do other problematic things, and all the other heresies, since there are many [heretics] here, especially those coming from the land of Galatia, and all those wanting to come over from them to orthodoxy we accept as we would pagans. On the first day we make them Christians[289] and on the second day catechumens; then on the third we exorcize them by breathing three times into their face and ears; and afterwards we catechize them and make them wait in the church and listen to the Scriptures, and then we baptize them.'[290]

Manichees, Valentinians, Marcionites,[291] and those who come over from similar heresies, we receive as we would pagans and rebaptize them.

Nestorians, Eutychians, Severians and those from similar heresies must compose petitions and anathematize both their heresy and also Nestorius, Eutyches, Dioscorus, Severus and the other originators of these heresies, those who hold their beliefs, and all the aforementioned heresies. They can then receive holy communion.

The concern of this canon is to distinguish between heresies so grave that converts from them needed to be rebaptized (since their original baptism was considered invalid), those of medium gravity, where those baptized in them needed simply to be confirmed, and those of least gravity, where

---

286 The so-called Canon 7 of Constantinople I (COGD 1, 69–70), dating in fact to the fifth century.

287 Canon 19 of Nicaea, COGD I, 30.

288 υἱοπατορία, the doctrine that the Father and the Son are a single person.

289 The implication is that what made someone a member of the church was not baptism, nor even actual entry into the catechumenate, but an application to enter the catechumenate. This will have derived from the practice in the fourth century whereby many postponed actual baptism out of respect for the strict rule of life the baptized were expected to follow. The most famous examples of this are Constantine the Great and St Augustine.

290 Canon 7 of Constantinople I, continued.

291 These three heresies as mentioned together in Canon 1 of Basil of Caesarea, in *ep.* 188, ed. Courtonne II, 122, 22–3, as being as seriously in error over the Godhead as (in his view) the Montanists.

converts from them needed simply to present a petition anathematizing their heresy and professing the orthodox faith.

The heretics who are specifically mentioned as needing rebaptism are the Paulianists, or followers of Paul of Samosata (who were accused of regarding Christ as a mere man), the Eunomians (who were Arians and did not practise the Trinitarian threefold immersion that the church insisted upon), the Montanists (accused of debasing the Holy Spirit to the same level as their own prophets)[292] and the Sabellians (who denied the distinction between the persons of the Trinity), Manichees (whom the mainstream church did not regard as even Christian), Valentinians (who added to the faith a highly complex mythology of their own) and Marcionites (who rejected the God of the Old Testament).

The heretics who are said here to need not rebaptism but a new bestowal of the Holy Spirit consist of Arians (who were accused of treating Christ as neither fully divine nor fully human), Macedonians (accused of denying the full Godhead of the Holy Spirit), Novatianists (who imposed a stricter penitential discipline than the mainstream church), Quartodecimans (who celebrated Easter on 14 Nisan, contrary to a decree of the Council of Nicaea) and Apollinarians (who accepted the Nicene Creed but were accused of denying that Christ has a human soul).[293]

The heretics who are here allowed to became members of the church simply through renouncing their heresies and presenting an orthodox profession of faith are the Nestorians and non-Chalcedonians (or Monophysites), who had fallen into heresy only in the fifth century and had always professed the faith of Nicaea.

This classification was conservative, in that the greater part of it simply re-enacts earlier canons dating, or thought to date (in the case of Canon 7 attributed to Constantinople I), to the fourth century. Many of these sects are unlikely to have been still in existence in the late seventh century. The only later additions are in the last section of this canon, which brings in the schisms resulting from the councils of Ephesus I (431) and Chalcedon (451), where the lack of canons issued by Constantinople II and Constantinople III left a gap to be filled. There will not have been any Nestorians within the

---

292 This charge is made in Canon 1 of Basil of Caesarea, in *ep.* 188, ed. Courtonne II, 122, 31–9.

293 For an example of the professions of faith that would be required of such converts, see those signed by Quartodecimans of Lydia on being received into the mainstream church by agents of Nestorius, as preserved in the Acts of Ephesus, ACO I.1/7, 100–105.

Byzantine empire, but the recovery of part of Armenia will have placed many non-Chalcedonians under renewed Byzantine rule.

St Athanasius, writing in the middle of the fourth century, had listed Arians, Paulianists and Phrygians and Manichees as among those who had to be rebaptized, since even when they used the correct baptismal formula their heresy was such as to make this meaningless (*Contra Arianos* III.43). It is somewhat surprising that the mainstream church later accepted Arian baptism, since the Arians rejected the Nicene Creed, the prime statement of the orthodox faith; but the term 'Arian' had come to be used so loosely, as a term of opprobrium applied to all who did not affirm unambiguously the equality of all three persons of the Trinity, that it had ceased to be a clear identifier of seriously erroneous theology.

Basil of Caesarea in his Canon 1 had also treated the question. He expresses doubt as to the validity of Novatianist (or Cathar) baptism, because he held that they had lost the valid priesthood and that only priests can baptize, but agrees to go along with the church in Asia (meaning the 'diocese' of Asia or the south-western half of Asia Minor), which had decided to recognize Novatianist baptism.[294] Similarly, as regards the 'encratites' (who preached marital continence), he expresses a preference for not recognizing their baptism, since they had concocted a baptismal rite of their own, but agrees that, if this were to deter them from returning to the true church, it would be better to accept it.[295] Basil was writing at a time when, as he says, practice and opinions varied. This Quinisext canon recognizes the clearer position that had developed in the post-Chalcedonian church. The entry into canon law of the so-called Canon 7 of Constantinople, cited here, enabled the Quinisext council to ignore the more fluid situation presented in Basil.

CANON 96

That men are not to braid their hair

[58] Those who have put on Christ in baptism have promised to imitate his life in the flesh. Therefore those who to the detriment of those who see them arrange and groom the hair on the head in elaborate braids and

294 Basil, *ep.* 188, ed. Courtonne II, 122–3, 46–65.
295 Ibid., 123, 65–80.

thereby set a trap for unstable souls, we treat, as the fathers did, with an appropriate penance, educating and teaching them to live sober lives, in such a way that, rejecting the deceit and vanity that come from things material, they may constantly redirect their minds to the imperishable and blessed life, maintain in fear a spotless pattern of life, draw as near to God as is possible through purity of life, and adorn the inner rather than the outer man with virtues and good and unimpeachable morals, [59] so that they no longer have in themselves any remnant of the crookedness of the adversary. If anyone persists in contravention of this canon, he is to be excommunicated.

This was new as a topic of a canon, but not without patristic and biblical precedent, for elaborately braided hair had received attention in some fourth-century writers, including Epiphanius.[296] Appeal could be made to Lev 19:27, which condemns elaborate hairdos and neatly trimmed beards immediately after condemning divination, and also 1 Pet 3:3, which condemns 'the outward adornment of braided hair' (with the word ἐμπλοκῆς as in the present canon).[297] Compare Canon 71, with its condemnation of showy dress.

CANON 97

About those who stay with their wives in churches without discrimination

[59] Regarding those who live with their wives [in churches] or who otherwise profane sacred places without discrimination, treating them with disdain by staying in them, we order that they are to be expelled even from the part of the venerable churches that is reserved for catechumens. If anyone does not observe this, if he is a cleric, he is to be deposed, and if a layman, excommunicated.

---

296 Epiphanius, *Panarion* 80.7, 1–2.
297 1 Tim 2:9 is also apposite, though with a different noun. Both these New Testament passages are speaking of women, but the rule in their regard would surely apply all the more to men.

Compare Canons 74, 76 and 88, all of which are concerned to protect the sacred character of a religious building from desecration. In the present case there was a particular danger arising from the impurity involved in sexual intercourse and menstruation, expressed in a number of patristic canons.[298]

CANON 98

About him who takes a betrothed woman while her fiancé is alive

[59] He who takes a woman betrothed to another in the communion of marriage when her fiancé is still alive is to incur the charge of adultery.

Compare Canon 92 on abduction. The present canon is striking for assimilating betrothal to marriage. Leo VI (886–912) later adopted it into civil law.[299]

CANON 99

About the Armenians offering pieces of cooked
meat within the sacred sanctuary

[59] We have learnt that this too happens in the land of Armenia: some people cook pieces of meat and offer them within the sacred sanctuaries, assigning pieces of them to the priests in Jewish fashion. Therefore, to protect the church from defilement, we decree that no priest is allowed to receive from those who offer them pieces of meat specially set aside, but they should be satisfied with what the one making the offering is happy with, and that this offering is to take place outside the church. If anyone does not do this, he is to be excommunicated.

This practice was a form of animal sacrifice, allowed by Gregory the

---

298   Ohme (2006a) 103–5.
299   Leo VI, *nov.* 74.109.

Illuminator when he won the Armenians over to Christianity. See Apostolic
Canons 3–4 (SC 336, pp. 274–6) for the banning of such sacrifices in the
mainstream church; they will have been a distinctive and treasured part of
the specifically Armenian tradition. The present canon does not, however,
ban the practice, but prohibits the use of it to express clerical status and its
celebration within a sacred building.

The reference to 'Jewish' fashion connects this canon to Canon 33 – the
concern being to remove the similarity of the Armenian priesthood to that
of the Old Testament.

CANON 100

About not painting on a panel things that incite to pleasure

[59] Wisdom gives the command, 'Let your eyes look straight and keep
your heart wholly under guard.'[300] For the senses of the body easily impress
themselves on the soul. We therefore order that henceforth there is in no
way at all to be any production of paintings, whether on panels or displayed
in some other way, that bewitch the sight and corrupt the mind, stirring it
to the excitement produced by shameful pleasures. If anyone takes it upon
himself to do this, he is to be excommunicated.

Novel as a topic for canonical legislation. According to Ohme we know
of no Byzantine art genuinely deserving to be called erotic. The reference
must be to scenes from Greek mythology, especially those representing
rape.[301]

300 Prov 4:25, 23.
301 For surviving examples see Ohme (2006a) 63.

CANON 101

That laymen are to receive communion in the
mouth[302] and not in a gold or silver receptacle

[60] The holy apostle declares loudly that man created in God's image is the body and temple of Christ.[303] He who has attained a heavenly dignity though the saving passion, eating and drinking Christ, is superior to the whole perceptible creation, and is steadily transformed into eternal life, sanctifying his body and soul though the reception of divine grace. Consequently, if anyone wishes to receive the spotless body at the time of the synaxis and to become one with it through participation, he is to form his hands into the shape of the cross and so approach and receive the communion of grace. Those who, to receive the divine gift, present receptacles of gold or another material and through them enjoy the privilege of the spotless communion we do not accept in any way, since they esteem soulless matter, which we handle, more than the image of God. If anyone is caught giving the spotless communion to those who present receptacles of this kind, he is to be excommunicated, as also is he who presents it.

This is another novel canon, and is one of the latest pieces of evidence for communion in the hand. Subsequently the West from the ninth century moved to communion in the mouth, while in Byzantium the reception of communion in the mouth and in a spoon gradually took over. Receiving communion in one's own valuable dish would be an obvious display of personal status, particularly shocking in this sacred context.

---

302   The actual canon speaks of communion in the hand. To avoid this, Joannou (1962a) 237 emends στόματι (mouth) to σώματι (body), and is followed in this in the translation in Nedungatt and Featherstone (1995) 181; but this correction has no manuscript authority (see the new ACO edition). This heading must date to the time when this had been replaced by communion in the mouth (with an attendant mixing of the eucharistic elements in the chalice), a change that occurred gradually, being universal by the twelfth century. No manuscript containing the headings is older. See Ohme (2006a) 114–15 and Ohme (2013) LII.
303   Cp. Gen 1:26, 1 Cor 12:27, 1 Cor 3:16.

CANON 102

That it is necessary to take into account the disposition
of the sinner and the character of the sin

[60] Those who have received from God the power to bind and loose must examine the character of the sin and the readiness of the sinner to repent, and so apply the appropriate cure to the disease, lest through excess in either direction he fails to save the sick person. For the disease of sin is not of one kind but various and multiple; it produces many harmful offshoots, as a result of which the evil spreads further and increases, until it is stayed by the power of the healer. Consequently the one exercising skill in spiritual healing must first examine the disposition of the sinner, and observe whether he is tending towards health or on the contrary through his own conduct drawing the disease upon himself; [he must observe] to what extent he is taking thought for his mode of life, and whether he is not resisting the expert, with the result that the wound of the soul actually increases through the medicines that are applied. He must measure out mercy in the right degree accordingly.

[61] For the intention both of God and of the one entrusted with the shepherd's role of direction is to bring back the sheep that has strayed and to cure him of the wound of the serpent, without either pushing him down the cliffs of despair nor so relaxing the bit as to produce dissolution and contempt of life. Instead, with total singleness of purpose, through remedies that are either more harsh and bitter or more tender and gentle, he must fight the disease and force the wound to form a scar, while he examines the fruits of repentance and directs with wisdom the man who is called to put on heavenly glory. 'It is therefore incumbent on us to know both strategies, that of strictness and that of custom, and to follow in the case of those who do not accept rigour the model that has been handed down,'[304] as the sacred Basil teaches us.

The insistence that the remedy to be applied must be adjusted according to the character and receptiveness of the particular patient derived from medicine, and had long been developed and practised in the context of spiritual direction, especially in monasteries. Monastically formed bishops

---

304 Canon 3 of Basil of Caesarea, in *ep.* 188, ed. Courtonne II, 125, §3, 18–21.

and pastors applied it to their own sphere of operation. The work most read in the West in the Middle Ages as a guide for bishops was Gregory the Great's *Book of Pastoral Rule*. The greater part of this work (Book III) is devoted to preaching, and Gregory's essential message is that (to quote from the preface to this book) 'the discourse of a teacher should be adapted to the character of the hearers, so as to be suited to the individual in his respective needs.' This therapeutic model for an understanding of the purpose of church law had already been expressed in Canon 2, which declares that the canons previously adopted by the church 'are from now on to remain firm and secure for the cure of souls and the treatment of the passions'.

To return to the Quinisext canons, to what extent do they respect the needs of individuals? They make a distinction between the penalty in a grave matter for clerics, who are to be deposed, and laymen, who are to be excommunicated.[305] The church, arguably, had to defrock scandalous clerics permanently, to preserve the integrity of the sacraments and the repute of the church, but excommunication was intended as a spur to laymen to demonstrate repentance and aspire to a return to the sacraments. In a few cases the length of this excommunication is laid down, varying from a trivial one week to seven years – with a much longer period, not clearly designated, for abortion.[306] Far more often it is left to the discretion of those imposing it in particular cases, whether bishops or spiritual fathers.

The present canon is able to quote Basil in favour of flexibility. The lines in Basil's Canon 3 that precede those quoted here make the essential point more clearly:[307]

> As a general rule, it is departure from sin that is the true remedy. In consequence he who has rejected grace for the pleasure of the flesh, but through mortification of the flesh and its total enslavement through self-control, has renounced the pleasures that had overpowered him, will display to us a perfect proof of his cure.

This implies that the length of penance imposed could be adjusted according to the speed and fullness of the penitent's contrition. The last sentence of Basil's Canon 2 is explicit on this: 'The length of their treatment

---

305 In a few cases 'anathematization' is specified, for which see p. 165 above.
306 These are Canons 27, 54, 58, 61, 68, 91.
307 Courtonne II, 125, §3, 13–18.

should be determined not by a period of time but by the character of their repentance.'[308]

Yet to describe this as a penitential system based on a therapeutic model of penance, aimed at healing, as contrasted to a punitive one, aimed at reparation, still more to contrast it to a supposed domination by the latter in western penitential theory and practice, is dubious.[309] How was exclusion from communion for a significant period of time thought to benefit the sinner? Holy communion is understood to be a medicine for the soul and not a reward for the righteous. The exclusion from full participation in the rites of the church that excommunication imposes is surely punitive, albeit with the intention of encouraging true contrition. Nor can we rule out in this situation an element of deterring potential sinners through humiliating those who have fallen into sin.[310]

308 In *ep.* 188, ed. Courtonne II, 124, §2, 10–11.
309 See Aquinas, *Summa Theologica* 3, qu. 89 for penance as a means of restoring the virtues.
310 For a contrasting view see the discussion of this in Ohme (2006a) 155–7.

III. THE SUBSCRIPTIONS

[62] The emperor, writing in vermilion:

Flavios Iustinianos, faithful in Christ Jesus God, emperor of the Romans, in agreement with, and abiding by, all the decrees: I hereby sign.[311]

(a)   of the most holy pope of Rome.[312]

(1) Paul unworthy bishop of Constantinople Rome: I hereby decree and sign.

(2) Peter unworthy bishop of the great city of Alexandria: I hereby decree and sign.

(3) [63] George insignificant bishop of Antioch or Theupolis: I hereby decree and sign.

(4) Anastasios insignificant bishop of Jerusalem: I hereby decree and sign.

(5) John unworthy bishop of Nea Iustinianupolis in the province of Hellespontus: I hereby decree and sign.[313]

(b)   of Thessalonica

(6) Kyriacos by the mercy of God bishop of the metropolis of Kaisareia in the province of Cappadocia Prima: I hereby decree and sign.[314]

(c)   of Sardinia

(7) Stephen unworthy bishop of the metropolis of Ephesos in the province of Asia: I hereby decree and sign.

(d) [64]   of Ravenna

(e)   of Herakleia in Thrace

(f)   of Corinth

---

311 The verbs, as is standard in documents of this kind, are all in the aorist, but this is not a genuine past tense but in effect a present performative. The same usage occurs in many of the canons.

312 In this line a space was left in the original text (as can be deduced from our manuscripts) in the hope that the pope's subscription would later be forthcoming; five further gaps of the same kind and same intention occur below. These names of sees, with their attendant gaps, are variously included or omitted in the manuscripts; even our best MS, Codex Patmensis 172, gives only three of them, while many MSS omit the names of the sees as well as of their holders. See Ohme (2009) 39–48 and (2013) LXXVI and LXXXI. This inclusion in the list of leading sees from the Roman patriarchate was misunderstood by Balsamon and many subsequent Orthodox commentators as evidence of their participation in the council and confirmation of its decrees as representatives of the Roman see (Ohme 1992b, 116–17).

313 This high position, immediately after the patriarchs, accorded to a new city founded by Justinian II (for which see Canon 39 above) is revealing of the man's vanity.

314 Kaisareia, Ephesos and Herakleia were the three senior sees in the patriarchate of Constantinople as the first cities of the Pontic, Asian and Thracian dioceses respectively.

(8) Basil bishop of Gortyna the metropolis of the Christ-loving island of Crete and representing the whole synod of the holy church of Rome:[315] I hereby decree and sign.

(9) Stephen insignificant bishop of the Christ-loving metropolis of Ankyra in the province Galatia Prima: I hereby decree and sign.

(10) Sisinnios by the grace of Christ our true God bishop of the metropolis of Dyrrachion: I hereby decree and sign.

(11) Stephen insignificant bishop of the metropolis of Sardeis in the province of Lydia: I hereby decree and sign.

(12) Peter unworthy bishop of the metropolis of Nikomedeia in the province of Bithynia: I hereby decree and sign.

(13) George unworthy bishop of the metropolis of Nikaia in the province of Bithynia: I hereby decree and sign.

(14) [65] John unworthy bishop of the metropolis of Chalkedon in the province of Bithynia: I hereby decree and sign.

(15) John unworthy bishop of the metropolis of Side in the province of Pamphylia:[316] I hereby decree and sign.

(16) Leontios unworthy bishop of Sebasteia in the province of Armenia Secunda: I hereby decree and sign.

(17) John unworthy bishop of the metropolis of Amaseia in the province of Helenopontus: I hereby decree and sign.

(18) John unworthy bishop of Pompeiupolis in the province of Cilicia Prima and the representative of Plato the most holy metropolitan of Tarsos: I hereby decree and sign.

(19) Isidore by the mercy of God bishop of the city of Anazarbos in the province of Cilicia Secunda: I hereby decree and sign.

(20) Makrobios insignificant bishop of the metropolis of Seleukeia in the province of Isauria: I hereby decree and sign.

(21) Justin unworthy bishop of the metropolis of Tyana in the province of Cappadocia Secunda: I hereby decree and sign.

(22) Sergios insignificant bishop of Gangra the metropolis of the province of Paphlagonia: I hereby decree and sign.

---

315 Basil had been one of the three representatives of the Roman synod (that is, of the bishops under direct Roman jurisdiction) at Constantinople III. He is here, quite falsely, attributed with the same authority at the Quinisext Council.

316 Side was the metropolitan see of Pamphylia I, while Perge (29) was that of Pamphylia II. But 'Prima' and 'Secunda' are omitted, since the two provinces formed a single province for secular purposes.

(23) **[66]** Kyprianos by the grace of Christ God bishop of the metropolis of Klaudiupolis in the province of Honorias: I hereby decree and sign.

(24) Constantine unworthy bishop of the metropolis of Neokaisareia in the province of Helenopontus:[317] I hereby decree and sign.

(25) John unworthy bishop of the city of Pisinus in the province of Galatia Secunda: I hereby decree and sign.

(26) Sisinnios insignificant bishop of the metropolis of Stauropolis in the province of Caria: I hereby decree and sign.

(27) Elias insignificant bishop of the metropolis of Ikonion in the province of Lycaonia: I hereby decree and sign.

(28) Stephen by the mercy of God bishop of metropolis of Antioch in the province of Pisidia: I hereby decree and sign.

(29) John insignificant bishop of Perge in the province of Pamphylia: I hereby decree and sign.

(30) Theopemptos insignificant bishop of the metropolis of Iustinianupolis or Mokissos in the province of Cappadocia Secunda: I hereby decree and sign.

(31) Theodore insignificant bishop of Phasis in the land of Lazica:[318] I hereby decree and sign.

(32) **[67]** Tiberios unworthy bishop of the metropolis of Hierapolis[319] in the province of Phrygia Pacatiana: I hereby decree and sign.

---

317 Since the time of Justinian I (*nov.* 28 of 535; Schöll–Kroll 212–18) Neokaisareia had been part of the province of Helenopontus, but it remained the metropolis of the ecclesiastical province of Pontus Polemoniacus, whence its position in this list.

318 'Land' (χώρα) because it was not a province of the empire but a client kingdom (Ohme 1990, 304).

319 Only one manuscript, Π (Codex Patmensis 172), admittedly the most reliable manuscript for the subscription list, has 'Hierapolis'; all the others have Traianupolis. There was a city of this name in Phrygia Pacatiana, but it was not a metropolis, while another Traianupolis was the metropolis of Rhodope (Thrace). Heinrich Gelzer surmised back in 1886 that there is a lacuna here, and that the original text ran: 'Tiberios unworthy bishop of the metropolis of Traianupolis in the province of Rhodope: I hereby decree and sign. <X> unworthy bishop of the metropolis of Hierapolis in the province of Phrygia Pacatiana: I hereby degree and sign.' This has the advantage of raising the total number of bishops signing to 227, the latter number being given at the end of the list in a large number of MSS (which, however, fail to list 227 bishops!). In addition, the absence from the emperor's council of the metropolitan of Rhodope, a province recently liberated by the emperor from the Slavs, would be surprising. Ohme (2009) 5 and (2013) XLII–XLIII and LIII–LVI is sympathetic to this suggestion, but does not adopt it in his text, since the number of 227 could be a pure mistake or have arisen from no. 18 in the list (Bishop John representing Bishop Plato) being counted as two bishops.

(33) Elias insignificant bishop of the metropolis of Dadima in the province of Armenia Quarta Justiniana: I hereby decree and sign.

(34) George insignificant bishop of the city of Bizye in the land of Thrace:[320] I hereby decree and sign.

(35) Theognostus unworthy bishop of the metropolis of Pompeiupolis in the province of Paphlagonia: I hereby decree and sign.

(36) Stephen unworthy bishop of the metropolis of Smyrna in the province of Asia: I hereby decree and sign.

(37) Zacharias by the mercy of God bishop of Leontopolis in Isauria: I hereby decree and sign.

(38) Theopemptos sinful bishop of the city of Apameia in the province of Bithynia: I hereby decree and sign.

(39) Moses unworthy bishop of the city of Theodoriu or Germia in the province [of Galatia Secunda]: I hereby decree and sign.

(40) Sisinnios insignificant bishop of the city of Mitylene on the island of Lesbos: I hereby decree and sign.

(41) [68] George insignificant bishop of the city of Miletos in the province of Caria: I hereby decree and sign.

(42) George unworthy bishop of the city of Selymbria the province of Europa: I hereby decree and sign.

(43) Theophylact insignificant bishop of the city of Methymna on the island of Lesbos: I hereby decree and sign.

(44) John by the grace of Christ our true God bishop of Kios in the province of Bithynia: I hereby decree and sign.

(45) George unworthy bishop of Cherson of Doras: I hereby decree and sign.

(46) Theodore unworthy bishop of Kotrada in the land of Isauria: I hereby decree and sign.

(47) Epiphanios unworthy bishop of Euchaita in the province of Helenopontus: I hereby decree and sign.

(48) George unworthy bishop of the city of Ainos in the land of Thrace: I hereby decree and sign.

The conjecture remains highly attractive, however, since a corruption of 'Hierapolis' to 'Traianopolis' is improbable.

320 The use of 'land' (χώρα) rather than 'province' (ἐπαρχία) for Thrace, as also occasionally for Isauria (§46) and Armenia Magna (§64), reflects the breakdown of the system of civil provinces and the appearance of 'themes' (under an official with both civil and military responsibility) in insecure frontier regions.

(49) Theodore by the mercy of God bishop of the city of Kamulianai: I hereby decree and sign.

(50) Mamalos unworthy bishop of the city of Mesembria in the province of Haemimontus: I hereby decree and sign.

(51) [69] Paul unworthy bishop of the city of Germe in the province of Hellespontus: I hereby decree and sign.

(52) John unworthy bishop of Abydos in the province of Hellespontus: I hereby decree and sign.

(53) Andrew unworthy bishop of the city of Miletupolis in the province of Hellespontus: I hereby decree and sign.

(54) Staurakios insignificant bishop of the city of Adraneia in the province of Hellespontus: I hereby decree and sign.

(55) Sisinnios insignificant bishop of the city of Lampsakos in the province of Hellespontus: I hereby decree and sign.

(56) Andrew sinful bishop of Philippoi: I hereby decree and sign.

(57) Silvanos sinful bishop of the city of Lemnos: I hereby decree and sign.

(58) Andrew sinful bishop of Amphipolis: I hereby decree and sign.

(59) Isidore insignificant bishop of the city of Edessa: I hereby decree and sign.

(60) Margarites sinful bishop of Stoboi:[321] I hereby decree and sign.

(61) Paul sinful bishop of the city of Nyssa in the province of Cappadocia Prima: I hereby decree and sign.

(62) Theodore unworthy bishop of the city of Thermai in the province of Cappadocia Prima: I hereby decree and sign.

(63) Plato insignificant bishop of the city of Kiskisos in the province of Cappadocia Prima: I hereby decree and sign.

(64) [70] George insignificant bishop of Kamache in the land of Armenia Magna:[322] I hereby decree and sign.

(65) Mamas by the mercy of God bishop of Tiberias: I hereby decree and sign.

(66) Zoetos unworthy bishop of Christupolis or Dioshieron in the province of Asia: I hereby decree and sign.

---

321 Stoboi had been the metropolis of Macedonia II (Salutaris). The implication of the listing of its bishop under the suffragans is that this province, submerged by a wave of barbarians, had effectively ceased to exist and Stoboi no longer counted as a metropolis.

322 In the Acts of 680–81 George appears as the bishop of 'the region of Daranalis in Armenia Magna'. Ohme (1991b) 347 suggests that Kamache (in this region) had been elevated to city status between 681 and 691. Although in the civil province of Armenia, its position in the list shows that for ecclesiastical purposes it was part of Cappadocia I (Ohme 2013, 118, n. 3).

(67) Paul unworthy bishop of the city of Priene in the province of Asia: I hereby decree and sign.

(68) Patrikios unworthy bishop of the city of Magnesia on the Meander in the province of Asia: I hereby decree and sign.

(69) Antony unworthy bishop of Hypaipa in the province of Asia: I hereby decree and sign.

(70) John unworthy bishop of the city of Anea in the province of Asia: I hereby decree and sign.

(71) George unworthy bishop of the city of Palaiupolis in the province of Asia: I hereby decree and sign.

(72) Sisinnios unworthy bishop of the city of Nysa in the province of Asia: I hereby decree and sign.

(73) John unworthy bishop of the city of Phokaia in the province of Asia: I hereby decree and sign.

(74) [71] John unworthy bishop of the city of Sion in the province of Asia: I hereby decree and sign.

(75) Zotikos unworthy bishop of the city of Bareta in the province of Asia: I hereby decree and sign.

(76) Myron insignificant bishop of the city of Tralleis in the province of Asia: I hereby decree and sign.

(77) Gregory unworthy bishop of the city of Kaloe in the province of Asia: I hereby decree and sign.

(78) Constantine bishop of the city of Myrine[323] in the province of Asia: I hereby decree and sign.

(79) Stephen unworthy bishop of Magnesia Aneliu in the province [of Asia]: I hereby decree and sign.

(80) Gregory unworthy bishop of the city of Euaza in the province of Asia: I hereby decree and sign.

(81) Niketas unworthy bishop of the city of Kydonia[324] on the island of Crete: I hereby decree and sign.

(82) Theopemptos unworthy bishop of the city of Kisamos on the island of Crete: I hereby decree and sign.

(83) Sisinnius unworthy bishop of the city of Chersonesos on the island of Crete: I hereby decree and sign.

---

323 This name is preserved only in Π (for which see p. 55 above) and in the corrupt form πο[λεως] Σμηρν[ης]. Smyrna comes above at 36 as a metropolis.

324 Ohme's emendation of 'Chalcedon' in the MSS.

(84) **[72]** Gregory unworthy bishop of the city of Tabia in the province of Galatia Prima: I hereby decree and sign.

(85) John unworthy bishop of Iuliupolis in the province of Galatia Prima: I hereby decree and sign.

(86) Michael unworthy bishop of the city of Aspone in the province of Galatia Prima: I hereby decree and sign.

(87) Andrew by the mercy of God bishop of the city of Mnizos in the province of Galatia Prima: I hereby decree and sign.

(88) Stephen unworthy bishop of Berinupolis in the province of Galatia Prima: I hereby decree and sign.

(89) John unworthy bishop of the city of Settai [Saittai] in the province of Lydia: I hereby decree and sign.

(90) Anastasios unworthy bishop of the city of Maionia in the province of Lydia: I hereby decree and sign.

(91) Theodotos by the mercy of God bishop of Aureliupolis in the province of Lydia: I hereby decree and sign.

(92) John unworthy bishop of the city of Daskylion in the province of Bithynia: I hereby decree and sign.

(93) **[73]** Sisinnius unworthy bishop of Basilinupolis in the province of Bithynia: I hereby decree and sign.

(94) George unworthy bishop of the city of Kadosia in the province of Bithynia: I hereby decree and sign.

(95) John insignificant bishop of the city of Helenupolis in the province of Bithynia: I hereby decree and sign.

(96) John unworthy bishop of the city of Neokaisareia in the province of Bithynia: I hereby decree and sign.

(97) Symeon unworthy bishop of the city of Theotokia in the province of Bithynia: I hereby decree and sign.

(98) Kosmas unworthy bishop of the city of Prainetos in the province of Bithynia: I hereby decree and sign.

(99) Theodore unworthy bishop of the city of Nea Iustiniane in the province of Bithynia: I hereby decree and sign.

(100) Isidore unworthy bishop of the city of Gordoserba[325] in the province of Bithynia: I hereby decree and sign.

---

325 This was a new see and the name is probably of Slavic origin. We may associate this see with the evangelization of the Slavs moved into the Opsikion theme (which included Bithynia) by Justinian II in 688, according to Theophanes 364, trans. Mango and Scott 508.

(101) Anastasios unworthy bishop of Linoe in the province of Bithynia: I hereby decree and sign.
(102) **[74]** Tates insignificant bishop of the city of Kolybrassos in the province of Pamphylia: I hereby decree and sign.
(103) Theodore insignificant bishop of the city of Orymna in the province of Pamphylia: I hereby decree and sign.
(104) Konon bishop of Kasai in the province of Pamphylia: I hereby decree and sign.
(105) Konon bishop of the city of Kotana in the province of Pamphylia: I hereby decree and sign.
(106) Theodotos insignificant bishop of the city of Karaleia in the province of Pamphylia: I hereby decree and sign.
(107) Konon by the mercy of God bishop of Korakesion in the province of Pamphylia: I hereby decree and sign.
(108) George insignificant bishop of the city of Syedra in the province of Pamphylia: I hereby decree and sign.
(109) Kallinikos by the grace of Christ bishop of the city of Koloneia in the province of Armenia Magna: I hereby decree and sign.
(110) Photios by the mercy of God bishop of the Christ-loving city of Nikopolis in the province of Armenia Magna: I hereby decree and sign.
(111) Gregory by the grace of Christ bishop of the city of Satala in the province of Armenia Magna: I hereby decree and sign.
(112) **[75]** Photius unworthy bishop of the city of Sebastopolis in the province of Armenia Secunda: I hereby decree and sign.
(113) Theodore unworthy bishop of the city of Amaseia in the province of Helenopontus: I hereby decree and sign.
(114) Sergios insignificant bishop of the city of Andrapa: I hereby decree and sign.
(115) Photios unworthy bishop of the city of Ibora in the province of Helenopontus: I hereby decree and sign.
(116) George unworthy bishop of the city of Zela: I hereby decree and sign.
(117) John unworthy bishop of the city of Korykos in the province of Cilicia Prima: I hereby decree and sign.
(118) Peter unworthy bishop of the city of Zephyrion in the province of Cilicia Prima: I hereby decree and sign.
(119) Basil sinful bishop of the city of Epiphaneia in the province of Cilicia Secunda: I hereby decree and sign.
(120) Paul unworthy bishop of the city of Eirenupolis in the province of Cilicia Secunda: I hereby decree and sign.

(121) Theodore insignificant bishop of the city of Kastabala in the province of Cilicia Secunda: I hereby decree and sign.

(122) [76] Sisinnios unworthy bishop of Klaudiupolis: I hereby decree and sign.

(123) Theodore unworthy bishop of the city of Olba in the province of Isauria: I hereby decree and sign.

(124) Paul insignificant bishop ... in the province of Isauria: I hereby decree and sign.

(125) Sisinnios insignificant bishop of the city of Siluana [Selinus] in the province of Isauria: I hereby decree and sign.

(126) Kosmas insignificant bishop of the city of Dalisandos in the province of Isauria: I hereby decree and sign.

(127) George unworthy bishop of Eirenupolis in the province of Isauria: I hereby decree and sign.

(128) Zacharias bishop of the city of Antioch in the province of Isauria: I hereby decree and sign.

(129) Stephen insignificant bishop of the city of Adrasos in the province of Isauria: I hereby decree and sign.

(130) Peter unworthy bishop of the city of Kelenderis in the province of Isauria: I hereby decree and sign.

(131) Kosmas by the mercy of God bishop of Dometiupolis: I hereby decree and sign.

(132) Basil by the mercy of God bishop of the city of Sbide in the province of Isauria: I hereby decree and sign.

(133) [77] Mark insignificant bishop of Zenonupolis in the province of Isauria: I hereby decree and sign.

(134) Dometios insignificant bishop of Titiupolis in the province of Isauria: I hereby decree and sign.

(135) George bishop of Arabissos in the province of Armenia Prima: I hereby decree and sign.

(136) John unworthy bishop of the city of Kukusos in the province of Armenia Prima: I hereby decree and sign.

(137) John unworthy bishop of Faustinupolis in the province of Cappadocia Secunda: I hereby decree and sign.

(138) Stephen unworthy bishop of the city of Sasima in the province of Cappadocia: I hereby decree and sign.

(139) George by the mercy of God deacon of the holy church of the city of Amastris in the province of Paphlagonia and the representative of Zoilos my most holy bishop: I hereby decree and sign.

(140) George by the mercy of God bishop of Iunupolis in the province of Paphlagonia: I hereby decree and sign.

(141) Phocas unworthy bishop of the city of Dadybra: I hereby decree and sign.

(142) [78] John unworthy bishop of the city of Sora in the province of Paphlagonia: I hereby decree and sign.

(143) George insignificant bishop of Kratia in the province of Honorias: I hereby decree and sign.

(144) Stephen unworthy bishop of the city of Herakleia in the province of Honorias: I hereby decree and sign.

(145) Narses unworthy bishop of the city of Kerasus in the province of Pontus Polemoniacus: I hereby decree and sign.

(146) Dometios insignificant bishop of the city of Polemonion the province of Helenopontus: I hereby decree and sign.

(147) Solomon unworthy bishop of Klaneos in the province of Galatia Secunda: I hereby decree and sign.

(148) Theodore unworthy bishop of the city of Amorion in the province of Galatia Secunda: I hereby decree and sign.

(149) Theodore unworthy bishop of the city of Troknada in the province of Galatia Secunda: I hereby decree and sign.

(150) [79] John unworthy bishop of the city of Germokoloneia in the province of Galatia Secunda: I hereby decree and sign.

(151) Segermas insignificant bishop of the city of Horkistos in the province of Galatia Secunda: I hereby decree and sign.

(152) George insignificant bishop of the city of Synodia in the province of Galatia Secunda: I hereby decree and sign.

(153) Elpidios insignificant bishop of the city of Thermai of Saint Agapetos in the province of Galatia Secunda: I hereby decree and sign.

(154) Zemarchos bishop of the city of Sidyma in the province of Lycia: I hereby decree and sign.

(155) George bishop of the city of Oinoanda in the province of Lycia: I hereby decree and sign.

(156) Theodore bishop of the city of Araxa in the province of Lycia: I hereby decree and sign.

(157) John insignificant bishop of the city of Tlatta in the province of Lycia: I hereby decree and sign.

(158) Menas insignificant bishop of the city of Pinara in the province of Lycia: I hereby decree and sign.

(159) [80] George insignificant bishop of the city of Xanthos in the province of Lycia: I hereby decree and sign.

(160) Theopemptos insignificant bishop of the city of Stratonikeia in the province of Caria: I hereby decree and sign.
(161) Constantine bishop of the city of Alabanda in the province of Caria: I hereby decree and sign.
(162) George unworthy bishop of the city of Hylarima in the province of Caria: I hereby decree and sign.
(163) George insignificant bishop of the city of Antioch in the province of Caria: I hereby decree and sign.
(164) Theodore unworthy bishop of the city of Herakleia Latmu in the province of Caria: I hereby decree and sign.
(165) Paul unworthy bishop of the city of Kibyrra in the province of Caria: I hereby decree and sign.
(166) Magnos unworthy bishop of the city of Eriza in the province of Caria: I hereby decree and sign.
(167) Eugenios bishop of Trapezopolis in [Phrygia] Pacatiana: I hereby decree and sign.
(168) Andrew bishop of the city of Eueragapes in Pacatiana: I hereby decree and sign.
(169) Kerikos unworthy bishop of the city of Ankyra in Pacatiana: I hereby decree and sign.
(170) **[81]** Plato bishop of the city of Sebaste in Pacatiana: I hereby decree and sign.
(171) Philip unworthy bishop of the city of Kadoi in Pacatiana: I hereby decree and sign.
(172) Theodore bishop of the city of Peltai in Pacatiana: I hereby decree and sign.
(173) Basil bishop of the city of Akmoneia in Pacatiana: I hereby decree and sign.
(174) Anastasios bishop of Tiberiupolis in Pacatiana: I hereby decree and sign.
(175) Kosmas bishop of the city of Kolassai in Pacatiana: I hereby decree and sign.
(176) Gregory unworthy bishop of the city of Aizanoi in Pacatiana: I hereby decree and sign.
(177) Constantine bishop of Iustinianupolis in Pacatiana:[326] I hereby decree and sign.

326 Omitted on our map, since its location is unknown.

(178) John unworthy bishop of the city of Synaos:[327] I hereby decree and sign.

(179) John presbyter of the holy church of God of the city of Anemurion and the representative of Mamas my most holy bishop: I hereby decree and sign.

(180) Leontios unworthy bishop of the city of Dorylaion in the province of [Phrygia] Salutaris: I hereby decree and sign.

(181) Alexander unworthy bishop of the city of Nakoleia in the province of Salutaris: I hereby decree and sign.

(182) Patrikios insignificant bishop of Prymnesos in the province of Phrygia Salutaris: I hereby decree and sign.

(183) [82] Theodore insignificant bishop of the city of Medaïon in the province of Salutaris: I hereby decree and sign.

(184) Agapetos insignificant bishop of the city of Augustopolis in the province of Salutaris: I hereby decree and sign.

(185) George insignificant bishop of the city of Otros in the province of Salutaris: I hereby decree and sign.

(186) John by the mercy of God bishop of the city of Polybotos in the province of Salutaris: I hereby decree and sign.

(187) Theophylact bishop of the city of Phyteia in the province of Salutaris: I hereby decree and sign.

(188) John deacon of the city of Kotyaion and the representative of my most holy bishop: I hereby decree and sign.

(189) Constantine insignificant bishop of the city of Barata in the province of Lycaonia: I hereby decree and sign.

(190) Eustathios unworthy bishop of the city of Amblada in the province of Lycaonia: I hereby decree and sign.

(191) Konon unworthy bishop of the city of Uasada in the province of Lycaonia: I hereby decree and sign.

(192) [83] Theodosios insignificant bishop of Berinupolis in the province of Lycaonia: I hereby decree and sign.

(193) Longinos insignificant bishop of the city of Misteia in the province of Lycaonia: I hereby decree and sign.

(194) Kyrikos insignificant bishop of the city of Derbe in the province of Lycaonia: I hereby decree and sign.

(195) Alexander insignificant bishop of the city of Umanada in the province of Lycaonia: I hereby decree and sign.

327 'Synaos' is Ohme's emendation. The MSS have 'Sombos' (or a slight variant thereof).

(196) Paul insignificant bishop of the city of Sozopolis in the province of Pisidia: I hereby decree and sign.

(197) Constantine unworthy bishop of the city of Tymandos in the province of Pisidia: I hereby decree and sign.

(198) Theodore insignificant bishop of Bindaios in the province of Pisidia: I hereby decree and sign.

(199) Marinos insignificant bishop of the city of Philomelion in the province of Pisidia: I hereby decree and sign.

(200) [84] Sisinnios insignificant bishop of Neapolis in the province of Pisidia: I hereby decree and sign.

(201) George insignificant bishop of the city of Sagalassos in the province of Pisidia: I hereby decree and sign.

(202) Constantine unworthy bishop of the city of Timbrias in the province of Pisidia: I hereby decree and sign.

(203) Konon insignificant bishop of Laodikeia in the province of Pisidia: I hereby decree and sign.

(204) John by the mercy of God bishop of the city of Adada in the province of Pisidia: I hereby decree and sign.

(205) Patrikios insignificant bishop of the city of Limenai in the province of Pisidia: I hereby decree and sign.

(206) Konon insignificant bishop of the city of Siniandos in the province of Pisidia: I hereby decree and sign.

(207) Stephen insignificant bishop of the city of Tityassos in the province of Pisidia: I hereby decree and sign.

(208) Peter insignificant bishop of the city of Seleukeia in the province of Pisidia: I hereby decree and sign.

(209) [85] Plato insignificant bishop of the city of Magydos in the province of Pamphylia: I hereby decree and sign.

(210) Zacharias insignificant bishop of the city of Lagina in the province of Pamphylia: I hereby decree and sign.

(211) George insignificant bishop of the city of Kodrula in the province of Pamphylia: I hereby decree and sign.

(212) Paul insignificant bishop of the city of Sylaion in the province of Pamphylia: I hereby decree and sign.

(213) Constantine insignificant bishop of the city of Eudokias in the province of Pamphylia: I hereby decree and sign.

(214) John insignificant bishop of the city of Adriane in the province of Pamphylia: I hereby decree and sign.

(215) Theodore insignificant bishop of the city of Doara in the province of Cappadocia Secunda: I hereby decree and sign.

(216) Konon insignificant bishop of the city of Koloneia in the province of Cappadocia Secunda: I hereby decree and sign.

(217) **[86]** Eustathios insignificant bishop of the city of Parnassos in the province of Cappadocia Secunda: I hereby decree and sign.

(218) Michael unworthy bishop of the city of Nazianzos in the province of Cappadocia Secunda: I hereby decree and sign.

(219) Faustinos unworthy bishop of the city of Zigana in the land of Lazica: I hereby decree and sign.

(220) John unworthy bishop of the city of Petrai in the land of Lazica: I hereby decree and sign.

(221) Stephen unworthy bishop of the city of Paros [Islands]: I hereby decree and sign.

(222) George unworthy bishop of the island of Thera: I hereby decree and sign.

(223) Isidore insignificant bishop of the city of Samos: I hereby decree and sign.

(224) John unworthy bishop of the city of Mosyna in the province of Phrygia: I hereby decree and sign.

(225) Stephen insignificant bishop of the city of Attuda in the province of Phrygia: I hereby decree and sign.

(226) Marianos unworthy bishop of the city of Kitharizon in the province of Armenia Quarta: I hereby decree and sign.

I give below a list of the sees represented at the council (the numbers are those of their place in the subscription list) arranged by patriarchate, diocese (i.e., group of provinces, where applicable) and ecclesiastical province. For each province the metropolitan see (there is occasionally more than one) comes in the first section of the list (5–33), after which come the autocephalous archbishoprics if any (34–50),[328] and finally the suffragans, which I give in the order in which they occur in the list. When the metropolitan did not attend the council, his absence is marked by a dash.

It is to be noted that, where the ecclesiastical provinces did not exactly correspond with the civil ones (most often where there was more than

---

328 These sees had earlier been given the title of 'metropolis', with a firm insistence (as laid down in Canon 12 of Chalcedon, COGD 1, 143) that this status was purely honorary and did not usurp any of the authority of the metropolis of a whole province.

one ecclesiastical province within a civil one), the lists normally give the name of the civil province rather than that of the ecclesiastical one, while in the list below I arrange the sees according to the latter. It is not credible, however, that a metropolitan of such an ecclesiastical province would have signed with the name of the civil province rather than that of his own ecclesiastical one. This suggests that the original subscriptions did not give the names of the provinces, and that these were added by the clerks who drew up the conciliar acts. This may likewise be detected in some of the other conciliar acts, where occasionally in a list recording the bishops' actual subscriptions bishops are assigned to a wrong province altogether.[329]

Under Rome, Diocese of Macedonia
Crete: (8) Gortyna; (81) Kydonia, (82) Kisamos, (83) Chersonesos.
Epirus Nova: (10) Dyrrachion.
Hellas: —; (57) Lemnos.
Macedonia: —; (56) Philippoi, (58) Amphipolis, (59) Edessa, (60) Stoboi.

(1) Constantinople
Diocese of Thrace
Europa: —; (34) Bizye, (42) Selymbria.
Haemimontus: —; (50) Mesembria.
Rhodope: ?Traianupolis (n. 319 above); (48) Ainos.

Diocese of Asiana
Asia: (7) Ephesos; (36) Smyrna; (66) Dioshieron, (67) Priene, (68) Magnesia
    on the Meander, (69) Hypaipa, (70) Anea, (71) Palaiupolis, (72) Nysa,
    (73) Phokaia, (74) Sion, (75) Bareta, (76) Tralleis, (77) Kaloe, (78)
    Myrine, (79) Magnesia Aneliu, (80) Euaza.
Caria: (26) Stauropolis; (41) Miletos; (160) Stratonikeia, (161) Alabanda,
    (162) Hylarima, (163) Antioch, (164) Herakleia Latmu, (165) Kibyrra,
    (166) Eriza.
Hellespontus: (5) Nea Iustinianupolis;[330] (51) Germe, (52) Abydos, (53)
    Miletupolis, (54) Adraneia, (55) Lampsakos.

---

329 For example, in the subscription list of the final session of the Acts of Constantinople III Daskylion and Adriani are wrong assigned to Hellespontus (ACO² II.2, 790, 12–16).
330 Technically this was not the metropolitan see of the province, but see Canon 39 with my annotation on pp. 119–21 above.

Islands: —; (40) Mitylene, (43) Methymna; (221) Paros, (222) Thera, (223) Samos.

Lycaonia: (27) Ikonion; (189) Barata, (190) Amblada, (191) Uasada, (192) Berinupolis, (193) Misteia, (194) Derbe, (195) Umanada.

Lycia: —; (154) Sidyma, (155) Oinoanda, (156) Araxa, (157) Tlatta, (158) Pinara, (159) Xanthos.

Lydia: (11) Sardeis; (89) Saittai, (90) Maionia, (91) Aureliupolis.

Pamphylia I:[331] (15) Side; (102) Kolybrassos, (103) Orymna, (104) Kasai, (105) Kotana, (106) Karaleia, (107) Korakesion, (108) Syedra.

Pamphylia II: (29) Perge; (209) Magydos, (210) Lagina, (211) Kodrula, (212) Sylaion, (213) Eudokias, (214) Adriane.

Phrygia Pacatiana I: —; (167) Trapezupolis, (168) Eueragapes, (169) Ankyra, (170) Sebaste, (171) Kadoi, (172) Peltai, (173) Akmonia, (174) Tiberiupolis, (175) Kolossai, (176) Aizanoi, (177) Iustinianupolis, (178) Synaos.

Phrygia Pacatiana II: (32) Hierapolis; (224) Mosyna, (225) Attuda.

Phrygia Salutaris: —; (180) Dorylaion, (181) Nakoleia, (182) Prymnesos, (183) Midaion, (184) Augustopolis, (185) Otros, (186) Polybotos, (187) Phyteia, (188) Kotyaion.

Pisidia: (28) Antioch; (196) Sozopolis, (197) Tymandos, (198) Bindaios, (199) Philomelion, (200) Neapolis, (201) Sagalassos, (202) Timbrias, (203) Laodikeia, (204) Adada, (205) Limenai, (206) Siniandos, (207) Tityassos, (208) Seleukeia.

Diocese of Pontica

Armenia I: —; (135) Arabissos, (136) Kukusos.

Armenia II: (16) Sebasteia; (109) Koloneia, (110) Nikopolis, (111) Satala (112) Sebastopolis.

Armenia IV: (33) Dadima; (226) Kitharizon.

Bithynia I: (12) Nikomedeia, (14) Chalkedon; (38) Apameia, (44) Kios; (92) Daskylion, (93) Basilinupolis, (94) Kadosia, (95) Helenupolis, (96) Neokaisareia, (97) Theotokia, (98) Prainetos.

Bithynia II: (13) Nikaia; (99) Nea Iustiniane, (100) Gordoserba, (101) Linoe.

Cappadocia I: (6) Kaisareia; (49) Kamulianae, (61) Nyssa, (62) Thermai, (63) Kiskisos, (64) Kamache.[332]

331 For secular purposes the two Pamphylias formed a single province.

332 Kamache was in the ecclesiastical province of Cappadocia I, even though it was separated from that province by Armenia II. See n. 322 above.

Cappadocia II: (21) Tyana; (137) Faustinupolis, (138) Sasima.

Cappadocia III: (30) Mokissos; (215) Doara, (216) Koloneia, (217) Parnassos, (218) Nazianzos.

Galatia I: (9) Ankyra; (84) Tabia, (85) Iuliupolis, (86) Aspona, (87) Mnizos, (88) Berinupolis.

Galatia II: (25) Pisinus; (39) Germia; (147) Klaneos, (148) Amorion, (149) Troknada, (150) Germokoloneia, (151) Horkistos, (152) Synodia, (153) Thermai.

Helenopontus: (17) Amaseia; (47) Euchaita; (113) Amaseia,[333] (114) Andrapa, (115) Ibora, (116) Zela.

Honorias: (23) Klaudiupolis; (143) Kratia, (144) Herakleia.

Lazica:[334] (31) Phasis; (219) Zigana, (220) Petrai.

Paphlagonia: (22) Gangra; (35) Pompeiupolis; (139) Amastris, (140) Iunupolis, (141) Dadybra, (142) Sora.

Pontus Polemoniacus: (24) Neokaisareia; (145) Kerasus, (146) Polemonion.

Zekchia: —; (45) Cherson.

(3) Antioch (Theupolis), *Diocese of Oriens*

Cilicia I: —; (18) Pompeiupolis,[335] (117) Korykos, (118) Zephyrion.

Cilicia II: (19) Anazarbos; (119) Epiphaneia, (120) Eirenupolis, (121) Kastabala.

Isauria: (20) Seleukeia; (37) Leontopolis, (46) Kotrada; (122) Klaudiupolis, (123) Olba, (124)?,[336] (125) Selinus, (126) Dalisandos, (127) Eirenupolis, (128) Antioch, (129) Adrasos, (130) Kelenderis, (131) Dometiupolis, (132) Sbide, (133) Zenonupolis, (134) Titiupolis, (179) Anemurion.

(4) Jerusalem

Palestina II:—; (65) Tiberias.

(2) Alexandria

The presence of the emperor's name at the very head of the list was unprecedented. The first acts of an ecumenical council that the emperor

---

333   This suffragan see had indeed the same name as the metropolis.

334   Lazica, like Zekchia below, was not a Roman province but a client kingdom.

335   The high position of this suffragan in the list is because he was representing his metropolitan, the bishop of Tarsos.

336   The MSS omit the name by accident, but tell us that this see was in Isauria.

himself signed were those of Constantinople III; there he signed after the bishops.[337] In the anti-Photian council of Constantinople (869–70) the emperors signed after the patriarchal representatives but before the other bishops.[338] Here the emperor signs first of all, even before the place reserved for the pope's subscription.[339] His subscription by name and with the novel title 'emperor of the Romans' (βασιλεὺς Ῥωμαίων) contrasts markedly with Constantine IV's subscription to the Definition of Constantinople III: simply the words (in Latin) *Legimus et consensimus*.[340] But in the present context the identification of the emperor necessitated the inclusion of his name.[341]

Apart from the names of bishops attending, the subscription list also gives the names of a number of sees whose bishops did *not* attend. The sees in question were all of exceptionally high rank. The first is the see of Rome, placed immediately after the emperor's subscription. Soon after it (though not all together) come the names of several major sees which were either in Italy or in East Illyricum (which was under Roman jurisdiction), namely Sardinia (Caralis), Ravenna, Thessalonica and Corinth; the bishop of Gortyna was the only bishop in this category who attended the council. Why were these additional names sought for, since they would in any case have added little weight to the pope's subscription? Justinian must again have been thinking of Constantinople III, which all the then bishops of these four sees attended. Almost at the end of this group comes (exceptionally) one see in the patriarchate of Constantinople, namely Herakleia, the principal see in the 'diocese' (group of provinces) of Thrace, doubtless for the same reason: for some unknown reason its bishop failed to attend and, since his see was so near Constantinople, it must have seemed that his belated subscription would be easy to obtain.

Gaps of this kind are not to be found in any of the other acts of ecumenical councils. How are we to account for them? The judgement of Heinz Ohme, repeated in his ACO edition of the text (LXXVI–LXXXI), is that the sees of Rome and of the principal sees under her in Italy and East Illyricum (as also of Herakleia) were included in the original text of the conciliar acts,

---

337 ACO² II.2, 829.
338 Acts of Constantinople IV, ed. Leonardi, 357.
339 For comment on this, see p. 40 above.
340 ACO² II.2, 796 *fin.*
341 For the varieties of imperial subscription in the seventh to ninth centuries see Ohme (2010b).

each one preceded by a gap, in the hope that the subscriptions of their bishops would be obtained later.

A rival explanation has been offered by Reinhard Flogaus.[342] He suggests that all these names of sees were inserted at a later date in order to make this subscription list more similar to that of Constantinople III, in support of the claim that the Quinisext Council was a continuation of its predecessor (see pp. 47–49 above). The intermingling in this first section of the subscription list of metropolitans of Constantinople with those of Rome, in contrast to their ordering in the subscription list of Constantinople III, where those of Constantinople come *after* those of Rome, is attributed by Flogaus to the transfer of East Illyricum to the patriarchate of Constantinople at the start of the iconoclast controversy, thereby adding to his argument that all these names of sees in the Roman patriarchate were only added subsequently. There are a number of difficulties in this proposal:[343]

(1) The *Liber Pontificalis* (as cited on p. 35 above) tells us that Justinian sent the conciliar acts 'to be confirmed and subscribed at the top by the pontiff Sergius as the head of all the bishops'. The entries for this period in the *LP* are agreed to have been written at the time – or at least immediately after the death of the pope in question. So this statement surely confirms that a space for Sergius' subscription was left at the top of the original subscription list.

(2) The transfer of East Illyricum to the jurisdiction of Constantinople in *c*. 730 may seem to explain the place of Corinth and Gortyna in the list, but provides no explanation for the placing of the sees of Sardinia (Calaris) and Ravenna in the midst of those of the patriarchate of Constantinople. A different explanation is called for, relating to all these names. Perhaps the point being made is that, although Constantinople did not dispute papal primacy, this did not make metropolitans under Rome of a higher rank than those under Constantinople.

(3) If the aim was to add entries to the subscription list to make it as similar as possible to that of Constantinople III, we would have expected the names of the bishops to have been added as well, and the manuscripts give no indication that this was ever the case.[344]

---

342 Flogaus (2009) 48–64.
343 For Ohme's own arguments against Flogaus' view, which are based on a meticulous scrutiny of the manuscript evidence, see Ohme (2009) 39–65.
344 Ohme (2009) 47–8.

(4) This hypothesis overestimates the circulation of the Acts of Constantinople III, especially after Justinian II called in the copies of its acts that were circulating privately and Philippicus tried to destroy what copies were left (see ACO² II.2, 886–7 and 899, 25–8). Tarasios was in a position to compare its subscription list to the Quinisext one, but very few other people would have been able to do so.

(5) Despite the uniqueness of this phenomenon of missing names and empty spaces, it was common for names to be added to a subscription list after the event. Some bishops who had not attended a council would add their names at a later date. For example, the subscription list to the dogmatic canons of Constantinople II ends with the names of ten bishops who did not attend the council.[345] This was easy for suffragans, since the names of the suffragans always came last in a list. The problem at the Quinisext Council was that it would have been improper to have at the very end of the list the names of metropolitans of the first rank (most of them with authority over several provinces), let alone the pope. The solution adopted was to leave gaps for their names in the first part of the list.[346]

How were the missing signatures to be obtained? Once the pope had signed, as intended, and kept one copy of the acts for himself, were the other five, invaluable and irreplaceable, to travel up north to Caralis and then across to Ravenna and then make a tour to Corinth, Thessalonica and Herakleia before returning to Constantinople? The last part of this tour is not incredible, or the intention could have been to make the three bishops from Greece and Thrace pay a visit to Constantinople. But the first part of this journey, braving the Lombards and pirates in the Adriatic, is not believable. A solution is suggested by Vienna papyrus P. Vindob. G 3, a fragment (with 35 signatures) of an original, official copy of the subscription list of the definition of faith approved at Session XVII of Constantinople III. The signatures are not the originals, but minutely and scrupulously imitate, for each signature, the original subscription.[347] It is more likely that the copies that were intended to go north were of this kind.

---

345 See Price (2009) II, 138–9 with the text and annotation. There were in the same way late subscriptions to the definition of Constantinople III: see Ohme (2009) 48–52.

346 Ohme (2009) 52 notes that, if the explanation of the absence of the patriarch of Jerusalem in the original proceedings of the Quinisext Council as sent to Rome (see p. 36 above) was indeed that he arrived and subscribed late, and yet his name is near the head of the list in virtually all the manuscripts, this implies that a space had been left for him.

347 Gregorio and Kresten (2009).

In all, Ohme's explanation of the incomplete subscriptions still holds the field: these additional names of sees must have been included in the hope that their bishops would add their signatures to the canons after the council. Once, however, the pope had refused to add his, obtaining the other missing signatures ceased to have purpose. The gaps in the subscription list where they would have come remained unfilled.

BIBLIOGRAPHY

1. Primary Sources

ACO II, Concilium universale Chalcedonense, 6 vols, ed. Eduard Schwartz (Berlin 1932–8). Trans. Price and Gaddis (2005).

ACO IV.1, Concilium universale Constantinopolitanum sub Iustiniano habitum, ed. Johannes Straub (Berlin 1971). Trans. Price (2009a).

ACO² II.1–2, Concilium universale Constantinopolitanum tertium, ed. Rudolf Riedinger (Berlin 1990–92).

ACO² II.4, Concilium Constantinopolitanum A. 691–2 in Trullo habitum (Concilium Quinisextum), ed. Heinz Ohme (Berlin 2013).

ACO² III.1–3, Concilium universale Nicaenum secundum, ed. Erich Lamberz (Berlin 2008–16). Trans. Price (2018).

Acts of the Council of Constantinople IV (869–70): Gesta sancti ac universalis octavae Synodi quae Constantinopoli congregata est, ed. Claudio Leonardi (Florence 2012).

Apostolic Canons: in Les Constitutions Apostoliques, ed. Marcel Metzger, vol. 3, SC 336 (Paris, 1987) 274–308.

Basil of Caesarea, Canons 1–84, in Lettres, ed. Courtonne, vol. 2 (1961) 121–31, 155–64, 209–17.

—, Lettres, ed. Yves Courtonne, 3 vols (Paris 1957–66).

Canons of Ancyra: Joannou (1962b) 56–73.

Canons of Antioch: Joannou (1962b) 102–26.

Canons of Carthage: Joannou (1962b) 197–436 or CCSL 148.

Canons of Chalcedon: ACO II.1 [354–9] or COGD 1, 138–51.

Canons of Constantinople (394): Joannou (1962b) 438–44.

Canons of Gangra: Joannou (1962b) 85–99.

Canons of Laodicea: Joannou (1962b) 130–55.

Canons of Neocaesarea: Joannou (1962b) 75–82.

Canons of Nicaea I: COGD 1, 20–30.

Canons of Nicaea II: ACO² III.3, 898–924 or COGD 1, 317–44.

Canons of Sardica: Joannou (1962b) 159–89.

Chronicon Paschale 284–628 AD, trans. Michael Whitby and Mary Whitney (Liverpool 1989).

Codex Iustinianus, ed. P. Krüger (Berlin 1877).

Codex Theodosianus XVI, SC 497 (Paris 2005).

Conciliorum Oecumenicorum Generaliumque Decreta (COGD), vol. 1, The Oecumenical Councils from Nicaea I to Nicaea II (325–787) (Turnhout 2006).

Constantine Porphyrogenitus, *De administrando imperio*, ed. G. Moravcsik (Budapest 1949).

Epiphanius, vol. 3, *Panarion 65–80*, ed. Karl Holl, GCS (Berlin 1985).

Gregory of Nazianzus, *Discours 1–3*, SC 247, ed. J. Bernardi (Paris 1978).

—, *Discours 32–37*, SC 318, ed. P. Gallay and C. Moreschini (Paris 1985).

Hadrian I, Pope, *Epistola ad Carolum regem*, in MGH *Epp.* V, Karolini aevi III (Berlin 1899) 5–57.

Justinian, *Novellae*, ed. R. Schöll and W. Kroll, *Corpus Iuris Civilis*, vol. 3 (Berlin 1928).

Leo VI, *Novellae*, in *Les Novelles de Léon le Sage*, ed. P. Noailles and A. Dain (Paris 1944).

Letter of the Three Patriarchs to Emperor Theophilos and Related Texts, ed. Joseph A. Munitiz and others (Camberley 1997).

Liber Pontificalis, ed. Louis Duchesne, vol. 1 (Paris, 1886).

Mansi, J.-D., ed., *Sacrorum Conciliorum nova et amplissima Collectio*, 31 vols (Florence and Venice 1759–98, repr. Paris and Leipzig 1901–6).

Michael the Syrian, *Chronicle. Chronique de Michel le Syrien Patriarche Jacobite d'Antioche (1166–99)*, ed. and trans. J.-B. Chabot, vol. 2, trans. of Bks VII–XI (Paris 1901).

La Narratio de rebus Armeniae, ed. Gérard Garitte, CSCO 132, Subsidia (Louvain 1952).

Step'anos Tarōnec'i, *Universal History*, trans. Tim Greenwood (Oxford 2017).

Theodore the Lector: Theodorus Anagnostes, *Kirchengeschichte*, ed. G.C. Hansen (Berlin 1971).

Theophanes, *Chronographia (Chronicle)*, ed. Karl de Boor (Leipzig 1883), trans. Cyril Mango and Roger Scott (Oxford 1997).

2. Secondary Literature

Auzépy, Marie-France, ed. (1997), *La Vie d'Étienne le Jeune par Étienne le diacre* (Aldershot).

Brock, Sebastian (1984), 'A Syriac fragment on the Sixth Council', in Brock, *Syriac Perspectives on Late Antiquity* (London) Essay XIII.

— (1992), 'Two Sets of monothelete Questions to the Maximianists', in Brock, *Studies in Syriac Christianity* (London) Essay XV.

Brunet, Ester (2011), *La ricezione del concilio quinisesto, 691–692, nelle fonti occidentali, VII–IX sec.: diritto, arte, teologia* (Paris).

Cameron, Averil (2002), 'Blaming the Jews: the Seventh-Century Invasions of Palestine in Context', *TM* 14: 57–78.

Charanis, Peter (1959), 'Ethnic Changes in the Byzantine Empire in the Seventh Century', *DOP* 13: 25–44.

Chrysos, Evangelos (1983), 'Konzilsakten und Konzilsprotokolle vom 4. bis 7. Jahrbundert', *AHC* 15: 30–40.

Clark, Gillian (1993), *Women in Late Antiquity: Pagan and Christian Life-styles* (Oxford).

Coleman-Norton, P.R., ed. and trans. (1966), *Roman State and Christian Church: A Collection of Legal Documents to A.D. 535*, 3 vols (London).

Dagron, Gilbert (1992), 'L'ombre d'un doute: l'hagiographie en question, VIe–XIe siècle', *DOP* 46: 59–68.

— (2003), *Emperor and Priest: The Imperial Office in Byzantium* (Cambridge).

Dictionnaire de droit canonique, 7 vols (Paris, 1924–65).

Durǎ, N. (1995), 'The Ecumenicity of the Council in Trullo: Witnesses of the Canonical Tradition in the East and the West', in Nedungatt and Featherstone (1995) 229–62.

Dvornik, Francis (1948), *The Photian Schism: History and Legend* (Cambridge).

Encyclopaedia Judaica, 16 vols (Jerusalem, 1971–2).

Engelzakis, Benedict, 'Cyprus, New Justinianopolis', in Engelzakis, *Studies on the History of the Church of Cyprus, 4th–20th Centuries* (Aldershot 1995) 63–82.

Esbroeck, Michel van (1992), 'Armenien und die Penthektè', *AHC* 24: 78–94.

— (1995), 'Le discours du Catholicos Sahas III en 691 et quelques documents arméniens annexes au Quinisexte', in Nedungatt and Featherstone (1995) 323–454.

— (1995/6), 'Justinian II. im Synaxar und das Konzil in Trullo', *AHC* 27/28: 103–8.

Evans-Grubbs, Judith (1989), 'Abduction Marriage in Antiquity: A Law of Constantine (CTh ix. 24. 1) and its Social Context', *JRS* 79: 59–83.

Flogaus, Reinhard (2009), 'Das Concilium Quinisextum (691/2). Neue Erkenntnisse über ein umstrittenes Konzil und seine Teilnehmer', *ByzZ* 102: 25–64 (and 889–90).

Fournier, Paul (1898), *Yves de Chartres et le droit canonique* (Paris).

Garitte, Gérard (1952), *La Narratio de rebus Armeniae*, CSCO 132, Subsidia 4 (Louvain).

Greenwood, T.W. (2008), 'Armenian neighbours (600–1045)', in Jonathan Shepard (ed.), *The Cambridge History of the Byzantine Empire* c. *500–1492* (Cambridge) 333–64.

Grégoire, Henri (1944/5), 'Un édit de l'empereur Justinien II daté de septembre 688', *Byz* 17: 119–24.

Gregorio, G. de and O. Kresten (2009), 'Il Papiro conciliare P. Vindob. G. 3: Un "Originale" sulla via da Constantinopoli a Ravenna (e a Vienna)', in L. Pani and C. Scalon, eds, *Le Alpi porta d'Europa* (Spoleto) 233–379.

Haldon, John (1990), *Byzantium in the Seventh Century* (Cambridge).

— (1994), 'Constantine or Justinian? Crisis and Identity in Imperial Propaganda in the Seventh Century', in Magdalino (1994) 95–107.

Hatlie, Peter (2007), *The Monks and Monasteries of Constantinople ca. 350–850* (Cambridge).

Head, Constance (1972), *Justinian II of Byzantium* (Milwaukee WI).

Hefele, C.J. and H. Leclerq (1911), *Histoire des Conciles d'après les documents originaux* IV. 1 (Paris).

Herrin, Judith (2009), 'The Quinisext Council (692) as a Continuation of Chalcedon', in Price and Whitby (2009), 148–68.

— (2013), '"Femina Byzantina": The Council in Trullo on Women', in Herrin, *Unrivalled Influence: Women and Empire in Byzantium* (Princeton NJ) 114–32. Originally in *DOP* 46 (1992) 97–105.

Hoffmann, L.M. and W. Brandes (2013), *Eine unbekannte Konzilssynopse* (Frankfurt am Main).

Humphreys, M.T.G. (2015), *Law, Power and Imperial Ideology in the Iconoclast Era, c. 680–850* (Oxford).

Irmscher, J. (1969), 'Die Bewertung der Prostitution im byzantinischen Recht', in M.N. Andreev and others, *Gesellschaft und Recht im griechischen-römischen Altertum* 2 (Berlin) 77–94.

Joannou, Périclès-Pierre (1962a), *Fonti*, Fascicolo IX, *Discipline générale antique (IIe–IXe s.)*: I. 1, *Les canons des conciles oecuméniques* (Grottaferrata/Roma).

— (1962b), *Fonti*, Fascicolo IX, *Discipline générale antique (IIe–IXe s.)*: I. 2, *Les canons des synodes particuliers* (Grottaferrata/Roma).

— (1963), *Fonti*, Fascicolo IX, *Discipline générale antique (IIe–IXe s.)*: II, *Les canons des pères grecs* (Grottaferrata/Roma).

Jones, A.H.M. (1964), *The Later Roman Empire 284–602* (Oxford).

Jungmann, Joseph (1955), *The Mass of the Roman Rite: Its Origins and Development (Missarum Sollemnia)*, 2 vols (New York).

Karlin-Hayter, Patricia (1992), 'Further Notes on Byzantine Marriage: Raptus— ἁρπαγή or μνηστείαι?', *DOP* 46: 133–54.

Kelly, J.N.D. (1995), *Golden Mouth: The Story of John Chrysostom, Ascetic, Preacher, Bishop* (London).

Konidaris, Ioannis M. (1982), 'Die Novellen des Kaisers Herakleios', *Fontes Minores* 5: 33–106.

— (1992), 'Das Mönchtum im Spiegel der Penthekte', *AHC* 24: 273–85.

Krausmüller, Dirk (2015), 'Contextualizing Constantine V's Radical Religious Policies: The Debate about the Intercession of the Saints and the "Sleep of the Soul" in the Chalcedonian and Nestorian Churches', *BMGS* 39: 25–49.

Krueger, Derek (1996), *Symeon the Holy Fool: Leontius's* Life *and the Late Antique City* (Berkeley CA).

Laurent, V. (1965), 'L'oeuvre canonique du Concile in Trullo (691–692). Source primaire du droit de l'église orientale', *RÉB* 23: 7–41.

Lewis, C.T. and C. Short (1879), *A Latin Dictionary* (Oxford).

L'Huillier, Peter (1991), 'Episcopal Celibacy in the Orthodox Tradition', *SVSQ* 35: 271–300.

— (1996), *The Church of the Ancient Councils: The Disciplinary Work of the First Four Ecumenical Councils* (Crestwood NY).

Liebeschuetz, J.H.W.G. (2001), *The Decline and Fall of the Roman City* (Oxford).

Magdalino, Paul, ed. (1994), *New Constantines: The Rhythm of Imperial Renewal in Byzantium, 4th–13th centuries* (Aldershot).

Mansi, J.-D., ed., *Sacrorum Conciliorum nova et amplissima Collectio*, 31 vols (Florence and Venice 1759–98, repr. Graz 1960–61).

Munitiz, J.A. (1974), 'Synoptic Accounts of the Seventh Council', *RÉB* 32: 147–86.

Nedungatt, George and Michael Featherstone, eds (1995), *The Council in Trullo Revisited*, Kanonika 6 (Rome).

Ohme, Heinz (1988), 'Das Quinisextum auf dem VII. Ökumenischen Konzil', *AHC* 20: 325–44.

— (1989), 'Der Terminus χώρα als Provinzbezeichnung in synodalen Bischofslisten des 6.-8. Jahrhunderts', *ByzZ* 82: 191–201.

— (1990), *Das Concilium Quinisextum und seine Bischofsliste*, Arbeiten zur Kirchengeschichte 56 (Berlin).

— (1991a), 'Zum Vorgang der kaiserlichen Subskription auf ökumenischen Konzilien', *ZKG* 102: 145–74.

— (1991b), 'Die "Armenia Magna" und die armenischen Reichsprovinzen am Ende des 7. Jahrhunderts', *Byzantina* 16: 339–52.

— (1992a), 'Das Concilium Quinisextum. Neue Einsichten zu einem umstrittenen Konzil', *OCP* 58: 367–400.

— (1992b), 'Zum Konzilsbegriff des Concilium Quinisextum (692)', *AHC* 24: 112–26.

— (1995a), 'Die sogenannten "antirömischen Kanones" des Concilium Quinisextum (692) – Vereinheitlichung als Gefahr dür die Einheit der Kirche', in Nedungatt and Featherstone (1995) 307–21.

— (1995b), 'The Causes of Conflict about the Quinisext Council: New Perspectives on a Disputed Council', *GOTR* 40.1–2: 17–43.

— (1999), 'Ikonen, historische Kritik und Tradition', *ZKG* 110: 1–24.

— (2006a), *Concilium Quinisextum. Das Konzil Quinisextum*. Fontes Christiani 82 (Turnhout).

— (2006b), 'Die Beziehungen zwischen Rom und Konstantinopel am Ende des 7. Jahrhunderts. Eine Fallstudie zum Conzilium Quinisextum', *AHC* 38: 55–72.

— (2009), *'In tempore.* Weichenstellungen für die Edition des Concilium Quinisextum (691/2), *AHC* 41: 1–68.

— (2010a), 'Die Quellen des Concilium Quinisextum (691/2)', *AHC* 42: 59–74.

— (2010b), *'Nisi fallimur.* Anmerkungen zu kaiserlichen Unterzeichnungsformen auf den Synoden des 7.-9. Jh.s', *AHC* 42: 241–90.

— (2012), 'Sources of the Greek Canon Law to the Quinisext Council (691/2): Councils and Church Fathers', in Wilfried Hartmann and Kenneth Pennington, eds, *The History of Byzantine and Eastern Canon Law to 1500* (Washington DC) 24–114.

— (2013), *Concilium Constantinopolitanum A. 691–2 in Trullo habitum (Concilium Quinisextum),* ACO² II.4 (Berlin).

Peri, Vittorio (1995), 'Le Chiese nell'Impero e le Chiese "tra I Barbari" – La territorialità ecclesiale nella riforma canonica trullana', in Nedungatt and Fatherstone (1995) 215–27.

Pitsakis, Constantine G. (1992), 'Le droit matrimonial dans les canons du Concile in Trullo', *AHC* 24: 158–85.

— (1995), 'Clergé marié et célibat dans la legislation du Concile in Trullo: le point de vue oriental', in Nedungatt and Featherstone (1995) 263–306.

Price, Richard (2004), 'Zölibat II: Kirchengeschichtlich', *TRE* 36: 722–39.

— (2009), *The Acts of the Council of Constantinople of 553,* 2 vols (Liverpool).

— (2017), 'East and West at the Ecumenical Councils: The Zernov Lecture 2017', *Sobornost* 39.2: 7–25.

— (2018), *The Acts of the Second Council of Nicaea (787),* 2 vols (Liverpool).

— (2018/19), 'Constantinople III and Constantinople IV: Minorities Posing as the Voice of the Whole Church', *AHC* 49: 127–37.

— (2019), 'The Virgin as *Theotokos* at Ephesus (AD 431) and Earlier', in Chris Maunder, ed., *The Oxford Handbook of Mary* (Oxford) 67–77.

Price, Richard and Michael Gaddis (2005, corrected edition 2010), *The Acts of the Council of Chalcedon,* 3 vols, TTH 45 (Liverpool).

Price, Richard and Mary Whitby, eds (2009), *Chalcedon in Context: Church Councils 400–700* (Liverpool).

Reynolds, Daniel (2017), 'Rethinking Palestinian Iconoclasm', *DOP* 71: 1–63.

Rochow, Ilse (1978), 'Zu "heidnischen" Bräuchen bei der Bevölkerung des Byzantinischen Reiches im 7. Jahrhundert, vor allen auf Grund der Bestimmungen des Trullanum', *Klio* 60: 483–97.

Rock, Stella (2007), *Popular Religion in Russia: 'Double belief' and the making of an academic myth* (London).

Sachot, Maurice (1994), 'Homilie', *RAC* 16: 148–75.

Sansterre, Jean-Marie (1984), 'Le pape Constantin Ier (708–15) et la politique religieuse des empereurs Justinien II et Philippikos', *Archivum historiae pontificiae* 22: 7–29.

Spieser, Jean-Michel (2015), *Images du Christ. Des catacombes aux lendemains de l'iconoclasme* (Geneva).

Treadgold, Warren (1997), *A History of the Byzantine State and Society* (Stanford CA).

Troianos, Spyros (1992), 'Die Wirkungsgeschichte des Trullanum (Quinisextum) in der byzantinischen Gesetzgebung', *AHC* 24: 95–111.

Trombley, F.R. (1978), 'The Council in Trullo (691–692): A Study of the Canons Relating to Paganism, Heresy, and the Invasions', *Comitatus* 9: 1–18.

— (1983), 'A Note on the See of Jerusalem and the Synodal List of the Sixth Oecumenical Council (680–681)', *Byz* 53: 632–38.

Vasiliev, A. (1943), 'An Edict of the Emperor Justinian II, September 688)', *Speculum* 18: 1–13.

Vogt, H.J. (1988), 'Der Streit um das Lamm: Das Trullanum und die Bilder', *AHC* 20: 135–49.

Wagschal, David (2015), *Law and Legality in the Greek East. The Byzantine Canonical Tradition, 381–883* (Oxford).

Winkelmann, Friedhelm (1980), *Die östlichen Kirchen in der Epoche der christologischen Auseinandersetzungen (5.–7. Jahrhundert)* (Berlin).

Wortley, John (1984), 'The Sixtieth Canon of the Council *in Troullo*', *StPat* 15.1: 255–60.

MAPS

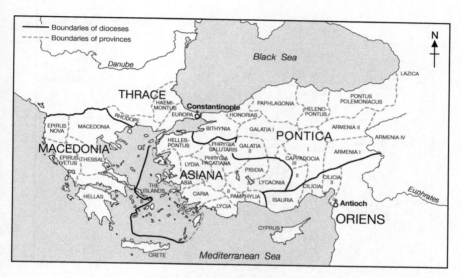

Map 1: Dioceses and Provinces

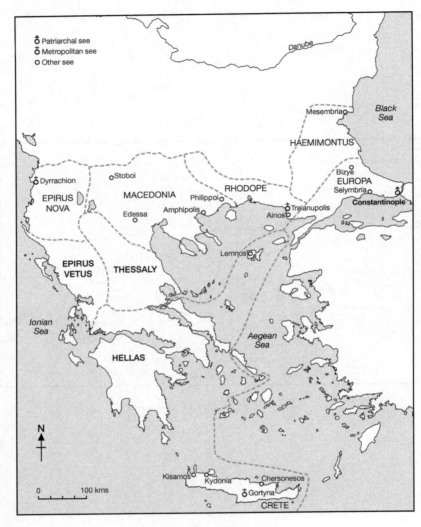

Map 2: The Balkans

Map 3: Western Asia Minor

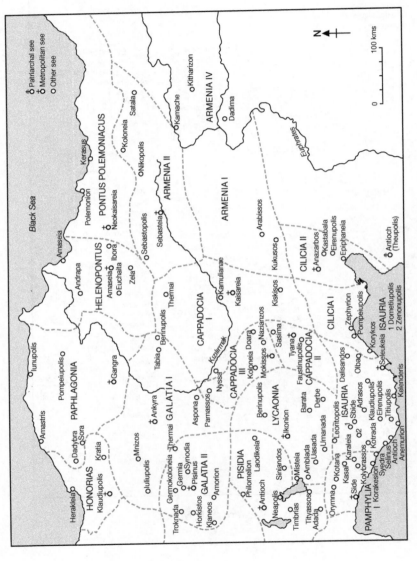

Map 4: Eastern Asia Minor

INDICES

1. TEXTS CITED IN THE ACTS

The figures in the right-hand columns in each case are the numbers of the canons where the citations occur.

Apostolic Canons

5	30
17	3
18	3, 40
26	6
42–43	50
64	55

Basil of Caesarea,
Longer Rules   40

Canons of Basil of Caesarea

1	95
3	102
8	91
9	87
18	40
27	3, 26
31	93
35	87
36	93
46	93
77	87

Canons of Carthage

3	13
18	83
25	13
37	32
41	29
72	84

Canons of Chalcedon

15	40
17	25, 38
18	34
19	8
24	49
27	92
28	36

Canons of Constantinople I

3	36
7	95

Canons of Laodicea

28	74
30	77
50	29
54	24

Canons of Neocaesarea

11	14
15	16

Canons of Nicaea

19	95
20	90

Constantinople I

Acts	Address to the emperor, p. 74

Gregory Nazianzus,

or. 2	1, 3
or. 32	64

John Chrysostom

hom. in Mt.	32

2. THE INTRODUCTION

For the content of the canons, the list of canons in thematic sequence on pp. 64–70 above takes the place of an index.